Campaigning for Children

Campaigning for Children

Strategies for Advancing Children's Rights

Jo Becker

Stanford University Press
Stanford, California

Stanford University Press
Stanford, California

Printed in the United States of America on acid-free, archival-quality paper

Library of Congress Cataloging-in-Publication Data

Names: Becker, Jo, author.
Title: Campaigning for children : strategies for advancing children's rights
    / Jo Becker.
Description: Stanford, California : Stanford University Press, 2017. |
    Includes bibliographical references and index.
Identifiers: LCCN 2016052825 (print) | LCCN 2016054148 (ebook) |
    ISBN 9781503601901 (cloth : alk. paper) | ISBN 9781503603035 (pbk. : alk. paper) |
    ISBN 9781503603042 (ebook)
Subjects: LCSH: Children's rights. | Human rights advocacy.
Classification: LCC HQ789 B43 2017 (print) | LCC HQ789 (ebook) |
    DDC 323.3/52—dc23
LC record available at https://lccn.loc.gov/2016052825

Typeset by Bruce Lundquist in 10/14 Minion

For Lois Whitman

Contents

Acknowledgments

While writing this book, I was privileged to speak with dozens of amazing activists who have helped advance the rights of children. I am grateful to each of them for sharing their work and insights: Amihan Abueva, Lauren Girard Adams, Bama Athreya, Veronique Aubert, Chernor Bah, Zama Coursen-Neff, Camilla Croso, Chris Dodd, Bernardine Dohrn, Steven Drizen, Ruth Dearnley, Courtney Erwin, Julia Freedson, Milena Grillo, Filipa Guinote, Om Prakash Gurjar, Thomas Hammarberg, Stephen Harper, Anne Jellema, Helena Karlen, Abby McGill, Molly Melching, Joe Mettimano, Peter Newell, Diya Nijhowne, Theo Noten, Elizabeth O'Connell, Mark Richmond, Dorothy Rozga, Bob Schwartz, Bede Sheppard, Ann Skelton, Jonathan Somers, Rachel Stohl, Ben Smith, Lakshmi Sundaram, and Beth Wood.

Many thanks to my editor, Michelle Lipinski, for her steadfast support and guidance, and to those who reviewed portions of the manuscript and offered helpful comments, including Lauren Girard Adams, Veronique Aubert, Heather Barr, Zama Coursen-Neff, Bernardine Dohrn, Julia Freedson, Peter Newell, Bede Sheppard, Beth Wood, and, most especially, Jim Ross. Thanks also to Jill Dearman for her coaching, encouragement, and fresh perspectives.

Finally, thanks to my colleagues at Human Rights Watch, and especially the Children's Rights Division, for inspiring me every day.

Campaigning for Children

Introduction

WALKING HOME FROM SCHOOL through the dusty streets of Sa'ana, Yemen's capital, Nujood Ali had no idea how her life was about to change. She was nine years old and loved going to school, drawing with colored pencils, and playing marbles with her best friend during recess. But when she arrived home that day in February 2008, her father had a startling announcement: "Nujood, you are about to be married."[1]

Child marriage was common in Yemen, a poor Middle Eastern country at the southern tip of the Arabian Peninsula. Nujood's mother had married her father when she was 16, and one in three girls married before the age of 18.[2] But Nujood was bewildered by her father's news because she was only in the second grade.

Nujood's family was poor and often didn't have enough to eat. Her father had struggled to find work, and when a man proposed to marry Nujood, the bride-price he offered—US$750—was too tempting for her parents to refuse. One night, Nujood overheard her father telling her older sister, "You know we haven't enough money to feed the whole family. So this will mean one less mouth." Her father made the man promise that he wouldn't touch Nujood until she was older, and without Nujood's knowledge, he signed the marriage contract.

Barely two weeks later, Nujood was married to a man three times her age. The ceremony was brief, but to Nujood, it seemed endless. After the wedding, her new husband took her to his home village, hours away from her parents. Despite his promise to her father, he raped her on the first night under his family's roof. She cried for help, but no one responded. "I realized that nothing would ever be the same again," she said.[3]

Every day, about forty-seven thousand girls marry before the age of 18.[4] For girls like Nujood, marriage means the end of schooling, heightened risk of domestic violence, and possibly pregnancy before their young bodies are ready. With less education and fewer economic opportunities, these child brides are more likely to live in poverty than other girls.

Well into the twenty-first century, childhood remains rife with peril. Around the world, 168 million children toil in child labor.[5] Sixty-one million primary-aged children do not go to school.[6] In most countries at war, schools are attacked and children are recruited to fight as soldiers. Every year, over half of the world's children—1 billion—experience violence,[7] including 3 million girls who may be subjected to female genital mutilation/cutting.[8]

The cruel irony of children's lives is that the same qualities that should elicit protection from harm—their young age and vulnerability—frequently make them targets for exploitation. They are forced to marry or enter the labor force instead of attending school, recruited as cannon fodder in the midst of conflict, manipulated into the commercial sex trade, and bear the brunt of adult violence. Too young to vote, they typically have little access to policymakers or political influence.

The abuses children suffer are unconscionable, yet remarkable change for the better is both possible and already taking place.

Compared to twenty-five years ago, children generally are much better off. Those born today are nearly twice as likely to make it to their fifth birthday. Since 2000, the number of children exploited in child labor has dropped by nearly one-third—from 255 million to 168 million[9]—and more than 110 million more children are in school.[10] Girls are nearly one-third less likely to be subject to female genital mutilation than they were three decades ago[11] and less likely to become child brides.[12] The number of conflicts where children are fighting as soldiers has dropped by more than one-third since the early 1990s, and in some countries, the use of child soldiers has ended entirely.[13]

This book takes you on a journey across continents to meet the extraordinary activists who are transforming children's lives. These individuals and their organizations show that far-reaching change is possible. The strategies they use show how it can be done.

You will discover trailblazing organizations that have used community dialogue to prompt thousands of villages across Africa to voluntarily abandon the practice of female genital mutilation/cutting. You will meet the woman who helped reduce the number of children in South Africa's prisons by nearly 80 percent and the campaigners who secured pledges from the world's largest chocolate companies to eliminate child labor from their products. You will meet activists working to end attacks on schools and to ensure that every child receives a good education.

Some of these dynamic individuals are children themselves, including Chernor Bah, who mobilized other children after Sierra Leone's devastating civil war to win their right to free education, and Basu Rai, who literally marched from one side of the globe to the other to press governments to commit to end the worst forms of child labor. Nujood Ali, whose story opened this book, found the courage at age 10 to seek out a judge and demand a divorce. She is now part of a global campaign that aims to end child marriage in a single generation.

Advancing the rights of children is a moral and human rights imperative as well as an extraordinary investment in society's future. Expanding children's access to education, for example, is one of the most powerful investments that countries can make. The United Nations estimates that if all children in low-income countries left school with basic reading skills, 171 million people could be lifted out of poverty.[14] Providing a child with just one year of extra education beyond the average is estimated to increase his or her eventual wages by 10 percent.[15] Children who are in school enjoy better health, better job prospects, and higher earnings as adults, and they are less likely to end up in child labor or child marriage or as child soldiers.

Similarly, ending violence against children has enormous payoffs for society. Economists have found that civil wars cost the global economy approximately US$170 billion annually, but that violence against children, primarily in the home, costs a staggering *US$3.6 trillion*.[16] Every $1 spent to end violence against children—for simple interventions such as home visitation programs—can save $14 over the long term, in medical and other treatment, child welfare costs, and lower future earnings.[17]

Despite a global consensus that children have fundamental rights and overwhelming evidence that investments in children have profound and long-lasting benefits, governments often fail to prioritize children. Providing every child in the world a quality education through secondary school would cost an additional US$39 billion per year[18]—just 2 percent of annual military expenditures[19]—yet efforts to achieve education for all face significant funding gaps. Governments show callous disregard for the lives of children by failing to enforce laws, refusing to hold perpetrators of abuses against children accountable, and neglecting the policies needed to help children thrive.

One of the most important lessons of the past is that change does not happen without the mobilization of concerned individuals, organizations, and even children themselves. Persistent and creative advocacy and campaigning by civil society have changed societal norms, contributed to a growing body of children's rights law, and forced governments and other entities to take concrete action to protect children and advance their rights.

Throughout most of history, children were regarded primarily as property, not as individuals with rights of their own, including the right to dignity, to protection from exploitation and abuse, to speak out, and to shape their own lives. Today the concept of children's rights has grown from a little-known idea to a body of international law embraced by virtually every country in the world. Experience and research have substantially increased our knowledge about the initiatives that enhance children's lives and prospects and those that don't. Thousands of civil society organizations now lead programs and advocacy to protect children from exploitation and abuse, improve their well-being, and hold governments accountable for their legal commitments.

This book has a dual purpose: it assesses the state of children's rights today, including the magnitude and severity of the violations that children endure and the impact of those abuses on their daily lives; and it examines the initiatives that have improved the lives of countless children—in particular, the vibrant civil society campaigns that have sparked action and had remarkable impact.

This book is meant to be simultaneously sobering and hopeful. The cases presented here give insight into the strategies and tactics that are helping to shape the children's rights movement and make a difference in children's lives. Not all have succeeded. Predictably, many efforts have encountered obstacles and setbacks. Both the successes and the failures can teach us about how transformation happens.

Change for children is possible. My hope is that this book will help policymakers make smarter policy decisions, enable advocates to strengthen their efforts to advance children's rights, and inspire others to join efforts to expand children's opportunities and help them thrive.

1 From Property to People

The Evolution of Children's Rights

EGLANTYNE JEBB was an unlikely champion for children. She never had children of her own and didn't even particularly like them. "I don't care for children . . . the little wretches," she once wrote.[1] Early in her career, she spent a year as a schoolteacher, but quickly realized she was ill suited for the job. In her diary, she wrote that she would prefer to go to the dentist than spend a day in the classroom.

Jebb was born in 1876 in Shropshire, England, and grew up on her well-to-do family's estate. After her ill-fated attempt at teaching, she became involved in charity work in Cambridge, but it was World War I that transformed her into an international children's advocate. During the war, a British economic blockade contributed to unprecedented deprivation across Central and Eastern Europe. Hundreds of thousands of people starved to death, and rates of infant and child mortality were appallingly high. While British propaganda minimized the level of suffering, Jebb worked to expose the humanitarian crisis and build support for an end to the blockade. In 1919, she was arrested in London's Trafalgar Square for distributing pamphlets depicting starving children in Austria. She also began an emergency relief fund to mobilize shipments of food and medicine for children affected by the blockade in Austria and Germany. This initiative became Save the Children, the international children's development organization that today works in 120 countries.[2]

Jebb became convinced that protecting the rights of children was essential to creating a better world order. "Every generation of children . . . offers mankind anew the possibility of rebuilding his ruin of a world," she said.[3] In 1922, she drafted a five-point Charter for Children that stated in part: "The child that is hungry must be fed; the child that is sick must be nursed; the child that is backward must be helped; the delinquent child must be reclaimed; and the orphan and waif must be sheltered and succoured."[4] Jebb took the charter to Geneva. In 1924, the League of Nations adopted it as the Declaration of the Rights of the Child, the first international statement of children's rights.

The concept of children's rights is relatively recent. For most of history, children were seen as the property of their parents or, at best, a vulnerable group in need of special care. Children were primarily valued for their labor and ability to contribute to their family's livelihood and survival. Nonetheless, children found ways to exercise their rights. In 1889, for example, children in England went on strike for better education,[5] and in 1903, striking child textile workers marched with Mother Jones from Pennsylvania to the home of President Theodore Roosevelt in New York to protest child labor.[6] From the 1970s, thousands of child protesters were at the forefront of South Africa's antiapartheid movement. Yet only in the last few decades have children been recognized as individuals with their own rights, including the right to speak out and participate in decisions that affect their lives.

The first formal legal protections for children emerged in nineteenth-century Europe as a reaction to the grueling and hazardous working conditions that many children endured. Children had long worked alongside their family members on farms or in family enterprises, but with the industrial revolution, many began working in factories. Children as young as five or six years old labored for twelve to sixteen hours a day in deplorable conditions, receiving little pay and subjected to harsh punishment. Social reformers began to advocate for legal restrictions, and for the first time in Europe, laws were enacted governing child labor. Reformers also established orphanages for abandoned and destitute children and reformatories or "industrial schools" for children found begging or engaged in theft. The purpose of these institutions was not necessarily to nurture the child, but to instill obedience and industriousness and to protect the child from negative influences.

The unprecedented suffering of children during World War I brought new attention to the vulnerabilities of children in the midst of disaster. The Declaration on the Rights of the Child, penned by Eglantyne Jebb and adopted in the wake of the war, was reaffirmed by the League of Nations in 1934. Heads of state pledged to incorporate it into national legislation, and in France, authorities ordered every school to display the text.[7]

In 1948, following World War II, the United Nations adopted the Universal Declaration of Human Rights, which for the first time set out fundamental human rights that apply to all people, including the right to life, liberty, dignity, nondiscrimination, freedom of expression, education, employment, an adequate standard of living, and freedom from torture and slavery. It gave special recognition to children as "entitled to special care and assistance."[8] In 1959, the United Nations adopted a new Declaration of the Rights of the Child, outlining ten nonbinding principles. It expanded on the 1924 declaration by recognizing children's right to nondiscrimination; a name and nationality; free education; and protection from all forms of neglect, cruelty, and exploitation.

Beginning in the 1960s, members of the United Nations negotiated legally binding treaties to elaborate the rights articulated in the Universal Declaration of Human Rights. In 1966, the United Nations adopted two parallel treaties: the International Covenant on Economic, Social, and Cultural Rights and the International Covenant on Civil and Political Rights (together known as the International Bill of Human Rights). These treaties include provisions specifically focused on children, including their right to a name and nationality, education, protection from economic and social exploitation (including hazardous work), and special procedures for children accused of criminal offenses that take their age into account. The Convention on the Elimination of All Forms of Discrimination against Women (adopted in 1979) addresses child marriage, stating that the betrothal and marriage of a child will not be legally recognized. The Convention on the Rights of Persons with Disabilities (adopted in 2006) affirms the rights of children with disabilities to inclusive education and other rights without discrimination.

In 1978, the government of Poland proposed the first legally binding convention devoted solely to children's rights, inspired by a Polish hero, Janusz Korczak. Korczak was a pediatrician and educator, and regarded by many as the father of children's rights. In 1911, he began an orphanage for Jewish children in Warsaw called Dom Sierot, which he directed for over thirty years. He helped the children of the orphanage create their own parliament and, in 1926, their own newspaper, *Maly Przeglad* (Little Review). He published books advocating for the rights of children and expressed his views on a regular radio program. He wrote of children as "a diminutive nation" that "had been forgotten in the great historical transformations from the struggle for the abolition of slavery to the struggle for equal rights for women."[9] In 1942, the Nazis came to the orphanage and collected over 190 children to transport to the Treblinka concentration camp. Korczak was reportedly offered sanctuary but refused to abandon the children. He and the children perished at Treblinka.

In proposing a children's convention, Poland hoped to honor and popularize Koczak's concepts of childhood. It submitted an initial draft to the UN

Commission on Human Rights in 1978 and a second draft a year later. This draft included the first provision recognizing a child's right to influence his or her own life, noting that the child "who is capable of forming his own views [has] the right to express his opinion in matters concerning his own person."[10]

Negotiations on the Convention on the Rights of the Child (CRC) lasted ten years and were shaped significantly by the dynamics of the Cold War. Eastern bloc countries focused on economic, social, and cultural rights, including the right of children to health, social security, and education. Western bloc countries focused more on civil and political rights. The United States participated actively in the negotiations during the Reagan administration and proposed seven new articles, more than any other country. These included articles guaranteeing children's rights to freedom of expression (article 13), freedom of religion (article 14), freedom of association and assembly (article 15), and the right to privacy (article 16).

Some nongovernmental organization (NGO) activists viewed the US role with suspicion, including Cynthia Price Cohen, an American lawyer and advocate who was intensely involved in the negotiations. She speculated that the US proposals to protect the civil rights of children "were inspired more by the desire to irritate the Soviet Union than from any grand philosophy regarding children's rights."[11] In fact, during the negotiations, a US representative stated that the United States had no intention of ratifying the convention but was participating in the negotiations to help create a "better convention" for other countries.[12]

Nongovernmental organizations played an unprecedented role in shaping the convention. Thirty NGOs formed the Ad Hoc Group on the Drafting of the Convention on the Rights of the Child, and the group proposed recommendations for the text before every session. According to Price Cohen, the group provided "a crucial buffer" between the East and the West. When negotiations bogged down between the two blocs, the NGO text often emerged as the basis for continued negotiations.[13] NGO representatives also participated in working groups of government representatives assigned to work on specific provisions.

One of the most contentious issues was the definition of child. Some delegations insisted that the child's rights came into being from the moment of conception, while others claimed that they began after birth. The final text sidestepped the issue by defining a child as "every human being below the age of eighteen years, unless under the law applicable to the child, majority is attained earlier."[14]

Governments also split over the issue of children's participation in armed conflict. The United States advocated that the minimum age for military recruitment and participation in hostilities should be 15, in line with existing laws of war.[15] Many other governments advocated for the age of 18, consistent with the standard used for all of the convention's other articles. The United States, which routinely deployed 17-year-old soldiers into combat, refused to budge. Because every article was adopted by consensus, the lower age prevailed despite other countries' objections.

The final text of the convention, adopted in 1989, combines economic, social, and cultural rights with civil and political rights—one of the first international treaties to do so. It affirms the child's right to education, social security, and the highest standard of health, as well as freedom of expression, religion, and association. It emphasizes four key principles: nondiscrimination; the best interests of the child; the right to life, survival, and development; and respect for the child's views. It prohibits violence and neglect, sexual and economic exploitation, and capital punishment, and it outlines standards for juvenile justice, adoption, and the treatment of children separated from their families, among other issues.[16]

The CRC was the first international agreement that treated children as rights holders rather than passive objects of care and protection—a significant shift. It affirms the child's right to express his or her own views, including in judicial and legal proceedings that might affect the child, and states that those views will be given "due weight" in accordance with the child's age and maturity.[17] The article guaranteeing freedom of expression also specifies that the child has the right "to seek, receive and impart information and ideas of all kinds . . . through any media of the child's choice."[18]

The CRC became the most widely ratified treaty in history, with 196 states that ratified it (known as "states parties"). By 2017, only one country, the United States, had failed to ratify the convention. Opposition to US ratification originated with conservative organizations that insisted that the convention would have a detrimental impact on American families. They believed that upholding the rights of the child, as articulated in the convention, would undermine the rights of parents to raise and discipline their children.[19] (In reality, at least nineteen of the convention's substantive articles give special deference to the parent-child relationship.) The United States signed the convention in 1995, but as of 2017, no administration had submitted it to the Senate for ratification.

In 2000, the UN General Assembly adopted two optional protocols to the CRC. One addressed its anomaly regarding children's involvement in armed conflict, raising to 18 the minimum age for conscription or direct participation in armed conflict and prohibiting any recruitment of children under the age of 18 by nonstate armed groups.[20] The second optional protocol dealt with the sale of children, child prostitution, and child pornography.[21] These instruments were also widely accepted: by 2017, each had been ratified by more than 160 countries. In 2011, the General Assembly adopted a third optional protocol, allowing children to bring individual complaints to the Committee on the Rights of the Child when states have violated or failed to protect their rights and when domestic remedies have been exhausted.[22]

The CRC established a committee of eighteen independent experts, known as the Committee on the Rights of the Child, to assess implementation of the treaty by individual countries. The UN General Assembly elects the members of the committee, who meet several times a year in Geneva. States that ratify the convention or its protocols, or both, must submit an initial report on their compliance within two years of ratification and every five years thereafter. NGOs and other "competent bodies" may also submit information to the committee. Based on these reports and a face-to-face dialogue with government representatives, the committee issues recommendations for ways that states can better protect the rights of children.

The Committee on the Rights of the Child and other treaty bodies also issue General Comments that interpret treaty provisions and give states guidance on implementing their legal obligations. By 2017, the Committee on the Rights of the Child had issued twenty General Comments covering issues such as corporal punishment, the child's right to play, the aims of education, the rights of children with disabilities, and the child's right to be heard.[23]

Some African nations believed that the CRC did not adequately address the economic, social, and cultural realities in Africa and that African countries had been underrepresented during the drafting process. (Only Algeria, Egypt, Morocco, and Senegal participated to a significant degree.)[24] In 1990, the Organization of African Unity (now the African Union) adopted the African Charter on the Rights and Welfare of the Child, the only comprehensive regional treaty to address children's rights.[25] The charter encompasses many of the rights enshrined in the CRC, but also emphasizes Africa's social and cultural values and history. For example, under the charter, the aims of education should include the "preservation and strengthening of positive African morals, traditional values and cultures." At the same time, the charter is clear that any customs, traditions, and cultural or religious practices that are inconsistent with the charter should be discouraged.[26] Some of the charter's provisions are stronger than the CRC's. For example, the charter defines a child as anyone under the age of 18 without exception and sets 18 as the minimum age for recruitment and participation in hostilities. The charter entered into force in 1999, and by 2017, forty-seven of the African Union's fifty-four states had ratified it.

Additional global standards addressing children have emerged in international labor law and criminal law. To address the use of child labor, the International Labour Organization (ILO) adopted the Convention on the Minimum Age of Employment (ILO C. 138) in 1973. The treaty sets age 15 as the minimum age of employment but allows so-called light work for children as young as 11. In 1999, the ILO adopted the Worst Forms of Child Labour Convention (ILO C. 182), obliging governments to take immediate action to eliminate slave-like practices, including trafficking, debt bondage, and forced labor; the use of children for prostitution or pornography; the use of children in drug trafficking or other illicit activities; and any work that would jeopardize the health, safety, or morals of children. Of nearly two hundred ILO treaties, the Worst Forms of Child Labor Convention became the most widely ratified.[27] The ILO designated both treaties, together with six others, as core labor conventions.

In 1998, governments negotiated the Rome Statute of the International Criminal Court, setting up a permanent international court with jurisdiction to prosecute individuals for war crimes, crimes against humanity, and genocide. The treaty includes several provisions relevant to children. Among its list of war crimes, it includes the conscription, enlistment, or use in active hostilities of children under the age of 15;[28] intentionally attacking schools;[29] and rape and other sexual violence.[30] The statute also considers the forcible transfer of persons under age 18 belonging to a national, ethnic, racial, or religious group intentionally targeted for whole or partial destruction, as genocide.[31] The court may issue arrest warrants, hold suspects in custody, conduct criminal trials, and sentence perpetrators to prison. In its first trial, concluded in 2012, it convicted Thomas Lubanga Dyilo, a rebel commander from the Democratic Republic of the Congo, of recruiting and using child soldiers.[32]

As the body of children's rights law has grown, individual states have also made legal reforms and adopted policies at the national level to recognize and protect children's rights. Countries have created and strengthened juvenile justice systems, improved children's access to education and health services, criminalized violence and exploitation of children, stepped up enforcement measures, and created avenues for children to participate in policy debates.

Many of these changes would not have happened without advocacy and campaigning by NGOs and children themselves. Across the globe, thousands of national, regional, and international organizations are working to promote and protect the rights of children. After the adoption of the Convention on the

Rights of the Child, for example, the NGOs active in its negotiation renamed their group the NGO Group for the Convention on the Rights of the Child (now Child Rights Connect). Its primary purpose is to support child rights groups and help them engage with the UN system, in particular, by providing independent information to the Committee on the Rights of the Child on government compliance with the Convention on the Rights of the Child.

Other key actors in the children's rights movement include the Child Rights International Network, which encompasses nearly three thousand organizations and serves as a primary information source on children's rights; major development and humanitarian agencies, including Save the Children, World Vision, Plan International, and ChildFund International; mainstream human rights organizations such as Human Rights Watch; child-led organizations; and issue-specific groups and networks, including many described in this book.

Child rights advocates have pressed for the development and adoption of international standards for children and used them to hold governments accountable for their commitments. They document and expose abuses and work for changes in policies and practices. They work with local communities to foster new social norms and ensure children can shape their own futures. They provide programs and services to children and ensure that children's voices are heard by decision makers at the highest level.

Children's rights are now an integral part of the human rights agenda, with a robust body of law and standards. Advocates continue to look for new and creative ways to advance children's rights, while governments increasingly recognize that a failure to address these rights will undermine not only children's futures but also their own.

2   Female Genital Mutilation/Cutting

The day I was cut, in Somalia, I had no idea what was about to happen. When I woke up there were so many people in the house I thought we were celebrating something. But it wasn't my birthday. The neighbor's daughter turned to me and said, "You must be really looking forward to this." As she spoke I heard my sister screaming. . . . Someone said: "Go get Leyla, it's her turn."

I was pinned onto the table by four women. They said, "It's not going to be painful, silly girl." Apparently they gave me an injection to numb it, but I felt everything, I felt my flesh being cut off. . . .[1] I was screaming so much I just blacked out. I didn't know what female genital mutilation was until the day it happened to me.[2]

LEYLA HUSSEIN WAS SEVEN when she underwent the practice known as female genital mutilation (FGM, or female genital cutting, FGC).[3] After the procedure, Hussein and her sister were given presents and sweets, but she was confused about why the people she trusted allowed her to go through such a painful ordeal.

Years later, Hussein confronted her mother about what had happened. She learned that as a child her mother had been cut not just once, but twice. A few days after the first procedure, members of the community saw Hussein's mother riding a bicycle. They concluded she had not been cut enough, and a few days later, she was forced to undergo the procedure again. It never occurred to Hussein's mother that Hussein and her sister could escape FGM/C. Women in their community believed that if their daughters weren't cut, they wouldn't be considered good Somali women. Hussein's mother thought that the best she could do to protect her daughter was pay the cutter not to perform the most severe type of FGM/C and to keep quiet about it.[4]

For generations, families, most often in Africa and the Middle East, have subjected their daughters to FGM/C, believing that it will secure their social status and marriageability. FGM/C takes several forms and is defined by the World Health Organization (WHO) as "all procedures involving partial or total removal of the external female genitalia or injury to the female genital organs for non-medical reasons."[5] UNICEF estimates that 200 million girls and women in thirty countries have been subject to FGM/C.[6] Each year, 3 million girls may be cut.[7] The prevalence of the practice varies significantly from country to country. The highest rates of FGM/C are in Mali, Guinea, Sierra Leone, Somalia, Gambia, and Egypt, where over 75 percent of girls are cut.[8] In Uganda and Cameroon, by contrast, only 1 percent of girls are cut.[9]

According to the WHO, FGM/C takes four forms.[10] Type I, also called clitoridectomy, involves the partial or total removal of the clitoris or prepuce (the fold of skin surrounding the clitoris), or both. Type II, known as excision, is more invasive and includes the partial or total removal of the clitoris and the labia minora and, sometimes, the labia majora. (The labia are "the lips" that surround the vagina.) Type I and Type II account for approximately 85 percent of all FGM/C worldwide.[11] Type III, known as infibulation, is the most extreme form of FGM/C. The labia minora or the labia majora, or both, are cut (with or without the excision of the clitoris) and then sewn together, sealing the vaginal opening. The opening is cut back open to allow sexual intercourse when girls marry, as well as for childbirth. Type IV includes all other harmful procedures to female genitalia, including pricking, piercing, incising, scraping, and cauterization.

FGM/C can cause severe bleeding and infection, sometimes leading to death. Long-term consequences include sterility, recurring urinary tract infections, difficult urination, decreased sexual pleasure, and complications during childbirth.[12] In communities where FGM/C is the norm, women and girls may not connect the health problems they experience to FGM/C. Pain, difficulty in childbirth, and the absence of pleasure during sex may all be considered the normal experience of being female.

FGM/C is a deeply rooted social norm, passed from one generation to another, and often an intrinsic part of cultural identity. It is linked to beliefs about female sexuality and concerns that girls' sexual desires must be controlled to preserve their virginity and family honor and to ensure marital fidelity. In many communities, FGM/C is perceived as a religious obligation and is variously linked to Christianity, Islam, and Judaism. In Togo, for example, 21 percent of Muslim women and girls have undergone FGM/C compared to only 1 percent of Christian girls and women. In Niger, it is the reverse: 55 percent of

Christian women and girls have undergone FGM/C compared to only 2 percent of Muslim girls and women.[13] According to religious scholars, however, FGM/C is not prescribed by any religious texts.

Parents subject their daughters to FGM/C primarily to ensure their acceptance and recognition in the community. Mothers in particular believe that by cutting their daughters, they are being a good parent. A daughter who is cut will be considered marriageable and respected within the community, whereas a girl who is uncut is likely to be ostracized and rejected and considered unmarriageable.

These beliefs help explain why some studies show that mothers do not support the practice yet still ensure their daughter is cut. They may recognize the pain and harmful effects of the practice, but still believe that it is in their daughter's best interest. For example, in Mali, the mothers of 59 percent of girls who have been cut oppose the practice.[14] This makes sense when considering that social acceptance is the primary reason behind families' decisions to cut their daughters. Even a parent who personally opposes FGM/C may cut her daughter to avoid social rejection.

Many efforts to end FGM/C have backfired. Advocacy by outsiders may be viewed as cultural imperialism and strengthen the resolve of communities to continue FGM/C. Focusing only on adverse health effects may unintentionally medicalize the practice, increasing the number of girls subjected to FGM/C performed by medical professionals but not necessarily decreasing the rate of FGM/C. Promoting less extreme forms of FGM/C has also been shown to be ineffective in reducing overall prevalence of the practice. Legal reform is not effective on its own in ending FGM/C either. Of the twenty-nine countries with the highest prevalence rate, twenty-six have laws prohibiting FGM/C.[15] In communities where FGM/C is practiced, the pressure to avoid social rejection outweighs the risk of prosecution or fines.

Providing a family with information about the negative health consequences of FGM/C or challenging assumptions that FGM is required by the family's religion may influence individual attitudes but is unlikely to change the practice as long as FGM/C is the norm in the community. As an observer in Sudan stated, "No matter how clever the public education message on the hazards of (FGM/C) or how authoritative the religious source that says it is unnecessary, parents know FGM/C is necessary if it is a prerequisite for their daughter's marriageability and long term security."[16]

Despite traditions going back centuries, ending FGM/C is possible. Through community dialogue, thousands of communities have collectively decided to abandon the practice in an amazingly short period of time. This chapter explores some of these efforts.

Creating Change

In China, foot binding was practiced for nearly a thousand years but ended in just one generation. Like FGM/C, foot binding was considered necessary to ensure a daughter's marriageability and social status. For a girl, the process began around the age of 6 or 8, when her toes would be broken, bent under toward the soles of her feet, and wrapped in position, eventually resulting in feet approximately 4 inches long. The process was extremely painful and often resulted in infection or gangrene, and sometimes death. Foot binding made it difficult for girls to walk, rendering them housebound. It was believed that their restricted mobility helped preserve their honor.[17]

Several attempts to end the practice failed, including prohibitions, edicts, and condemnations by missionaries and literary elite. Ultimately a successful campaign was initiated by a group of anti-foot-binding reformers. The effort had three components: an education campaign that explained that the rest of the world did not bind women's feet; awareness raising around the disadvantages of bound feet and benefits of natural feet; and, most crucial, the establishment of natural-foot societies. People who joined the societies pledged not to bind their daughters' feet or allow their sons to marry a woman with bound feet.[18] The Anti-Footbinding Society established in Shanghai in 1897, for example, drew 300,000 members. Spurred by these pledge societies, change happened quickly. A sociologist found that in Tinghsien, a rural area south of Beijing, the prevalence of foot binding plummeted from 99 percent in 1889 to zero in 1919.[19]

The sociologist Gerry Mackie used social convention theory to explain why practices like foot binding and FGM/C were resistant to change but also how they can be abandoned surprisingly quickly: "What one family chooses to do depends upon what other families in that community choose to do. No one family has an incentive to deviate: if they do, their daughter is destined not to be married or to have a poor marriage."[20] He explains that while education about the harms of a practice is essential, a change in individual attitudes is not sufficient for behavioral change. "A *public commitment* is required so that each member of the intramarrying community can see that most others in the community not only would abandon, but *do* abandon."[21]

Decades later, the same principles that ended foot binding in China have been used successfully to end FGM/C in parts of Africa.

Ethiopia: Kembatti Mentti Gezzima

Gobaletch Gebre was about 12 years old when she was cut in the 1960s. She recalls that a man held her from behind, blindfolded her, and put a rag in her mouth. While he held Gebre's legs apart, a woman sliced off her genitals. Gebre nearly bled to death and required two months to recover. But after she healed, she was considered ready for marriage.

Gebre holds no bitterness over what happened to her: "When they were taking me out to be cut, it was celebratory. My mother though, was crying—she was saying, 'I wish they could do away with it.' But my mother didn't have a choice. Her role as a mother was to prepare a proper girl for marriage, to prepare a daughter to be a good wife. Otherwise no one would marry her."[22]

Ethiopia's constitution, adopted in 1994, prohibits practices that cause bodily harm and says that the state is responsible for eliminating "the influences of harmful customs."[23] Ethiopia's 2005 criminal code specifies that anyone who circumcises a woman of any age can be punished with imprisonment of at least three months and a fine of at least 500 birr (US$45).[24] Despite the legal prohibitions, approximately 74 percent of women and girls between 15 and 49 in Ethiopia have undergone FGM/C.[25] The practice is common in both Christian and Muslim communities, and over half the girls in Ethiopia who undergo FGM/C are cut before their first birthday.[26] Others, like Gebre, are cut during adolescence, as part of celebrations inducting them into womanhood. The most common form of FGM/C is extreme: it involves removing the clitoris, the labia minora, and the labia majora. Traditionally it is known as "removing the dirt."[27]

Gebre, known as "Boge," pursued her education and eventually went to Israel and the United States to study. She earned a PhD in epidemiology, and in 1997, she returned to the community where she grew up and began an organization called Kembatti Mentti Gezzima—Toppe (KMG), which means "women of Kembata working together." Local people trusted her: "People admire her because of all people of this area who went abroad and got educated," said an elderly member of the community, "it is Boge who designed such projects that addressed people's problems. She is heard more than anybody, even the government."[28]

In Gebre's home community, the predominantly Christian Kembatta/Tembaro Zone, girls typically were cut between the ages of 12 and 18 as part of their initiation into womanhood. Cutting is performed in August and September as part of a special ceremony involving many relatives and members of the community.

Using community dialogue as a core strategy, KMG helped facilitate dramatic change in Ethiopia. In just five years, support for FGM/C in Ethiopia dropped by nearly half, from 60 percent among women and girls ages 15 to 49 in 2000 to 31 percent in 2005.[29] More important, practices also changed: in 2000, 52 percent of women in Ethiopia reported that at least one of their daughters had been cut. Five years later, the rate was 38 percent.[30]

Gebre initially focused on community development projects to address practical issues identified by the community, such as health and education. KMG developed projects to prevent HIV/AIDS and malaria, created health centers for women and children, constructed classrooms and supported community schools, helped build bridges and wells, and initiated reforestation projects. These projects built community confidence and trust in KMG.

At the same time, KMG began a range of awareness-raising activities to address violence against women, FGM/C, abduction, and rape. It trained women from different districts in democracy and women's rights and community members to sensitize their neighbors. These trainings focused on groups perceived to have particular influence: circumcisers, traditional birth attendants, traditional leaders (including elders, religious leaders, mothers, and leaders of mutual support groups known as *edirs*). It conducted awareness-raising efforts in local schools to provide students with information about HIV/AIDS, FGM/C, and other harmful practices, using school clubs, theater groups, and student media groups. The student clubs became an important force in promoting the abandonment of FGM/C, mobilizing students to demonstrate against harmful practices at public weddings and during days dedicated to ending FGM/C and HIV/AIDS.

The awareness-raising activities informed communities about the harm of FGM/C, and by 2004, they had reached nearly 100,000 residents. But Gebre believed that additional strategies were needed to bring about actual abandonment: "You must allow the community to decide for themselves rather than condemning," she said. "It has to come from inside the community. It has to be discussed over and over again, in the African tradition. That's how change comes."[31]

In 2002, KMG initiated a community conversation program. Local communities chose facilitators—both men and women—who were then trained by KMG. Twice a month for at least a year, the facilitators led discussions with groups of about fifty participants, covering issues such as human rights, democracy, good governance, reproductive health, HIV/AIDS, and harmful practices. In each case, the groups were encouraged to identify the community's problems and needs and eventually reach consensus on how they would be addressed. Each member was also expected to share results of the community conversation with at least five other households in their community. At the end of the year, the group selected ten members to form a committee that would continue activities to influence people in their village. By June 2008, nearly eight hundred facilitators were working throughout the zone, holding community conversations involving over twenty thousand people.

KMG also trained adolescent girls to facilitate community conversations for other girls. During these conversations, girls identified rape, abduction, FGM/C, and polygamy as harmful practices that should be abandoned. Empowered by the discussions, some refused their parents' attempts to have them cut or intervened on behalf of other girls. One girl said, "If our parents attempt to force us into FGM/C, we tell them with patience that this should not happen."[32]

Religious and *edir* leaders were important to the process of abandonment. *Edir* leaders, who are in charge of village mutual assistance groups that help needy families and support community projects, held intensive discussions and decided as a group to abandon a set of harmful practices, including FGM/C. They made public declarations regarding their decision and threatened expulsion to members who failed to comply. In their sermons, religious leaders emphasized that FGM/C had no basis in scripture and was not a religious obligation.[33]

In 2002, KMG organized its first public wedding of a girl who had refused to be cut. During the ceremony, the bride wore a sign that read, "I will not be circumcised. Learn from me." The groom also wore a sign saying, "I am happy to marry an uncircumcised woman." Some two thousand people attended the wedding, including local officials and 317 girls who served as bridesmaids. The wedding received broad media attention, and by 2007, at least seventy-eight similar weddings with uncut brides were held in one district alone.[34]

Beginning in 2004, KMG organized a special day to celebrate uncut girls with the theme "whole body, healthy life." One hundred thousand people reportedly attended the first celebration, held in a soccer stadium in late October, the end of the traditional cutting season. At the event, uncut girls received a silver pendant that said, "I am whole."[35] Subsequent annual celebrations featured marches, dances, songs, and speeches by local officials.

The participation of both influential *edir* leaders and government officials in the community conversations helped ensure that the decisions to abandon FGM/C were enforced. Their public declarations regarding abandonment not only strengthened community resolve to abandon FGM/C but also encouraged law enforcement officials to take action when the law was violated. Violations were monitored and reported by community conversation members, uncut girls, and the committees that had been established to follow up the community conversations.

A 2008 UNICEF evaluation of KMG found that FGM/C had been almost completely abandoned in areas where the organization had programs. Girls reported that they generally had no fear that parents would force them into FGM/C or worries about finding a husband. Open marriage of uncut girls had become common, circumcisers had stopped practicing, and women were more able to talk openly and discuss their rights. Before KMG began working in the area, nearly 97 percent of villages said they would maintain the practice, according to the local tradition. Less than a decade later, less than 5 percent of villagers said they would cut their daughters.[36]

Senegal: Tostan

In 1974, a young American named Molly Melching arrived in Senegal. Raised in Illinois, she had long been fascinated with other cultures and had a gift for languages. She had been accepted into an exchange program, but on her arrival in Dakar, the nation's capital, she discovered the program had been canceled. She was determined to stay in Senegal and talked the university into giving her a spot in its master's program.

Melching studied Wolof, the language spoken by the majority of people in Senegal, and began to work as a translator for development organizations, traveling with their staff to local villages where the organizations were implementing projects. What she saw during these visits to local villages discouraged her: "There was little true dialogue happening, no deep inquiry into what was working for the villagers and what they thought should be changed."[37] Not surprisingly, many of the projects she observed failed.

In 1991 Melching founded an NGO she called Tostan (the Wolof word for "breakthrough," as in the hatching of an egg). She hoped to use local languages and informal education as part of a problem-solving approach to address health, literacy, and other issues in rural communities. In each village, the three-year program urged participants to envision their own and the community's future. Facilitators asked participants, "What do you want your village to look like in five years? How can we achieve our goals as a community? What problems must we solve in order to achieve our vision?"[38] Within three years, the program was running in 350 villages, contributing to increased rates of birth registration, prenatal and postnatal care, child vaccinations, and use of latrines.

After several years, Melching decided to incorporate human rights education into the program. She said:

> I have learned many lessons during the decades I've been doing this work, but none as important as this: if you want to help empower people to positively transform their communities and their lives, human rights education is key. For many years, our education program did not include discussions on basic human rights. We were successful, but it was only after introducing human rights learning that an amazing thing happened. I can't explain it. It felt like magic.[39]

The first village in Senegal to abandon FGM/C was Malicounda Bambara. In 1996, a group of thirty-five women participating in Tostan's Community Empowerment Program began discussing human rights, including the rights of women and girls to live in health and be free from all forms of violence. Over a period of several months, the women discussed the tradition of FGM/C, its health effects, and whether it helped achieve their dreams for their community. When their Tostan facilitator informed them that FGM/C was not required by their religion, they went to their local imam. He confirmed that FGM/C was not a religious obligation and was not even mentioned in the Koran. Eventually every woman in the class agreed not to cut her daughter that April, when cutting typically takes place. They also began to speak about their decision with other women in the village. In July 1997, the women of the village held a meeting, attended by twenty journalists, and announced publicly their decision to abandon FGM/C.

Not surprisingly, Tostan found that the first collective agreement in a region was the most difficult. Each successive one became easier. Villages sent representatives to other villages to discuss their decision and welcomed others to visit to verify that an alternative was possible. For example, villages in Guinea-Conakry sent delegates to a Senegalese village making an abandonment declaration. The delegates reported they were "much relieved" by the experience, and as a result, they soon pursued collective abandonment in their own villages.[40] Over time, villages even saw public declarations as a way to boost their village's popularity or status.[41]

Through the work of Tostan, over eight thousand communities across eight African countries have publicly abandoned FGM/C.[42] An evaluation of Tostan's efforts in Senegal found that ten years after making public declarations to abandon FGM/C, prevalence in participating villages had fallen by more than half, with 30 percent of girls cut, compared to 69 percent in villages that had not made declarations. Another study found that in villages that had publicly abandoned FGM/C, 24 percent of women who had been cut said they intended to subject their daughters to FGM/C; in other villages, it was 44 percent.[43]

The Senegalese government supported Tostan's efforts and set a goal of total abandonment of FGM/C by the year 2017. In 2014, Melching acknowledged that goal might be overly ambitious but said, "I see change happening in a big way. There are still pockets of resistance, I know that's normal, but I'm very optimistic. I think that by 2020, the numbers will have gone way down, that it will be amazing."[44]

The United Kingdom

Leyla Hussein, who was cut at age seven in the story opening this chapter, eventually settled in the United Kingdom and had a daughter. "I knew the moment my daughter was born that I wanted a different fate for her," Hussein said. "I wished to create an environment where she feels safe—physically and emotionally."[45] Hussein said it was only during her pregnancy that she began to come to terms with what had happened to her. During medical exams, she would often black out. A specialist nurse finally asked her if she had been cut and explained that her body was experiencing flashbacks. "Until that day, I had never made the association," said Hussein.[46]

A 2014 study found that more than 137,000 women and girls in England and Wales had been subjected to FGM/C.[47] London hospitals reported that between 2009 and 2014, nearly four thousand women and girls were treated for FGM-related medical issues.[48] Most, like Hussein, were from families who had moved to the United Kingdom from countries such as Somalia, Sudan, Senegal and Egypt, where FGM/C is widespread. Although most women and girls with FGM/C in the United Kingdom had the procedure before their arrival in the new country, those from immigrant communities where FGM/C is common often feel pressure from family members, in either the United Kingdom or in their countries of origin, to continue the practice.[49] As a result, some girls are sent back to their home community during school vacation to be cut.

Hussein began working with women and girls who had experienced FGM/C and received a degree in psychotherapy. "I was lucky to have the right services around me when I became pregnant," she said. "No one can go on this journey without specialist support. That is why I continue to offer counseling for women today, even when funding is scarce or non-existent. I can't turn women away."[50] She cofounded the organization Daughters of Eve to conduct awareness raising and other activities to protect girls and young women at risk of

FGM/C, and began the Dahlia Project, the first counseling service for FGM/C survivors in the United Kingdom.[51]

Hussein believes that many people in the United Kingdom were afraid to speak out against FGM/C because they didn't want to be seen as criticizing another culture. Conducting an experiment in Northampton, she approached shoppers with a petition supporting FGM/C, telling them she wanted to protect her "culture, traditions and rights." In just thirty minutes, nineteen people signed the petition. The experience left Hussein in tears.[52] Some of the signers said they believed FGM/C was wrong but would support the petition because it was part of Hussein's culture. Only one person refused to sign. UK studies found that among young women from affected communities, however, most wanted to see the practice stopped and supported a more interventionist approach by the UK government.[53]

FGM/C has been a criminal offense in the United Kingdom since 1985, and in 2003, the Female Genital Mutilation Act made it illegal for a British resident to travel abroad to have FGM/C carried out on a child. Anyone found guilty of either offense faces a maximum penalty of fourteen years in prison.[54] It was nearly thirty years after FGM/C was criminalized in the United Kingdom before anyone was charged under the law. In 2014, a doctor from North London was charged with carrying out FGM/C on a woman shortly after she gave birth in 2012. The victim's husband was charged with aiding and abetting the doctor.[55]

Hussein began a petition campaign entitled Stop FGM in the UK Now, calling on the UK Home Office to take responsibility to develop and implement a national action strategy to eliminate FGM/C in the United Kingdom. In just a few months, over 100,000 people signed the petition. It triggered a March 2014 debate in Parliament on FGM/C, the first such debate since the law on FGM/C had previously been amended in 2003. The Home Affairs Committee initiated an inquiry into the issue and invited Hussein to speak. The debate and inquiry considered a special report, "Tackling Female Genital Mutilation in the UK," prepared by Royal Colleges of medicine, trade unions, and Equality Now. The report made a range of recommendations, including awareness campaigns, empowering frontline professionals to identify and protect girls at risk of FGM/C, and incorporating FGM/C as a form of child abuse into all child safeguarding procedures.[56]

After a series of hearings, the Home Affairs Committee called the government's failure to address FGM/C in the United Kingdom a "national scandal" and concluded that the failure to respond adequately had likely resulted in "the preventable mutilation" of thousands of girls.[57] The committee called on the government to implement a comprehensive national action plan that would ensure active prosecutions of FGM/C; equip professionals, including teachers and medical personnel, to identify and protect girls at risk of FGM/C; strengthen laws to make failure to report FGM/C a crime; and provide better services for women and girls affected by FGM/C.[58]

Less than three weeks later, the UK government hosted a global Girl Summit, aimed at mobilizing efforts to eliminate FGM/C and child marriage within a generation. At the summit, Prime Minister David Cameron, together with the home secretary and international development secretary, announced a package of action and funding designed to address FGM/C both internationally and within the United Kingdom. It included a £1.4 million FGM/C prevention program to help care for survivors and safeguard those at risk; police guidance and inspections of how the police handle cases of FGM/C; new legislation to enable prosecution of parents who allow their daughter to be cut; specialized social services to identify and respond to FGM/C; new programs to prevent child and forced marriage in twelve developing countries; and an international charter calling for the eradication of FGM/C and child marriage within a generation.[59]

Challenges

Deeply ingrained and long-held traditions do not change overnight, particularly when a community believes that a practice like FGM/C protects a girl's "honor" and improves her status and future prospects. Denunciations from outsiders are doomed to fail and likely to be perceived as an attack on a community's values.

Education or appeals on an individual level are also unlikely to succeed. If only one family abandons FGM/C, it is left worse off, with its daughters losing both status and marriageability. But if most or all families in a community abandon FGM, they retain their status and daughters preserve their health, their human rights, and their marriageability. Tostan has found that the tipping point where change can begin to happen is when fifty people in a village of eight hundred resolve to abandon FGM/C.[60] In Ethiopia, KMG has also found that a primary core group of fifty can influence the broader community.[61]

Community dialogue can change attitudes, but it takes time. A UNICEF evaluation examined several projects in Ethiopia addressing FGM/C and found some important differences in both approach and result. For example, a community dialogue project in the Wolayta Zone was not nearly as successful as the KMG project in the Kembatta/Tembaro Zone. The Wolayta project brought together several villages for a single dialogue session, lasting from one to three days. The dialogues addressed the health, religious, and legal aspects of traditional practices, including FGM/C. At the end, most groups decided by either majority vote or acclamation to abandon harmful practices. The decisions were not respected, however, and cutting continued clandestinely. One religious leader who participated in the dialogue said, "It is not easy to abandon an age old tradition in a day or two of activities. You know that people are circumcising secretly. During the night men take the women and she does her job. The practice has gone underground."[62] Other participants reported that they were not convinced of the information they had received during the dialogue, and mothers continued to believe that their daughters would be stigmatized if they were uncut. The evaluation concluded that decisions to abandon were not truly collective. The dialogues were too short, and because they were held at the subdistrict instead of the village level, the decisions were seen as coming from the government, not the communities themselves.[63] "Villagers had not decided that FGM/C was wrong, but instead that they should take precautions to not get caught practicing."[64]

On their own, legal efforts to end FGM/C also are largely ineffective in communities where the practice is the norm, as families perceive the social inclusion that FGM/C offers to outweigh potential prosecution. In West Africa, Melching said that initially, she was strongly against the 1999 law that prohibited FGM/C: "I was really concerned. People would say that they were ready to die for their tradition."[65] An assessment of criminalization efforts in Senegal, for example, concluded that where FGM/C has community support, criminalization efforts are ineffective or force the practice underground.[66]

The Way Forward

Successful efforts to end FGM/C have relied on several key components: building trust and confidence through community development projects, using community conversations to foster dialogue about FGM/C, encouraging public commitments to abandon FGM/C and events to celebrate uncut girls, and developing community-government alliances to enforce abandonment.

Collective abandonment requires genuine debate within practicing communities regarding the merits of continuing or abandoning FGM/C. "Families involved in abandonment are not changing their most basic values at the behest of outsiders," says sociologist Gerry Mackie. "Rather, in response to credible new information, and thanks to the opportunity to reflect upon it together, they are choosing to change their ways so as to realize their basic values more coherently and more fully."[67]

Successful programs in Africa have endeavored to be nonjudgmental and to appeal to a community's deepest values. "I worry about denunciation," says Melching, Tostan's founder. "We've all seen that when you denounce someone, you use a method that really tears apart society. Our goal is to help people align with their values and maintain the unity of the family."[68] Tostan also sought to build on villages' religious values. "We ask, what are the values of human rights and of religions?" said Melching. "By doing that, we get religious leaders on board, so that they see this is really about reinforcing and giving value to religion."[69]

Melching found human rights education to be an effective accelerator in the abandonment process. Initially she put the human rights module at the end of Tostan's Community Empowerment Program's curriculum, but later moved it to the beginning. "It had a huge impact," she said. "They learned they had the right to speak out, and to form organizations. We couldn't believe it. The people became more active than we had ever seen."[70] Tostan found that a holistic approach to human rights worked best. "When we did women's rights, the men were upset," said Melching. "When we did children's rights, the parents were upset. By separating the groups, it caused conflict. . . . [So] with every human right we chose, we started looking at what it meant for women, for men, and for children. We said that everyone has rights. If as a man you want your rights respected, you need to respect women and children. We saw a real change of attitude, including by men, in the process."[71]

When change has begun to take place, legal frameworks can play an important role in supporting that change and providing legitimacy to new behaviors. The same study that found that criminalization on its own is ineffective also found that when FGM is actively being debated, legislation can create an "enabling environment" and help to strengthen the stance of those favoring abandonment.[72] Melching, for example, said that she eventually came to change her view about Senegal's law but is careful to frame discussions of the law in terms of the state's responsibility to protect its citizens.[73] In the United Kingdom, surveys of young women from communities with a tradition of FGM/C found that they welcomed more intervention from the state, perhaps because they realized that FGM/C was not the norm or required for marriageability or social status.

In many countries, girls have been cut for hundreds of years. The work of Tostan, KMG, and other organizations, however, shows that deeply ingrained traditions are not immutable. Careful education and community dialogue based on a community's core values can spark collective decisions to pursue new practices. Like the successful efforts to end foot binding in China, dramatic change can happen within just one generation.

3 Juvenile Justice

CHRISTIAN BRACAMONTES grew up in Fontana, California, a rapidly growing suburb east of Los Angeles, bordering the San Gabriel Mountains. Attending high school in the 1990s, he dreamed of becoming a professional baseball player and had already earned several baseball trophies. He lived in a comfortable two-story house with his parents and three younger sisters, who looked up to him.

Christian's plans for the future ended disastrously one day when he was 16. He and an older friend, Jose, age 19, decided to ride their bikes to a concrete storm drain not far from their homes to paint some graffiti on its walls. When they arrived and got off their bikes, Jose showed Christian a gun inside his backpack. Christian was surprised and asked Jose why he had the gun. Jose replied, "For protection."

While Christian and Jose were painting graffiti, a group of kids arrived and offered to sell them some marijuana. Christian and Jose had no money and declined the offer. But then Jose suggested to Christian that they rob the kids. Christian agreed. Years later, he reflected on his impulsive decision: "What was I thinking? I don't know why I followed him."[1]

When they approached the other youth, Jose pulled out his gun and demanded the marijuana. One of the kids challenged him, saying, "If you don't kill me, I'll kill you." Christian never dreamed Jose would actually shoot. Believing Jose would back down, he turned to pick up his bike. "I thought that it was over, we were leaving." But then Jose shot the gun, killing 15-year-old Thomas Williams.

Christian paid dearly for his lack of judgment; for participating in the crime, he was sentenced to spend the rest of his life in prison with no possibility of parole. Prosecutors offered Christian several plea bargains, which would have allowed his release after fifteen years, but he turned them down. He couldn't comprehend that he could spend fifteen years in prison, much less the rest of his life, for a crime he physically didn't commit. "Taking a deal—it's like admitting I did the murder." Jose, however, took the plea deal, making him eligible for parole after fifteen years.

Years later, while serving his sentence, Christian said, "I think about the family who lost the man killed. I think about their pain, and I wish I could take it away, or do something for them. If I could do that day over, I would have told Jose, 'No,' and stopped him from robbing them."[2]

On any given day, an estimated 1 million children are locked up in jails, prisons, or other correctional facilities.[3] While Christian Bracamontes was involved in a serious crime that cost a boy's life, the overwhelming majority of children are held for petty, nonviolent crimes, including what are called "status offenses" that would not be illegal if committed by an adult—crimes such as truancy, running away from home, curfew violations, or possessing alcohol. Most—nearly six in ten—have not been convicted of any crime but are simply awaiting trial.[4] Others have been convicted of an offense and are sentenced to a prison or other correctional facility.

When children break the law, international law requires governments to detain children only as a last resort, for the shortest appropriate period of time, and, whenever possible, to use nonjudicial means to deal with offenses.[5] The treatment of child offenders must also prioritize rehabilitation and reintegration into society. In reality, however, countries often detain children as their first, rather than last, resort when children come in conflict with the law and subject them to cruel and punitive treatment in a harsh, unforgiving system.

In some countries, the law allows children as young as 7 to be sentenced to life imprisonment. In at least forty countries, legal systems permit sentencing of children to include whipping, flogging, caning, or amputation.[6] Prosecutors and judges may have broad discretion in charging and sentencing children for ill-defined offenses. In Saudi Arabia, for example, prosecutors can hold children for up to six months before referring them to a judge, and girls can be detained indefinitely for "guidance."[7]

Conditions of detention can be abysmal, with overcrowding, physical and sexual violence, poor sanitation, inadequate food, and lack of access to education or recreation. Detention facilities are often marked by violence, including sexual abuse, perpetrated by other detainees and staff. In a 2010 survey of nine thousand youth in 195 US juvenile detention facilities, 12 percent of youth reported experiencing one or more incidents of sexual victimization during a twelve-month period. Facility staff perpetrated 80 percent of the reported sexual abuse.[8] In secure US juvenile detention facilities, 42 percent of children said they were somewhat or very afraid of being physically attacked.[9]

Children often are confined with adults because separate juvenile detention facilities are lacking or because laws allow children to be tried as adults and held in adult facilities. Such commingling with adults charged with crimes results in higher recidivism rates among youth offenders and renders children more vulnerable to rape and other extreme violence.

Decades of research have shown that detaining or incarcerating children is both harmful and counterproductive. Children who are confined in criminal justice facilities end up with less education, lower rates of employment, and higher suicide rates than their peers.[10] Contact with the criminal justice system also increases the chances of future criminal behavior. In the United States, 70 to 80 percent of juvenile offenders who are incarcerated are rearrested within two to three years after their release.[11] A Canadian longitudinal study found that involvement in the juvenile justice system was by far the strongest predictor of adult criminal behavior. Youth who were incarcerated were thirty-eight times more likely to be involved with the criminal justice system as adults, compared to other youth with similar backgrounds and self-reported offending histories.[12]

A strong body of research has shown that community-based alternatives to detention are more effective and often far less costly than incarceration. The most successful youth programs employ therapeutic counseling, intensive family interventions, and skills building, and they address specific risk factors that are linked to criminal behavior, including anger, lack of self-control, weak supervision from parents, and poor academic skills. Multisystemic therapy, for example, involves multiple visits to a child's home each week to support improvements in all aspects of the child's environment: parenting skills and family functioning, educational performance, job skills, and recreational activities. In the United States, the program results in rearrest rates that are 25 to 70 percent lower than for other youth and costs US$6,000 to $9,500 per youth. In contrast, the average annual cost to incarcerate one youth in the United States is over US$88,000.[13]

Given the research showing that overuse of detention is both costly and ineffective, why do so many countries lock up so many children? Many lack programs and services that can intervene more effectively. When social workers or other assistance programs are in short supply, police may pick up children who are simply in need of protection and put them in jail as the only available option. Without alternatives, judges may sentence even petty offenders to detention or prison. In some countries, high crime rates have created punitive attitudes that erroneously perceive incarceration as the best way to protect public safety and deter future crime. Research has found, however, that most places that have dramatically reduced rates of youth incarceration have not experienced a corresponding rise in crime.

Some countries have begun to reevaluate their approach to juvenile justice. Some have managed to dramatically reduce the number of children in detention or incarceration, and others only exceptionally incarcerate children.[14] Others have abandoned extreme forms of sentencing. This chapter examines two examples of successful reforms: a wholesale transformation of the child justice system in South Africa that led to dramatically lower incarceration rates and the successful campaign in the United States to abolish the juvenile death penalty.

Creating a New Child Justice System in South Africa

In October 1992, a 13-year-old boy named Neville Snyman broke into a shop with a group of friends in Robertson, South Africa, to steal some cold drinks, chips, and candy. The police soon arrested Neville. Because his mother was unable to get off work to attend his court hearing, the magistrate refused to release Neville and placed him in a cell with other offenders under the age of 21. Neville's cellmates raped him and then bludgeoned him to death.[15]

Neville Snyman's death provoked an outcry in South Africa about the treatment of children in conflict with the law. Thousands of children were detained without trial in the late 1970s and 1980s, often for protesting South Africa's apartheid system, and in the early 1990s, over thirty-two thousand children each year were subjected to whipping as a sentence.[16] The proportion of incarcerated children in South Africa was one of the highest in the world and, in 2002, was second only to the United States.[17] A decade later, South Africa had adopted a transformative Child Justice Law that dramatically reduced the number of children in South Africa's prisons by nearly 80 percent.[18]

Ann Skelton was a leader in South Africa's juvenile justice reform. She had attended an all-white school under South Africa's apartheid regime, and as a teenager, she saw black children her age who protested apartheid being jailed or even shot. She got her first job as a prosecutor in 1986. "I saw many children appear in court, arrested and beaten up by police, bitten by police dogs with their wounds still open," she said. "They were often very young, being detained without a trial and kept in police cells. . . . I realized that the system was very bad for children who got into trouble with the law and that we needed to change it."[19]

After Neville Snyman's death, Skelton and Lawyers for Human Rights started the Free a Child for Christmas campaign and called on hundreds of other lawyers and advocates to work for the release of children. That year, they got 260 children out of jail. That same year, nongovernmental organizations (NGOs) including the Community Law Centre, Lawyers for Human Rights, and NICRO (National Institute for Crime Prevention and Reintegration of Offenders) published a report calling for reform of the juvenile justice system: "Justice for the Children: No Child Should Be Caged."

The apartheid era was ending, and NGOs saw an opportunity to put forward proposals for a new juvenile justice system. They organized seminars and conferences and in 1993 invited a group of juvenile justice lawyers from the United States to consult with them. One of the American lawyers, Robert Schwartz, later recalled, "It was very exciting to be there early on to think about how to design a system, especially when you can avoid the mistakes that others, like the US, have made."[20] In 1994, Skelton and two other advocates published a paper presenting policy and legislative proposals outlining a new vision of a juvenile justice system that would focus on alternatives to detention.[21]

In 1994, Nelson Mandela was elected president. In his first speech to parliament, he declared his intention to "empty our prisons of children."[22] The brutal treatment of children under apartheid had increased awareness that the justice system needed to operate differently. The new South African constitution, adopted in 1996, explicitly stated that every child had the right not to be detained except as a measure of last resort.[23] That same year, Mandela appointed Skelton to chair a special committee under the auspices of the South African Law Commission to write a new law on child justice.

The creation and adoption of the Child Justice Law took a long time. Skelton and her colleagues began by consulting with children who had been in prison. The children told stories of violence, despair, and anger, and shared concrete ideas of how children should be treated. The committee published a comprehensive discussion paper with a draft child justice bill in 1998. After consultations with government and NGOs, the proposed draft bill was presented to the minister of justice and constitutional development in 2000. The Child Justice Alliance formed that same year to advocate on behalf of the bill, bringing together nongovernmental and civil society organizations, academic institutions, and others who had a common interest in juvenile justice reform.[24]

The child justice bill, introduced into parliament in 2002, envisioned a radically different way of treating children in conflict with the law. Its fundamental aim was not punishment but restorative justice. It was designed to hold children

responsible for crimes they committed but to avoid the stigma of criminalization or the negative consequences of incarceration. One of its key elements was
to require preliminary inquiries for all children who came into contact with
the law to assess the child's circumstances (including family, educational, and
social background) and best interests. It created a pretrial process to divert children from criminal procedures and resolve their cases through informal means.
When children were sent to trial, it obliged the courts to consider alternatives to
detention, including home-based supervision, counseling, community service,
or placement into Child and Youth Care Centres. The draft law also raised the
minimum age of criminal capacity of children from 7 to 10 years, meaning that
children under age 10 could not be arrested or charged with a crime.

Skelton described the philosophy behind the bill:

> It accepts that children make mistakes and that teenagers tend to break the
> rules. If we treat them like criminals there is a danger that they will come
> into contact with real criminals, become hardened and grow up to commit
> really serious crimes. If we realize that they have done wrong, but give them
> a second chance to put things right without taking them into the courts and
> prisons, then it is likely they will learn from their mistakes and grow up to
> be law-abiding citizens who respect the rights of other people.[25]

The idea of diverting children from the criminal justice system was not new.
In 1992, NGOs including NICRO began pilot programs offering alternatives to
detention. These included diversion, where a child offender avoids a trial entirely, and noncustodial sentences, allowing a child to stay in his or her home.
Both options became widely accepted by the courts.[26] A NICRO study found
that only 6.7 percent of child offenders committed new offenses within twelve
months after participating in a diversion program and less than 10 percent
reoffended during the first twenty-four months. In contrast, criminal justice
analysts estimated that South Africa's overall recidivism rate (for adults and
children) was approximately 66 percent.[27]

Skelton's committee commissioned a unique "costing exercise" to assess the
economic impact of the child justice bill. Two economists concluded that
the new bill's emphasis on diversion and alternatives to incarceration would
reduce annual spending on children in conflict with the law by over 20 percent.
This was the first time such an economic assessment had ever been undertaken
during the development of South African legislation.[28]

Although hearings were held on the child justice bill in 2003, it fell off the
parliamentary agenda for several years. During this period, the Child Justice

Alliance worked to keep child justice issues alive in the mainstream media, through a journal devoted to child justice issues (titled *Article 40*) and targeted advocacy with politicians and key officials. In 2007, the Department of Justice presented a new version of the bill that was dramatically different from the 2002 version. Although the new bill retained key features such as the preliminary inquiry, diversion, and alternative sentences, it excluded certain children from the process based on their age and the type of offense. These changes reflected an increasing public concern about rising crime rates and a punitive backlash fueled by media reports of crimes committed by children who had been released on bail.[29] Under the new bill, children over age 14 who were charged with serious offenses would not benefit from the new system.[30]

The Child Justice Alliance actively lobbied in favor of the original bill. They made extensive submissions to stress their opposition to a "bifurcated system" that excluded some children from the application of restorative justice processes.[31]

In 2008, public hearings were held on the revised bill. In a dramatic change, the Portfolio Committee on Justice and Constitutional Development indicated that it was prepared to revert to the original child justice bill and ensure that its processes were applicable to all children, regardless of age or offense. Civil society's unanimous support for the original 2002 bill was a major factor in the shift.

The child justice bill was adopted in 2008, signed into law in 2009, and implemented on April 1, 2010. A 2012 assessment identified a number of areas of concern, including inadequate services and educational opportunities for children sentenced to detention. But the overall number of children in South Africa's prisons had declined rapidly, from 4,500 in 2003 to just 846 in February 2011.[32]

In 2013–2014, over twenty-one thousand preliminary inquiries were held for children in conflict of the law, but the vast majority of cases were resolved through informal means or alternative sentences, including fines, community-based programs, restorative justice, and correctional supervision. Only forty-nine children were sentenced to prison, compared to 536 just three years before.[33] In a short period of time, South Africa had made remarkable shift in its treatment of children in conflict with the law and great progress towards ensuring that detention was only used as a measure of last resort.

Ending the Juvenile Death Penalty in the United States

Gary Graham was born in Houston, Texas, to a mentally ill mother and an alcoholic father. As a child, he was passed from relative to relative while his mother was repeatedly institutionalized. He began abusing drugs and alcohol and dropped out of school with only a seventh-grade education. At age 13, he began stealing bicycles, and soon he was stealing cars. By the age of 15, Graham had fathered two children and had a juvenile record for theft.

In May 1981, 17-year-old Graham went on a week-long crime spree of armed robberies and assaults. One night at a gas station, he abducted Lisa Blackburn, a 57-year-old taxi driver, and took her to a vacant lot, where he raped her. She was able to grab his gun, hold it on him, and call the police. Graham was arrested and charged with aggravated assaults and armed robberies. Prosecutors also charged him with the murder of 53-year-old Bobby Grant Lambert, a white man who had been killed in the parking lot of a local Safeway supermarket a week earlier. From the day of his arrest, Graham acknowledged the assaults and robberies but claimed that he was innocent of Lambert's murder. No physical evidence tied Graham to the crime, and his conviction was based on a single eyewitness, who claimed that she saw Graham for a few seconds in the dark parking lot where the murder was committed. Nevertheless, a Houston court sentenced him to death.

From prison, Graham apologized verbally and in writing to the victims he had robbed and assaulted. He learned to read and write and earned his GED and paralegal certification. He cofounded a prison newspaper titled *Endeavor*. Through letters from prison, he tried to reach out to young people to urge them to stop violence and work for change in their communities.[34]

The media wrote about Graham's case, and prominent individuals such as Coretta Scott King, Bishop Desmond Tutu, and various celebrities advocated for Graham's life, arguing that he had poor legal representation at trial and that there were serious doubts about his guilt for Lambert's murder. Thousands of people wrote to the Texas governor, urging him to grant Graham clemency. After an execution date was set in 1993, the alleged victim's widow, Loretta Lambert, appealed to the Texas governor to spare Graham's life, saying, "I do not want the execution of a possibly innocent man on my conscience. I do not believe in capital punishment."[35] The governor granted a reprieve, but in 2000, another execution date was set. Graham was put to death by lethal injection on June 22, 2000.

The International Covenant on Civil and Political Rights and the Convention on the Rights of the Child strictly prohibit capital punishment for crimes committed before the age of 18.[36] The vast majority of countries have abandoned the practice, but between 1990 and 2005, eight countries worldwide—China, the Democratic Republic of Congo, Iran, Nigeria, Pakistan, Saudi Arabia, Yemen, and the United States—were known to have carried out executions of juvenile offenders. During this period, Graham was one of nineteen juvenile offenders put to death by the United States—more than the other seven countries combined.[37]

In 1999, eighty-one juvenile offenders were awaiting execution on death row in the United States. A group of juvenile justice lawyers realized that five of those individuals, including Graham, were scheduled for execution in 2000. The lawyers were scattered across the country, but decided to do what they could to stop the executions, case by case. They organized appeals for clemency from the European Union, the American Bar Association, and even Pope John Paul II, who asked Governor George W. Bush to commute a Texas offender's sentence from death to life in prison. Despite their efforts, four of the juvenile offenders were executed. "It was a rocky start," said Steven Drizin, a law professor from Northwestern University in Chicago. "We had much higher hopes than were realistic at the time. But over the course of that year, we developed a strategy."[38] They decided to continue to work on individual cases while mounting a more ambitious campaign to abolish the juvenile death penalty altogether. This was the genesis of the Juvenile Death Penalty Initiative.

In November 2000, the lawyers organized a meeting in Chicago with other juvenile justice activists to map out a strategy to end the juvenile death penalty in the United States. They decided on a plan of action with several components: a grassroots campaign to win legislation in several states to end the juvenile death penalty; building a substantial national coalition of educational, child-serving, medical, psychological, psychiatric, religious, and rights organizations; educating the public about child development and youth crime; working for clemency on behalf of individual juvenile offenders on death row; and mobilizing international pressure to highlight the country's isolation in its use of the juvenile death penalty.

Initially the core organizers of the campaign met skepticism. During the previous decade, all but a handful of states had passed increasingly draconian laws that allowed juvenile offenders to be tried as adults and receive harsher sentences. Other activists as well as potential funders felt that it was a poor use of resources to focus on the juvenile death penalty—and the relatively small number of juvenile offenders on death row—when hundreds of thousands of youth each year were being tried by adult courts. Drizin saw it differently: "I felt that as long as the juvenile death penalty was on the table, we couldn't talk about issues like juveniles sentenced to life without parole, or other extreme sentences. Ultimately, we persuaded more and more people in the room that this was a campaign worth undertaking."[39]

The campaign focused on a message that "kids are different" and therefore less culpable than adults for their behavior. New studies in neurobiology had found that adolescent brains are significantly different from adults' brains and that areas of the brain that govern impulse control, risk assessment, and moral reasoning are not fully developed until individuals reach their mid-20s.[40] Laurence Steinberg, a prominent researcher and psychologist, explained the findings in this way: "The teenage brain is like a car with a good accelerator but a weak brake."[41] These differences in the brain mean that adolescents are more likely than adults to engage in risky behavior, less likely to consider the long-term consequences of their actions, and far more susceptible to peer pressure. These findings became a centerpiece of the campaign against the juvenile death penalty. "Instead of only expressing our moral outrage at the juvenile death penalty," said Drizin, "we used science and rational arguments based on common sense."[42]

Campaign organizers believed it was critical that nonlawyers speak out on the issue. Lauren Girard Adams, a lawyer and core member of the campaign, said:

> We focused on determining which voices would have the greatest impact. We knew that it probably wasn't going to be death penalty abolitionists or juvenile justice advocates. We knew we couldn't rely solely on moral outrage, not when horrible crimes had been committed. What we were looking for was that piece that you can't debate, that piece that shows that kids are less culpable than adults, so you can't treat them as the worst of the worst, you can't subject them to the most extreme punishment. That's hard to argue with. That allowed us to reach out to unlikely allies.[43]

The campaign made contacts in the medical and psychological community, asking professional associations to adopt formal policy positions opposing the juvenile death penalty. Among the first to do so were the American Academy of Child and Adolescent Psychiatry, the American Psychiatric Association, and the American Society of Adolescent Psychiatry. Others followed, including the American Medical Association and the National Mental Health Association. Physicians for Human Rights helped mobilize a public call to abolish the death penalty that was signed by over four hundred health professionals, scientists, and medical associations and health organizations. Their statement said that on the basis of their medical and scientific knowledge, "children under the age of 18 do not possess the maturity and mental capacities required to justify the imposition of the ultimate adult punishment."[44] The campaign also sought allies from among religious leaders, Nobel Peace Prize laureates, local children's advocates, families of murder victims, and individuals from the law enforcement community. According to Drizin, "We picked up the phone, we called people, we networked. We found people who would be really good spokespeople."[45]

Efforts to abolish the juvenile death penalty at state level were essential to the campaign. Although a relatively small number of states actively implemented the death penalty on juvenile offenders, twenty-three jurisdictions in the United States legally allowed the execution of children in the year 2000. The activists believed that increasing the number of abolitionist states was necessary to convince the Supreme Court that "evolving standards of decency" rejected the juvenile death penalty as a constitutional violation of the Eighth Amendment's prohibition of "cruel and unusual punishment." In 2003 alone, fourteen states introduced legislation to ban the juvenile death penalty: Alabama, Arkansas, Arizona, Delaware, Florida, Kentucky, Mississippi, Missouri, Nevada, Pennsylvania, Oklahoma, South Dakota, Texas, and Wyoming.[46]

"On paper, many states looked good, but didn't pan out," said Bernardine Dohrn, director of the Children and Family Justice Center at Northwestern School of Law. "We kept trying. As we met a roadblock in one state, we tried somewhere else. We kept reaching out to more and more people."[47] Between 2000 and 2005, Indiana, South Dakota, and Wyoming passed legislation raising the age for the death penalty to 18, while Missouri's juvenile death penalty was abolished by the state supreme court.[48] Measures were narrowly defeated in Florida and Nevada, and in New Hampshire, legislation banning the juvenile death penalty passed both houses, only to be vetoed by the governor.

The psychological and medical community was key to these state-level initiatives. Doctors and psychologists testified before state legislatures and spoke to the press. According to one medical professional who was active in the effort, these statements "made all the difference" in South Dakota's decision to change its law. In New Hampshire, the call signed by four hundred scientists and medical professionals was read out in the Senate before the body voted to end the execution of juvenile offenders.[49]

Organizers used the media to place strategic opinion pieces in state and national newspapers. They approached psychologists, pediatricians, religious leaders, local child advocates, judges, state prosecutors, and former law enforcement, as well as victim families against the death penalty and other prominent individuals to write opinion pieces, particularly for state newspapers where legislation to prohibit the juvenile death penalty was under consideration. Former president Jimmy Carter, former first lady Roslyn Carter, and even the former director of the Federal Bureau of Investigation were among those to publish pieces calling for an end to the juvenile death penalty.[50]

The campaign highlighted the isolation of the United States compared to the rest of the world in using the juvenile death penalty. Pope John Paul II, the European Union, the Council of Europe, the United Nations high commissioner for human rights, and leaders from individual countries in Europe conveyed their strong opposition to the juvenile death penalty. At a Rome summit in 2003, a group of Nobel Peace Prize laureates issued a statement saying, "The death penalty is a particularly cruel and unusual punishment that should be abolished. It is especially unconscionable when imposed on children."[51]

Although campaign organizers were unable to stop most of the executions scheduled in 2000, they continued to pull out all the stops to prevent subsequent executions of juvenile offenders. "Any time there was an imminent execution, we all stopped what we were doing and did what we could," said Lauren Girard Adams. "We tried to think outside the box to identify every single person we could call."[52] They involved the Vatican and the European Union, and they used back channels to try to reach the wives of governors who had the power to grant clemency. The day Scott Allan Hain was scheduled for execution in Oklahoma in 2003, Adams was in touch with the office of Desmond Tutu, the Nobel Peace Prize laureate, trying to organize a call from Tutu to the governor. When Tutu finally got through, the governor refused to take his call. Hain was executed shortly after.

Five juvenile offenders, including Hain, were executed between 2001 and 2003. But organizers believed that the attention they generated around the cases helped raise awareness on the juvenile death penalty. The case of Napoleon Beazley in particular captured public attention. Beazley was a straight A honor student and senior class president when he killed a 63-year-old businessman during a carjacking. His friends, family, and classmates were all shocked by the crime. On the eve of his execution, Beazley acknowledged, "The act I committed to put me here was not just heinous, it was senseless."[53] Beazley might not have gotten the death penalty but for two facts: his victim was the father of a federal judge, and he lived in Texas, which had carried out over half of the country's juvenile executions.

Beazley's case garnered coverage on CNN and multiple articles in the *New York Times*. An unlikely array of individuals urged the governor to commute his sentence to life imprisonment, including the judge who presided over Beazley's trial, the district attorney in Beazley's home county, and the former warden on death row. Despite the appeals, Beazley was executed on May 28, 2002.

In two other cases, the campaign helped lawyers win clemency: Alexander Williams's sentence was commuted in 2002, and Kevin Stanford's sentence was commuted in 2003. Perhaps more significant, juries were becoming much more reluctant to impose the death penalty on juvenile offenders. During the decade before 2000, 103 juvenile offenders had been sentenced to death, an average of about 10 each year. Beginning in 2000, however, the rate of death sentences began to drop. In both 2000 and 2001, 7 juvenile offenders were sentenced to death; in 2002, 4 received the sentence. In 2003 and 2004, only 2 individuals in each year were sentenced to death, the lowest rate since 1989.[54] Public opinion also weighed against the execution of juvenile offenders. A May 2002 Gallup poll found that while 72 percent of Americans supported capital punishment in general, only 26 percent supported juvenile executions.[55]

On January 26, 2003, the Supreme Court agreed to hear the case of *Roper v. Simmons.* Christopher Simmons was 17 when he committed a heinous murder. He and a 15-year-old friend broke into the home of Shirley Crook, used duct tape to cover her eyes and mouth, and drove her to a railroad trestle, where they tied her hands and feet together with electrical wire, wrapped her whole face in duct tape, and threw her off the bridge. She drowned in the water below.[56] "Nothing about the facts of the case were sympathetic," said Dohrn. "Simmons bragged about the crime the next day in school. The case was not good, but it was the case we had."[57]

Campaign organizers weren't sure if they could win the case before the Supreme Court, not only because the crime committed was so horrible but also because they weren't sure their campaign had made enough progress. Only a few states had abolished the juvenile death penalty during the preceding few years, and activists weren't sure it was enough to persuade the court that public sentiment had evolved on the issue.

The campaign carefully organized an amicus curiae (literally, "friend of the court") strategy, preparing a series of briefs for the Supreme Court, ensuring that all the important issues were covered and key constituencies were represented. One, filed on behalf of fifty child advocacy organizations, focused on the national consensus in the United States against executing child offenders, highlighting the legislative trend against the juvenile death penalty, and other legal restrictions on children under age 18 that demonstrate that society considers them less culpable then adults.[58] A second, on behalf of seventeen Nobel Peace Prize laureates, including former president Jimmy Carter, focused on the prohibition of the juvenile death penalty in international law.[59] A third, on behalf of the American Medical Association and other medical and mental health organizations, argued the differences in adolescent brain development compared to that of adults.[60] Additional briefs were submitted by the European Union and nearly thirty major religious denominations in the United States.

Organizers continued their outreach to the media, focusing on newspaper editorial boards. During 2004, more than fifty newspapers across the country published editorials supporting abolition of the juvenile death penalty. Virtually all cited the relative immaturity of juveniles compared to adults as the basis for their position, with many also noting the increasing isolation of the United States in continuing the practice.[61]

On March 1, 2005, the US Supreme Court ruled that executing individuals who were under 18 at the time of their offense was unconstitutional, effectively abolishing the juvenile death penalty in the United States. The Court found that juveniles are "categorically less culpable" than adults who commit the same crimes, stating that "retribution is not proportional if the law's most severe penalty is imposed on one whose culpability or blameworthiness is diminished, to a substantial degree, by reason of youth and immaturity."[62] The Court also found that "evolving standards of decency" determined that sentencing juvenile offenders to death was so disproportionate as to be cruel and unusual punishment. It cited the rejection of the death penalty for juvenile offenders in the majority of states, the infrequent use of the punishment, and "the consistency of the direction of change" in state legislation as signaling a national consensus against the practice. It also noted the overwhelming rejection of the juvenile death penalty by other countries and its specific prohibition in international treaties, including the Convention on the Rights of the Child.[63]

The work of the campaign was evident in the Supreme Court's decision. The Court found persuasive the arguments that juveniles are different from adults, stating they "cannot . . . be classified among the worst offenders."[64] The Court agreed with amici that juveniles demonstrate lack of maturity, they are more vulnerable or susceptible to negative influences and peer pressure, and their characters are still developing. In noting the isolation of the United States from both international law and the rest of the world, the Court cited the amicus briefs from the European Union, the Nobel Peace Prize laureates, and the bar of England and Wales.

The decision created a new framework for looking at juvenile justice issues that resonated far beyond the juvenile death penalty. The Court used the same rationale just a few years later to ban life without parole as a mandatory sentence for juvenile offenders for nonhomicide crimes.[65] Advocates also used the Court's decision to win broader juvenile justice reforms at the state level. In California, for example, advocates used the "kids are different" argument to win legislation allowing thousands of individuals who had received adult sentences for crimes committed before age 18 to file for early release.[66] This legislation allowed Christian Bracamontes, whose story began this chapter, to go before a judge and secure a new sentence that will allow for his eventual release.

Challenges

The campaigns in both the United States and South Africa faced challenges related to public perceptions of youth offenders and youth crime rates. In the United States, juvenile offenders on death row were rarely regarded with sympathy. "The biggest obstacles were your clients themselves, because of what they did," said Robert Schwartz, former executive director of the Juvenile Law Center. "All murders are horrible."[67]

In the United States, perceptions that juvenile crime was on the rise led many policymakers to adopt a tough-on-crime stance that led to extreme sentences for youth offenders. In the 1990s, social and political scientists warned of a wave of remorseless juvenile "superpredators" that would bring a "bloodbath" of violence. In 1995, for example, a professor at Princeton University predicted that the number of juvenile offenders in custody would triple in the coming years and that over a quarter-million more young "predators" would be on the streets by 2010 compared to 1990.[68]

These predictions turned out to be false. The rate of violent juvenile crime in the United States began to drop in the mid-1990s and by 2000 was below the level of 1985.[69] Nevertheless, the media and politicians adopted increasingly punitive rhetoric, typified by statements like, "Adult time for adult crime." By 1999, nearly every state in the country had passed legislation that expanded the treatment of juveniles as adults for trial and sentencing. The campaign to abolish the juvenile death penalty bucked a strong public perception that penalties for violent child offenders should be toughened, not eased.

Similarly, South Africa's high crime rate prompted some policymakers to push for more punitive measures. The South African Child Justice Alliance coordinated its media strategy to respond to high-profile cases and any false reports about juvenile crime rates. Although child advocates pushed for a cap of fifteen years for sentences for serious crimes, the final law allowed children from age 14 to be sentenced to up to twenty-five years in prison. "That's nothing to brag about," says Skelton. "But before, we had life imprisonment, and so far, no court has imposed the maximum 25 years."[70]

The Way Forward

For policymakers, accumulated experience and research are clear on two key points. First, children are different from adults. Their brain development makes them more likely to act impulsively, especially influenced by peer pressure, without regard for the long-term consequences of their actions. This difference makes them both less culpable for criminal offenses and more amenable to rehabilitation. Social scientists have also found that adolescents often grow out of criminal behavior and that committing offenses as teenagers does not necessarily predict adult behavior.

Second, a wealth of research shows that putting children in prison is both detrimental and counterproductive. According to the Annie E. Casey Foundation, the incarceration of children "can be neatly summarized in five words: dangerous, ineffective, unnecessary, wasteful and inadequate."[71] Alternatives to detention—including community service, intensive family interventions, and therapeutic counseling—are usually cheaper and result in lower rates of future crime and higher rates of education and employment.

In both South Africa and the United States, the involvement of civil society was crucial in winning change. For US activists, building a broad-based campaign of disparate voices to speak against the juvenile death penalty was key, whether in the context of legislative campaigns, clemency cases, or arguments to the Supreme Court. Similarly, South African activists used every opportunity to shape the Child Justice Act through research, media work, submissions to the Law Reform Commission, consultations, and coordinated campaigns. According to Skelton, civil society's key role was to take advantage of opportunities to make the problem visible and the public aware: "We didn't have loads of money, we just had good instincts."[72]

Both campaigns looked for messages that would resonate with policymakers and the public. In the United States, the campaign focused on the "kids are different" theme, bolstered by recent neuroscience findings and voices from the medical and psychological community. In South Africa, advocates found that the concept of restorative justice resonated with African society and the postapartheid transition. The interim constitution, adopted in 1993, said, "There is a need for understanding but not for vengeance, a need for reparation but not for retaliation, a need for *ubuntu* but not for victimization."[73] *Ubuntu* is an African philosophy that embodies the ideas of connection, community, and mutual caring for all. It loosely means "a person is a person through other people."[74] According to Ann Skelton, "We didn't present it [restorative justice] as something new. It's very African, it's always been there."[75]

One significant difference between the United States and South Africa was South Africa's apartheid era and subsequent political transformation, which created the context and opportunities for reform. During the apartheid regime, large numbers of children had been detained for political acts, and civil society groups actively advocated on their behalf. Many leaders in the postapartheid government had spent time in prison and were vocal about the treatment of children in the criminal justice system, putting it high on their political agenda. The drafting of a new constitution and new laws presented opportunities to look at juvenile justice in a new way.

While advocates in South Africa sought to reform the entire juvenile justice system, advocates who worked to abolish the juvenile death penalty in the United States decided to focus on a very narrow issue with the expectation that it would have an impact beyond the few dozen juvenile offenders on death row. According to Bernardine Dohrn, "Every time you challenge and change the outer boundaries of sentencing, you move the whole system in a different direction."[76] This has proven true: the key principles that were established in the Supreme Court decision abolishing the juvenile death penalty—that children are less culpable for their actions and more amenable to change than adults—have been applied to other aspects of the juvenile justice system, including sentences of life without parole and extreme prison sentences, benefiting thousands of child offenders.

For both campaigns, a well-planned and well-executed strategy, based on a clear message that children are unique and need to be treated accordingly, was key. Reflecting years later on the abolition of the juvenile death penalty in the United States, Stephen Harper, one of the core organizers, said, "One of the things I find most gratifying is that it was a small group of juvenile justice lawyers that came up with a strategy and followed up on it without any egos getting in the way. Kids are indeed different. We won because we emphasized that most basic fact."[77]

4 Child Marriage

THIS BOOK BEGAN with the story of Nujood Ali, a girl who was forced to marry when she was only nine years old. In the small village where Nujood was born, child marriage was common. "Women were not taught how to make choices," she said.[1]

Nujood's village was in a green river valley in northwest Yemen, a poor country bordering Saudi Arabia. Nujood thought it was paradise. Her father had eighty sheep and enough cows to provide the family with plenty of butter, yogurt, and cheese. A river ran just a few yards from their house. But after a violent dispute between Nujood's father and others in the village, her family left the valley and moved to Sana'a, Yemen's dusty capital, four hours to the south.

In Sana'a, Nujood made new friends and enrolled in school. She played marbles during recess and learned to draw with colored pencils. But her father struggled to find work, and the family often didn't have enough to eat. When a man three times her age offered to marry Nujood, her father saw a way to alleviate the family's desperate financial situation. The bride price the man offered, US$750, was too much to refuse. Her father also believed the arrangement would protect Nujood. "This way she won't be raped by a stranger and become the prey of evil rumors," he said.[2]

Nujood was in second grade and bewildered by her father's decision. Her sister tried to convince her father that Nujood was too young, but his mind was made up. The wedding took place in her parents' home just two weeks later. The guests danced and clapped, but Nujood was miserable, her face puffy from crying.

After the wedding, Nujood's new husband took her to his home village, far from Sana'a, where she had lived with her family. During the journey, she thought of only one thing: how she might escape and return home.

Her new husband had promised Nujood's father that he would not touch her until she reached puberty, but the first night under his family's roof, he raped her. She cried for help, but no one responded. The rapes continued almost nightly, and he soon began beating her, first with his hands and a stick and later with his fists. Bruised and distraught, Nujood begged her in-laws to allow her to return home. They not only refused, but her mother-in-law urged Nujood's husband to beat Nujood even more. "She must listen to you—she's your wife," her mother-in-law said.

After several weeks, Nujood convinced her husband to let her visit her family. She asked her parents to let her return home, but they refused, insisting she had to stay with her new husband. Her father's second wife, however, suggested she go to court and ask a judge for help. The next morning, Nujood took money her mother had given her for bread, and hailed a cab to take her to the courthouse. She had never seen so many people but was resolved: "I'm a simple village girl who has always obeyed the orders of my father and brothers. Since forever, I have learned to say yes to everything. Today I have decided to say no."[3]

She waited in a courtroom all day. When a judge finally approached her, she told him, "I want a divorce." The judge was shocked that a girl so young was already married and arranged temporary shelter for her. Shada Nasser, a human rights lawyer who represented women prisoners, heard about Nujood's case and offered to defend her. At the time, Yemen had no minimum age for marriage, but the law forbade sex with young brides until they were "suitable for sexual intercourse." Nasser argued that since Nujood was so young and had been raped, her marriage violated the law. At the trial, the judge asked Nujood if she would like to wait a few years and then "resume" the marriage. She refused, and said, "I hate this man, and I hate this marriage. Let me continue my life and go to school."[4]

A week later, a judge granted Nujood a divorce. At 10 years old, she was perhaps the youngest divorcee in the world. Her case made international news and prompted national debate and proposals in parliament to raise the minimum age for marriage. Her case inspired other girls to challenge their circumstances, including an 8-year-old bride who requested a divorce in Saudi Arabia. Nujood returned home to her family and resumed school, saying, "When I grow up, I'll be a lawyer, like Shada, to defend other little girls like me."[5]

In Yemen, nearly one in three girls are married by their 18th birthday.[6] Worldwide, over 15 million girls a year—about 47,700 a day—are married before they turn 18.[7] In the developing world, one in nine girls is married by age 15,[8] and in some countries, children may be engaged at birth or even married as babies or toddlers. Child marriage, defined as marriage before the age of 18, may involve boys or girls but overwhelmingly affects girls. The impact of early marriage is profound: girls are typically forced to leave school, are at heightened risk of domestic violence and HIV, and become pregnant and have children before their bodies are ready. With little education and fewer economic opportunities, they are likely to live in poverty.

The health consequences of child marriage are particularly severe. Girls under 15 are five times as likely to die in childbirth as women in their early 20s.[9] Complications from pregnancy and childbirth are the second leading cause of death for girls between ages 15 and 19 in developing countries.[10] Because their bodies are not fully developed, girls who give birth often experience prolonged or obstructed labor, which can result in obstetric fistula, a hole between the vagina and rectum or bladder. The fistula often leaves the girl incontinent, leaking feces or urine. Her husband and family may reject her because of the foul smell. Sixty-five percent of all cases of obstetric fistula occur in girls under the age of 18.[11]

Girls who are already married account for an estimated 90 percent of adolescent pregnancies in the developing world.[12] These early pregnancies put not only the mothers at risk but their babies as well. Women and girls who give birth before the age of 20 have a 50 percent higher rate of stillbirths and newborn deaths.[13] Child brides tend to have less access to reproductive health information and have larger families than women who marry later.

The roots of child marriage lay in custom, poverty, and deeply rooted beliefs about the value and role of girls. A boy is often expected to provide income for families and care for his parents in their old age, while a girl may be considered an economic burden who will join—and "belong to"—the family of her husband. In India, for example, girls are referred to as *paraya dhan* or "wealth of another."[14] When parents perceive a girl as just one more person to feed, clothe, and educate, without a future benefit to them, they may believe it is in their best interests to marry her off as soon as possible. Families struggling simply to stay alive may see marrying off daughters as a way to improve their food security—and perhaps for their daughter to have better nutrition after marriage.

When a dowry, or bride-price, paid to the girl's family is customary, poor families welcome the additional income that marrying a daughter can provide. In areas where the bride's family pays the groom a dowry, marrying a girl who is very young may require less money than an older girl.[15] Families may also marry off their daughters while young to protect their daughter's "honor" and avoid any speculation about sexual activity before marriage. In areas with high rates of violence and sexual assault, including during conflict or following disaster, they may see marriage as providing a measure of security.[16]

Lack of access to information about sexual and reproductive health and to contraceptive supplies and abortion limits the ability of young people to make their own choices about relationships and sex. The same pressures that encourage parents to marry off their children sometimes contribute to children deciding for themselves to marry young or agreeing to a child marriage because they see it as helping their family.

The countries with the highest rates of child marriage are primarily in Africa. In Niger, for example, 75 percent of girls are married before age 18.[17] In total numbers, however, the most affected countries are in South Asia. India accounts for nearly as many child brides as all other countries put together. In Bangladesh, nearly 30 percent of girls are married before age 15.[18]

Children also marry in the Western world. Many US states, for example, allow 16- and 17-year-old girls to marry with parental consent and younger children to marry with approval from a judge. In New York State, nearly four thousand children married between 2000 and 2010. In 2011 alone, New York judges approved the marriage of at least four 14- or 15-year-old girls to men at least ten years older. Girls in the United States who marry are from diverse social, cultural, and religious backgrounds, and immigrant and nonimmigrant families alike.[19]

The first treaty to address the issue of child marriage, the Convention on Consent to Marriage, Minimum Age for Marriage and Registration of Marriages, was adopted by the UN General Assembly in 1962. It stated, "No marriage shall be legally entered into without the full and free consent of both parties," and it obliged governments to set a minimum age of marriage, though it did not stipulate a specific age.[20]

The Convention on the Elimination of All Forms of Discrimination against Women states that women should have the same right as men to "freely choose a spouse and to enter into marriage only with their free and full consent" and that the "betrothal and marriage of a child shall have no legal effect."[21] The Convention on the Rights of the Child obliges states to take measures to abolish "traditional practices that are prejudicial to the health of children."[22] In a joint general comment issued in 2014, the Committee on the Rights of the Child and the Committee on the Elimination of Discrimination against Women explicitly identify child marriage as a harmful practice, and emphasize states' obligation to prevent and eliminate it.[23] The committees recommend a minimum legal age of marriage of 18 for girls and boys, with or without parental consent. They also say that a marriage at an earlier age may be allowed "in exceptional circumstances" that are defined clearly in law; in such cases, the child must be at least 16 and give his or her full, free, and informed consent; permission can be granted only by a court of law.[24]

Ending child marriage would have dramatic benefits for society, including higher education rates, better child health, lower infant and maternal mortality, reduced population growth, and lower rates of poverty. One study found that just a 10 percent reduction in child marriage could reduce a country's maternal mortality rates by 70 percent.[25] Another study estimated that for Niger, a country that has both the highest rate of child marriage and is also the poorest in the world, ending child marriage could result in economic gains for households of $6 billion between 2014 and 2030.[26] Globally, lower birth rates as a result of ending child marriage could reduce the world's population by 120 million people by 2030.[27]

Ending child marriage requires a range of actions. According to the United Nations Population Fund (UNFPA), five interventions can make the biggest impact: empowering girls with information, life skills, and support networks; improving girls' access to quality education; mobilizing communities to transform detrimental social norms; improving the economic situation of girls and their families; and generating an enabling legal and policy environment.[28]

A program in Maharashtra state in India demonstrates the value of empowering girls. A life skills program brings together unmarried girls between ages 11 and 19 twice a week for six months to learn about their rights and health, including sexual reproductive health. Adolescent girls' clubs and leadership training for girls who work as peer educators help influence parents and the community to prevent child marriage. After eighteen months, an evaluation of the program found that the proportion of girls marrying before age 18 had dropped from 81 percent to 62 percent.[29]

Expanding girls' access to education is one of the most powerful avenues to ending child marriage. Families often see education or marriage as a binary choice for a girl—she can either continue to study, or get married, but not both—so staying in school delays marriage, and dropping out heightens the risk of marriage. The longer a girl stays in school, the less likely she is to get married before age 18. Education can empower a girl to make her own decisions, resist pressures to marry, and boost her income potential. Research shows that girls with secondary education are six times less likely to marry early compared to girls with little or no education.[30]

Cash transfers, an effective tool to reduce rates of child labor (see chapter 5), can also prevent child marriage by enhancing a family's economic situation and providing incentives to keep girls in school and delay marriage. In Malawi, a cash transfer program in Zomba district paid for girls' secondary school fees and provided a cash payment of approximately US$10 per month (representing about 15 percent of monthly household consumption). Thirty percent of the payment went to the girl's guardian and the remainder to the girl. After only one year, girls who were out of school at the beginning of the program were 40 percent less likely to marry and 30 percent less likely to become pregnant. Three out of five girls who had previously dropped out had returned to school.[31]

Changing social norms around child marriage requires the engagement of influential figures, sometimes referred to as gatekeepers, including parents, religious leaders, community elders, and local authorities. Sensitizing these community stakeholders to the harms of child marriage can lead parents to decide to delay marriage for their daughters, prompt others to intervene on behalf of girls, and shift attitudes around child marriage. Interventions take the form of community dialogues, education and information sessions, and media campaigns. Local government officials and police play a critical role in shaping community perceptions regarding child marriage; they have considerable power to prevent and discourage child marriage or fatally undermine efforts to combat child marriage by condoning or being complicit in such marriages.

In Ethiopia, where one in two girls marry before her 18th birthday and one in five girls marry before the age of 15, the Berhane Hewan (Light of Eve) program effectively combines each of the strategies noted. The program offers families school supplies worth US$6 per year for each daughter to encourage school attendance. It also provides a sheep or goat to each family whose daughter is still unmarried at the end of two years of school, improving the family's livelihood. Both married and unmarried girls attend girls' groups supported by local mentors, where they receive social support, informal education and opportunities for skills building, and information about sexual and reproductive health. Community dialogues help to sensitize local communities to the risks associated with child marriage and promote alternatives. An evaluation of the program three years after it began found that younger girls (age 10 to 14) were 90 percent less likely to marry and three times more likely to remain in school compared to girls not in the program and that married girls were three times more likely to use family planning methods.[32]

Law reform is another important element in ending child marriage. On its own, it is usually insufficient to change practices. In the face of economic and cultural pressures, many parents are willing to defy the law. Enforcement is often weak, and authorities regularly turn a blind eye to early marriage. India, for example, accounts for the largest number of child marriages in the world, but authorities convicted only eleven individuals in 2010 for violating laws that prohibit child marriage before age 18.[33] However, setting 18 as the minimum age of marriage for both men and women sets a clear standard, facilitates changes in social norms, and enables enforcement efforts. Law reform gives activists, including children themselves, the opportunity to press for enforcement of the law on the local level.

The majority of countries have established 18 as the legal age for marriage, but 146 countries have exceptions that allow girls to marry at younger ages with the consent of their parents or other authorities.[34] Such exceptions are often used to marry children without their consent. A study of sub-Saharan countries found that countries that set their legal minimum age of marriage and sexual consent at 18 or older, without exceptions for parental consent, had rates of child marriage that were 40 percent lower than countries where these laws contradicted one another.[35]

Girls Not Brides:
The Global Partnership to End Child Marriage

In the early 1990s, Mabel Wisse Smit, a young Dutch college graduate, became involved in peace efforts during the Bosnian war. She often visited Sarajevo and was impressed with how people there continued to organize cultural events and maintain an independent media, even while under siege: "I learned from its courageous citizens that resistance and change are possible, even in the most dire circumstances."[36]

Wisse Smit, who later married a member of the Dutch royal family and became Mabel van Oranje, continued to devote herself to peace, human rights, and development. From 2008 to 2012, she was the chief executive officer of the Elders, a network of global leaders convened by Nelson Mandela to use their collective experience and influence to tackle some of the world's toughest problems.

During her work with the Elders, van Oranje became aware of the extent of child marriage. "What surprised me when I started looking at this issue," she said, "was that the world was really not paying attention."[37] She decided that the first task was to raise awareness of the issue and convinced members of the Elders, including former UN secretary-general Kofi Annan; Graça Machel, the former first lady of South Africa; and Archbishop Desmond Tutu to work on the issue.

Van Oranje and some of the Elders visited communities where child marriage was common and spent a year conducting consultations to discover what organizations were working on the issue and what strategies were working and to explore the potential for a global partnership. They found that organizations were doing good work on the issue but were often small and quite isolated. Van Oranje said, "It became clear that an effective effort to end child marriage would require a bottom-up movement, bringing together those organizations that are working to bring about change at the local level."[38]

In early 2011, the Elders held a meeting in Ethiopia with nearly three hundred people working on child marriage to discuss forming a formal global network and determine its purpose and activities. They secured core funding from the Ford Foundation, and in September launched Girls Not Brides: The Global Partnership to End Child Marriage. Its goals were to bring child marriage to global attention; build an understanding of what it will take to end child marriage; and call for the laws, policies, and programs that could make it happen.[39] The launch took place at the annual meeting of the Clinton Global Initiative, where Archbishop Desmond Tutu declared, "I'm confident that change can happen very quickly . . . we can end child marriage in a generation."[40]

Girls Not Brides grew quickly. By 2017, it had over 650 members in eighty-five countries, ranging from small local groups to large international organizations. Lakshmi Sundaram, who joined Girls Not Brides as its global coordinator in 2012 and later became its executive director, said, "Many of our members have faced resistance, hostility and in some cases outright threats to their personal safety. When you know you're not the only one trying to do this work, it does bring strength. The other main advantage is the opportunity to build a community of practice, learning from the experiences of those outside one's silo and sharing best practice."[41]

One of Girls Not Brides' member organizations is the Girls Empowerment Network (GENET) in Malawi, where half of all girls are married before age 18.[42] The network was formed in 2008 to empower girls and young women to advocate for justice and gender equality. Members of the network trained over two hundred girls in one district of southern Malawi to become advocates. These girls then lobbied sixty village chiefs to enact local by-laws to protect girls from early marriage and harmful sexual initiation practices. Under the bylaws, men who marry girls under the age of 21 are fined seven goats and forced to give up land. The bylaws also impose penalties on parents who marry off their underage daughters, including mandatory janitorial service in the local health clinic. The network campaigned for change in Malawi's national laws, which allowed children as young as 15 to marry with parental permission. Using the slogan "No to 15: Yes to 18," the network held policy forums and collected letters from girls to the president, urging revisions to the law. In early 2015, Malawi's parliament raised the minimum age of marriage to 18.[43]

Girls Not Brides organized meetings in South Africa, Turkey, Morocco, India, and other countries for members to share experiences and knowledge about ending child marriage. The secretariat, a small staff based in London, developed tool kits, infographics, and videos; organized webinars and meetings; and established a website, girlsnotbrides.org, to share case studies from member organizations, reports, and other resources.[44]

An early focus for the global Girls Not Brides network was the first International Day of the Girl Child, held on October 11, 2012. Fifty members of the partnership organized activities in twenty-nine countries, including public debates, film screenings, text message campaigns targeting local members of parliament, petitions to government authorities, media outreach, and community sensitization campaigns. In Uganda, girls developed a memorandum outlining the role of government and parents in protecting their rights and delivered it to the speaker of parliament. In India, girls put on a play for their parents, highlighting the benefits of delaying marriage. In Ethiopia, members invited community and religious leaders to a fistula hospital to meet with fistula patients and gain a better understanding of the dangers of early pregnancy. New national networks were launched in Turkey and Tanzania.[45]

At the global level, Girls Not Brides worked with UN Secretary-General Ban Ki-moon, UN agencies, and individual governments to mobilize support. After a meeting with Archbishop Desmond Tutu, US Secretary of State Hillary Clinton announced new US initiatives to prevent child marriage and promote girls' education, including mandatory reporting on child marriage in the State Department's annual human rights reports. Both the Ford Foundation and UNFPA announced new funding, totaling US$45 million, for efforts to prevent child marriage.[46] A group of UN human rights experts issued a new joint statement calling on states to raise the minimum age of marriage to 18 without exception and adopt "urgent measures" to prevent child marriage.[47]

Girls Not Brides used other designated days and events to bring attention to child marriage, including the Day of the African Child (June 16), International Youth Day (August 12), and the first global Girls' Summit, organized in 2014 by the UK government and UNICEF to mobilize commitment to end child marriage and female genital mutilation. The network was instrumental in starting an African Union campaign to end child marriage. It succeeded in getting the first General Assembly and Human Rights Council resolutions on child, early, and forced marriage adopted in 2013,[48] requesting UN reports and panel discussions on the issue. In 2014, Canada and Zambia initiated another General Assembly resolution, cosponsored by 116 countries, marking the first time that UN member states had agreed on concrete steps to end child marriage.[49] In July 2015, another Human Rights Council resolution followed.

In 2014, Girls Not Brides began working intensively to influence the Sustainable Development Goals (SDGs), a new set of international goals for the year 2030 that governments planned to adopt in September 2015. According to Girls Not Bride's policy and advocacy officer Ommera Zafar, "When you have a once-in-a-generation opportunity to shape the face of global development, you want to make sure you make the most of it."[50]

Girls Not Brides worked to ensure that a specific target to end child, early, and forced marriage by 2030 was included in the SDGs. It argued that the international community would not be able to make progress on pressing world issues without tackling child marriage. Governments had largely failed to meet a previous set of goals for the year 2015, the Millennium Development Goals, related to poverty, maternal and child health, HIV/AIDS, and primary education. Girls Not Brides argued that a failure to adequately address child marriage was one reason and that child marriage had directly hindered the achievement of six of the eight goals.

To influence the SDGs, Girls Not Brides members worked at the national level to influence government officials and participate in national consultations on the goals. At the global level, Girls Not Brides conducted advocacy with the UN secretary-general and members of a high-level panel tasked with making recommendations for the SDGs, issued press releases, and engaged in ongoing consultations of UN member states in New York, tracking the positions of various governments to inform their advocacy. In October 2014, 176 member organizations of Girls Not Brides sent a joint letter to the UN secretary-general urging a strong target on child, early, and forced marriage in the SDGs.[51] They sent a similar letter to governments chairing the deliberations on the SDGs. Members of the Elders wrote op-eds about the importance of including child marriage in the new goals. In its advocacy, Girls Not Brides stressed that ending child marriage was not only the right thing to do; it was in governments' economic interests. It highlighted research from its members showing that investments to end child marriage contributed to better health, higher levels of education, growth in the labor force, and overall economic development.[52]

In September 2015 at a high-level summit in New York, the 193 UN member states adopted the new SDGs, intended to end poverty, protect the planet, and ensure prosperity for all by 2030. Included in the fifth goal, devoted to gender equality and the empowerment of women and girls, was a specific target to "eliminate all harmful practices, such as child, early, and forced marriage and female genital mutilation."[53] According to Mabel van Oranje, the new goals changed the terms of the debate. With this commitment, she said, "We can start talking with governments about what policies they will develop, how much money will mobilize. . . . Now the real work starts, now we need to get it implemented."[54]

Girls Not Brides immediately launched a new global campaign calling on governments to fulfill their new commitment to end child marriage. The campaign, #MyLifeat15, invited individuals to use social media to post photos and describe their hopes and dreams at age 15, along with the hashtags #MyLifeat15 and #EndChildMarriage. A tool kit encouraged individuals to meet with policymakers and reach out to the media and their networks regarding the new 2030 goal. In Pakistan, activists approached people with blank paper and a camera, asking them to think back to when they were 15, what they wanted to do then, and whether they were ready for marriage, and photographed the people with what they wrote. "This is the first time that we have had so many people join in," said Qamar Naseem, a lead organizer. He reported that the campaign helped reach new allies and that political parties, government department heads, and journalists saw the campaign photos and wanted to join. "People got the message very clearly. At 15, nobody wants to be married."[55]

Although many member organizations of Girls Not Brides had been working to end child marriage for years, the creation of a new global partnership helped catalyze international attention to the problem and secure new commitments to tackle the issue. Change also took place at national levels. In 2015 alone, Chad, Guatemala, and Malawi each raised their legal age for marriage to 18. Gambia, Tanzania, and Zimbabwe followed in 2016.

Challenges

Ending child marriage is a difficult endeavor. It's a complex problem, fueled by poverty, tradition, lack of alternatives, and long-standing gender discrimination. Leaders of Girls Not Brides emphasize that there is no one-size-fits-all solution. "Ultimately, we must accept that there exist fundamental differences in local contexts," says van Oranje. "There is no one approach that can work across all levels and countries to change attitudes to towards child marriage."[56]

Advocacy to end child marriage may be perceived to be in conflict with local values. In northern Nigeria, for example, religiously devout women argued that advocates against child marriage were hypocritical for "promoting promiscuity" through reproductive health and sex education projects.[57] Scholars and experts rightly argue that the socioeconomic conditions that lead to child marriage have to be identified and addressed to develop effective and culturally appropriate responses. "Simply to 'ban early marriage,'" warns scholar Annie Bunting, "risks exacerbating, not alleviating, the underlying socio-economic problems facing girls and adolescents."[58]

For families under economic strain, it may be difficult to consider other courses of action. Lakshmi Sundaram, the executive director of Girls Not Brides, says:

> Often, the toughest question we face from parents is: "What alternative do we have?" When we are able to have these conversations directly with parents, it is a good sign: a dialogue has started, a key step in the process of communities deciding to stop the practice of child marriage. But when a community lacks safe, accessible, quality schooling or opportunities for girls to earn an income, it is hard for parents to imagine a viable alternative to child marriage. The challenge, therefore, is to make sure that we can link community-level work on changing attitudes with efforts to address more structural challenges, such as insecurity, poor schooling and a lack of economic opportunity.[59]

The Way Forward

Experience on the ground shows that several strategies can make a profound difference in ending child marriage. As noted, five interventions can make the biggest impact: improving girls' access to quality education; providing girls with information, life skills, and support networks; mobilizing communities to consider the harms of child marriage; improving the economic situation of girls and their families; and ensuring strong laws and policies.

The Population Council has evaluated programs in several hot-spot countries and found that child marriage can be prevented for as little as US$44 per girl. In Ethiopia, Burkino Faso, and Tanzania, programs implemented three of the strategies above. First, they provided economic incentives to families that kept their girls unmarried. For example, girls received chickens or goats if they remained unmarried and in school for the two years of the project. Second, they provided school uniforms and school supplies to help make it easier for families to keep their girls in school. Third, they used community meetings and the engagement of religious leaders to inform communities about the dangers of child marriage. They found that when these tactics were combined, girls were two-thirds less likely to get married.[60]

Considering the enormous costs to society of child marriage, the relatively low cost of these interventions makes them a smart investment with enormous dividends. Regardless of any economic cost-benefit analysis, they also allow girls to enjoy their fundamental rights to health, education, and freedom from violence and to control their decisions over when and who to marry.

One key lesson is the importance of community-based, rather than top-down, change. "Tackle harmful practices, not one family at a time, but one community at a time," says Mabel van Oranje. "If they collectively decide something is a bad practice, it can be changed." She noted that community dialogue about child marriage needs to be done in a respectful way, initiated by respected individuals: "It can't be done by outsiders like me."[61]

While community-level efforts to change practices are crucial, ultimately governments are responsible for passing laws on child marriage that comply with their international obligations, enforcing those laws, and implementing effective policies. Civil society must hold governments accountable for addressing issues such as gender discrimination, lack of access to education, and the economic conditions that encourage child marriage.

Like other social movements, broad alliances are needed to strengthen efforts on the ground to end child marriage, enable groups to share effective strategies, and bring together organizations to more effectively place child marriage on the international agenda and mobilize resource and policy commitments from governments. While local and national organizations are usually best placed to work directly with affected communities, international members of Girls Not Brides, such as the International Center for Research on Women and Human Rights Watch, are able to conduct research and advocacy at an international level. Graça Machel, one of the Elders who founded Girls Not Brides, said, "If I were to share one piece of advice with those looking to make a positive difference, it would be that you cannot do it alone. I have always tried to listen to and learn from the experiences of others and to think creatively about how we can come together to achieve lasting change."[62]

In the face of traditions that are centuries old, child marriage activists also must believe in the potential for change. "You need a big vision and the conviction that the impossible is possible," says van Oranje. "Ending child marriage might seem like a daunting task. . . . [But] look at other traditions that people thought couldn't be changed, like foot binding in China or the change in people's attitudes over recent decades towards gay rights. It is fascinating to see how traditions and attitudes can and do evolve. . . . You won't achieve your vision unless you're committed for the long haul, so you need determination, stamina and perseverance. Accept that you'll have setbacks but keep your eye on that long-term goal."[63]

5 Child Labor

OM PRAKASH GURJAR was only 5 years old when he was bonded into labor in Rajasthan, in northwestern India. "Where I was born and raised, the notion of child rights does not exist," he said. "If a family is able to save money, their children may be able to attend school. More often, however, the children have no option but to join their parents in farming and caring for cattle."[1]

Om Prakash's family was very poor. Out of desperation, his father borrowed 15,000 rupees (about US$250) from their landlord, agreeing that in return, he and his son would work on the landlord's farm. Instead of going to school, Om Prakash got up early in the morning to work in the fields or take cattle into the jungle to graze. He got little food and no wages, and said the farm owner beat him so many times that he lost count.

When Om Prakash was 8, activists from Bachpan Bachao Andolan (BBA, Save the Childhood Movement) came to his village. They were conducting a survey to identify children who were attending school and those who were not. One of the activists located Om Prakash on the farm. Om Prakash recalled, "The activist asked me if I wanted to go to school and to play."[2] He said yes. When the activists approached the farmer, he insisted that he would release Om Prakash only if he was repaid the money he had loaned Om Prakash's father. Because debt bondage was illegal in India, the activists filed a complaint at the local police station. Only then did the farmer let Om Prakash go. BBA took him to Bal Ashram, a rehabilitation center for child laborers. "I was so happy," he said. "There were so many children playing, not working."[3] He received new clothes and was enrolled in a nearby school.

During visits to his home village, Om Prakash saw other children working instead of going to school and observed that many of them were in poor health. He decided that he wanted to work against child labor. When he found a local school illegally charging families 100 rupees for each student, he raised the issue with a local magistrate and helped petition the Jaipur Court, which ruled that the school had to return the money to the families. He helped five hundred children formally register with the government to get birth certificates, which were necessary to enter school. When he learned that the Second Children's World Congress on Child Labour and Education was being organized in New Delhi in 2005, he bicycled for over thirty-six hours to attend. He also began working with BBA to establish child-friendly villages, known as Bal Mitra Gram, that are free of child labor and where children's assemblies organize on their own behalf.

In 2006, at age 14, Om Prakash received the International Children's Peace Prize in recognition of his work against child labor. He traveled to Amsterdam to collect the prize, where he told journalists that adults must listen to children: "This is our right. They have to listen. These are children's rights. And if they are not abiding with that right, we will work harder to make them hear."[4]

According to the International Labour Organization (ILO), 168 million children were engaged in child labor in 2012, accounting for more than one in ten children worldwide. Among these were 73 million under the age of 12 and 85 million engaged in hazardous work that put their health or safety directly at risk.[5] Many, like Om Prakash, labor long hours in fields and with livestock, often working in extreme temperatures with sharp tools and dangerous pesticides. Others work in brick kilns or mines, in garment factories, or as street vendors, or they pick through trash heaps to find items to sell. Millions are lured into drug trafficking or commercial sexual exploitation.

Child labor is often associated with factory sweatshops, but the vast majority—59 percent—of child labor is found in agriculture. Industry, including factory work, construction, and mining, accounts for 7 percent of child labor. Twelve percent of child laborers work in the service industry, including 11.5 million children, overwhelmingly girls, who labor as domestic workers in private homes to cook, clean, and perform child care and other household tasks.[6] Hidden from the public eye, child domestic workers are particularly vulnerable to physical and sexual abuse by their employers.

It is no surprise that the highest rates of child labor are in poor countries. Children from poor households that struggle to meet basic needs, including food and housing, are most likely to enter the workforce. Although keeping children in school is much more likely to lead to long-term economic stability and better job prospects, many families feel that they have no choice but to seek the immediate income that a child can provide. Child labor is also highly associated with a parent's loss of a job or events such as drought, floods, and crop failures. Poor families often do not have the credit or the savings to withstand such financial setbacks and send children into the workforce to cope financially. In Cambodia, for example, one study found that children in areas that had experienced crop failure in the previous year were 60 percent more likely to go to work than children unaffected by crop failures.[7]

Child labor's costs to society are considerable. Children who enter the workforce at an early age end up with less education, poorer health, and lower earnings as adults.[8] They are then more likely to send their own children to work, perpetuating the cycle of poverty. In 2003, the ILO estimated that eliminating child labor could contribute $5.1 trillion to the global economy, based on the greater productivity of children who have stayed in school longer.[9] According to the Center for Global Development, providing a girl with just one year of extra education beyond the average is estimated to increase her eventual wages by 10 to 20 percent. An extra year of education for boys increases future wages by 5 to 15 percent.[10]

Although millions of children are still engaged in child labor, governments and activists have made significant progress in reducing their numbers. Between 2000 and 2012, the ILO estimates that the number of child laborers fell from 245 million to 168 million, a decline of 30 percent.[11] This encouraging drop is due to several factors, including global economic development, stronger legislative frameworks, government policies designed to increase school enrolment and cushion the economic desperation of poor families, and heightened mobilization, by both governments and civil society, against child labor.

The link between poverty and child labor suggests that as countries develop economically, child labor will decline. For example, the economic growth in Vietnam between 1993 and 1998 is believed to account for a 70 percent drop in child labor.[12] While reducing poverty alleviates the pressure on families to send children to work, economic growth is not a panacea. Economic growth can also drive up the demand for child labor and increase the number of children at work, at least in the short run.[13] Even as countries develop economically, persistent income inequality may still leave poorer families without sufficient resources to meet basic needs. The fact that child labor continues to occur in even the most developed countries shows that economic development on its own is not sufficient to end child labor. The creation and enforcement of strong child labor policies, combined with targeted measures to assist vulnerable families, are also necessary.

The Convention on the Rights of the Child recognizes the right of children "to be protected from economic exploitation and from performing any work that is likely to be hazardous or to interfere with the child's education, or to be harmful to the child's health or physical, mental, spiritual, moral or social development."[14] In 1999, the ILO adopted the Worst Forms of Child Labor Convention (Convention 182), which became the most widely ratified of all ILO conventions, securing 180 ratifications by 2017. The treaty obligates governments to take immediate steps to eliminate slavery and slavelike practices, forced labor, illicit activities including drug trafficking and commercial sexual exploitation, involvement in armed conflict, and any work that is considered hazardous (i.e., harmful to a child's safety, health, or moral development). Under the convention, countries are required to devise time-bound national action plans to eliminate the worst forms of child labor and identify specific areas of work that it considers hazardous for children and are prohibited before age 18.[15]

ILO Convention 138 on the minimum age of employment, adopted in 1973, is the other core international child labor standard, obliging governments to set a minimum age of employment of not less than 15 years (or 14 years for developing countries), while permitting "light work" for children between ages 12 and 14.[16] By 2017, 169 countries had ratified the treaty. These sister conventions have prompted governments to create prevention and monitoring mechanisms, strengthen penal sanctions for child labor, and develop strategies to identify and withdraw children from the worst forms of child labor.[17] These international standards do not prohibit all work by children. Work that is safe and performed at an appropriate age can be positive and help children develop new skills, earn extra income, contribute to their development, and prepare for the responsibilities of adulthood. The term child labor is reserved for work performed by children under the minimum age of employment or that is likely to jeopardize their health, safety, or morals.[18]

One of the most effective government policy strategies to reduce child labor is to increase school enrollment. Children are much less likely to work if they are in school, but many do not attend because schools are too costly or too far away, the quality of available education is poor, or they (or, more likely, their parents) believe that schooling is not worth the investment. Proven strategies to increase school enrollment (discussed further in chapter 9) include eliminating school fees; providing school meals; improving school transportation; and covering the costs of books, uniforms, and other associated school expenses. Such initiatives can lead to significant reductions in child labor. For example, in little more than a decade, Morocco used several of these strategies to boost the number of children completing primary school by more than 20 percent and reduced child labor rates from 9.7 percent to 2.5 percent among children ages 7 to 15.[19]

Programs that provide poor families with a guaranteed monthly income, often known as cash transfer programs, are another successful means to increase school enrollment and reduce child labor. These programs work on the simple theory that providing monthly stipends to poor families will provide an incentive to keep children in school and will discourage child labor by offsetting their lost income. In some cases, the stipends are conditional on school attendance, but even programs without conditions have shown positive results. Meta-analyses have found that beneficiaries of such programs are 23 to 41 percent more likely to be in school than their counterparts.[20]

Cash transfer programs not only encourage schooling, but also help reduce child labor rates. In Ecuador, child labor dropped by 17 percent in poor families that received cash transfers, and in Cambodia, conditional cash transfers resulted in a 10 percent drop in child labor rates.[21] Even modest stipends can be effective. For example, Morocco's *Tayssir* cash transfer program provided only US$7 per month for a primary school child (representing only 5 percent of average household consumption), but helped reduce school dropout rates by nearly 70 percent and reduce child labor rates by one-third.[22]

In some cases, cash transfers have brought unintended consequences. In Malawi, for example, households received stipends of US$4 to US$13 per month, with a bonus for school attendance. An evaluation found that the program resulted in a redistribution rather than a reduction in child labor. The stipends enabled families to better invest in livestock or microenterprise, leading children to shift their labor from work outside the family to work within the family.[23] Although their impact varies from country to country, cash transfers nevertheless are considered one of the most promising interventions to reduce child labor, particularly when combined with other measures to increase access to education and health services.

The private sector, including both local businesses and multinational corporations, may also be implicated in the use of child labor. In 2011, the UN Human Rights Council adopted the UN Guiding Principles on Human Rights and Business (also known as the Ruggie Principles), outlining the responsibilities of businesses to identify, prevent, and remedy the negative human rights impacts of their operations. Under the principles, businesses have a responsibility to conduct due diligence and address child labor and other human rights abuses throughout their supply chains. The principles are voluntary rather than binding, but they are increasingly recognized as the standard for responsible business.

Although sound government laws and policies are critical to reduce child labor rates, mobilization by civil society has often been essential to move governments to act and help ensure that laws are enforced. Public and consumer pressure has also prompted corporations to address child labor in the creation of their products. This chapter focuses on initiatives to address child labor at the community level, drive government action, and influence multinational corporations to eliminate child labor from their supply chains.

The Global March against Child Labor

In 1980, at the age of 26, Kailash Satyarthi gave up a promising career as an electrical engineer to campaign against child labor. In his native India, millions of children were trapped in slavelike conditions, often to pay off debts incurred by their parents. He was determined to do something about it.

He first became aware of bonded labor as a 6-year-old schoolboy. Every day when he entered his school, he saw a boy about his own age sitting on the steps outside the school with his father, cleaning and repairing shoes. One day Satyarthi asked the cobbler why his son did not attend school. He recalled that the cobbler replied, "Young man, my father was a cobbler and my grandfather before him, and no one before you has ever asked me that question. We were born to work, and so was my son."[24]

India has some 5.8 million children between 5 and 17 engaged in child labor.[25] Children in India weave carpets and saris, work in the fields, pick rags in city streets, make bricks, polish gemstones, roll cigarettes, package firecrackers, sell goods in the streets and in shops, and labor as domestic workers in private homes, cooking, cleaning, and caring for children.

Satyarthi formed Bachpan Bachao Andolan, the organization that would eventually rescue Om Prakash Gurjar and more than eighty thousand other children from bonded labor. But when he began organizing in 1980, he found it difficult to convince others that slavery still existed. "When I brought this issue to the United Nations Human Rights Commission, nobody believed it," he said. "They said, 'What nonsense are you talking about?'"[26]

He began mounting raids on factories and other worksites where children, and sometimes their entire family, were held captive as bonded laborers. At the time, many forms of child labor were still legal under Indian law, but bonded labor was prohibited.[27] Activists posing as buyers or laborers first determined the location of child laborers; then Satyarthi mobilized groups of activists, the police, and media to participate in the raids. The work was sometimes dangerous. During a 2004 raid on a circus that employed trafficked teenagers from

Nepal, Satyarthi and his team were attacked by men with iron rods, knives, and guns. The attackers fractured Satyarthi's leg and left him bleeding profusely from a head injury. A local magistrate had tipped off the circus owner of the impending raid.

Conducting raids to rescue child workers is a controversial tactic. Interviews with rescued children found that many children experienced the raids as scary and confusing. A study of children rescued through government raids in Mumbai found that without adequate initiatives to transition children back into school and address their family's poverty, many of the children ended up back in child labor.[28]

In the 1990s, Satyarthi decided to mount a global march to mobilize international action against child labor. Within six months, he had garnered support from over 350 organizations around the globe. The march began on January 17, 1998, and covered almost 50,000 miles across 103 countries. A core group of marchers began in the Philippines, flew to Vietnam, and then crossed Asia, while other contingents traveled across the Americas or Africa.[29] Thousands of individuals joined the marchers for short periods along the way. Organizers called it the largest single social intervention in history for the benefit of children.[30]

The youngest core marcher, a boy from Nepal named Basu Rai, was only 9 years old. Basu was orphaned and had ended up on the streets at age 4. He joined a street gang and spent the next three years begging, picking pockets, stealing bicycles, and working a series of jobs. He worked in a bicycle shop and a private home as a domestic worker and delivered meat for a butcher and bread for a baker. He was beaten by street thugs and employers and often went hungry. When he was 7 years old, activists from Child Workers in Nepal found him and brought him to one of their rehabilitation centers, where he studied for the first time and attended child rights workshops.

Child Workers in Nepal chose Basu to represent the organization in the global march. With the other core marchers, he traveled across Asia and Europe, marching through villages, towns, and cities with placards and banners and participating in public meetings and rallies everywhere they went. "We were full of enthusiasm, potential and with fire in our hearts," he said. "We wanted to bring justice for children from every corner of the world."[31]

The core contingents converged in Geneva in June 1998 during the International Labour Conference, where delegates from around the world were deliberating over new child labor standards. Children from the Philippines, India, and Brazil led about ten thousand people through the streets of Geneva, shouting "Stop Child Labour! End it Now! Education for all Children!" The following day, some 150 children entered the conference's assembly hall. For the first time in the history of the ILO, children took the platform during the opening plenary of the conference. They gave speeches about the aims of the global march and the significance of the convention being debated by the ILO delegates, receiving a standing ovation from the thousands of government, worker, and employer delegates assembled.[32] According to a senior ILO official, "The voices of those children echoed throughout the debate" around the convention.[33] The following year, the conference unanimously adopted the Worst Forms of Child Labor Convention, obliging ratifying states to take immediate action to prohibit and eliminate such labor by children under the age of 18.

In India, BBA continued to conduct raids to rescue bonded child laborers and advocate for stronger laws and policies. Satyarthi, Om Prakash Gurjar, and their colleagues also began to develop another strategy. "A few years after we started BBA, we realized that to combat child trafficking and labour we must address the source of the problem: villages, since nearly 70 percent of child labourers came from villages," said Satyarthi.[34] Om Prakash explained, "My experience is that children and poverty occurs in the rural areas. Poor families move to big cities, where children often work in the street and in hotels and industry. Why not work in villages and stop child labor from there?"[35]

BBA began to develop the idea of child-friendly villages, known as Bal Mitra Grams (BMG). According to Satyarthi, "We decided to create an environment where children are withdrawn from the workplaces, attend school, voice their opinions and ensure that authorities hear them out."[36] The model aims to address not only child labor but illiteracy and poverty. In a BMG village, all children have been withdrawn from work and attend school. Children's assemblies (known as *Bal Panchayets*) work with village assemblies to identify problems in the village and ideas for how to address them. The model is dependent on the active participation of all sectors of the village: children, families, the village council (*panchayet*), and local officials.

To establish a child-friendly village, BBA activists first conduct surveys to determine the number of children attending school and those who are working. They then approach children and their parents to discuss the value of education and engage village leaders in dialogue about the links between child labor and poverty and the importance of education. Over a period of several months, BBA conducts awareness-raising activities for the entire community, through rallies, street theater, and community meetings, about the ill effects of child labor. BBA then takes the idea of a Bal Mitra Gram to the village *panchayet* for a formal decision. If a village *panchayet* agrees to create a Bal Mitra Gram, a BMG board is put into place.

BBA holds orientation programs with children to help them understand their rights and gain confidence in expressing their opinions. Children in the village then elect a children's assembly to voice their concerns and develop concrete proposals to address them. The village *panchayet* gives official recognition to the children's assembly and includes its proposals in the village's decision making.

The biggest challenge, says Om Prakash, is that many village leaders are uneducated themselves and do not appreciate the importance of schooling: "We have to go many times to explain. Little by little, they begin to understand."[37] Village authorities also claim that they do not have the funds to implement the children's assemblies' proposals, and in many cases, they are not aware of government programs that can benefit the village. BBA investigates how funds allocated to the village are dispersed and identifies government programs that can increase local funding for education and village projects.

Since the program's inception in 2001, child-friendly villages have been established in more than 350 villages in eleven states in India, and in 2012, they reached approximately 200,000 people.[38] In addition to transitioning children from work to school, child-friendly villages have improved village infrastructure by installing hand pumps, toilets, and sewer lines; constructing school classrooms; setting up libraries; and repairing playgrounds. Observing its success, organizations including World Vision, Oxfam, and BASE in Nepal have begun replicating the model in other countries. A 2012 evaluation of the program for the US Department of Labor found that the model was easily adaptable for any village, substantially increased school enrolment, developed "community capital," and facilitated changes in community attitudes, in particular toward the value of education.[39]

Sugarcane Production in El Salvador

In the early 2000s, child labor was rampant on El Salvador's sugar plantations. Children worked for hours every day in the hot sun, using machetes and knives to cut sugarcane and strip leaves off the stalks. Accidents were common, and child sugarcane workers often bore scars from gashing their arms and legs with the sharp tools. Despite legal prohibitions on hazardous labor before age 18, children made up over one-third of all workers in the sugarcane harvest,[40] identified by labor experts as the most dangerous of all forms of agricultural work in El Salvador.[41] The sugar industry is also one of the most important in the country, employing tens of thousands of people and contributing to hundreds of thousands of other jobs.[42] El Salvador's sugar is exported around the world and bought by major multinationals, including the Coca-Cola Company.

Efforts to grapple with child labor in the sugar industry began in 2002, when the Sugar Association of El Salvador (FUNDAZUCAR, the social arm of El Salvador's sugar industry) signed an agreement with the ILO and the Ministry of Labor and Social Welfare to address the issue. FUNDAZUCAR undertook a baseline study, conducting interviews with five thousand young workers, examining issues including age, the health risks of sugarcane work, school attendance, labor conditions, and the factors encouraging children to work. One of the survey's findings was that that nearly 20 percent of children working in sugarcane did not attend school, often because their parents did not encourage them to or because the costs, including tuition, transportation, and clothing, were prohibitive.[43]

In 2004, Human Rights Watch published a damning report on child labor in El Salvador's sugar plantations. The organization found that children as young as 8 years old worked for up to nine hours a day, and nearly every child interviewed had scars from cutting themselves with machetes. Human Rights Watch claimed that El Salvador's sugar mills and the businesses that purchased or used Salvadoran sugar, such as Coca-Cola, knew or should have known that the sugar was in part the product of child labor. The organization urged both the government and the industry to adopt a remedial approach, establishing alternatives for child sugarcane workers before taking any action that would deprive children and their families of needed income.[44]

After Human Rights Watch's report became public, some international buyers threatened to stop buying Salvadoran sugar, concerned that their products would be linked to child labor.[45] The sugar guild acknowledged that it faced a "critical" situation.[46] The initial response to the report was not promising, however. Instead of establishing alternatives for child workers, the Ministry of Labor instructed sugar plantations to simply fire children. The government and industry set up some pilot job training projects for the following season, but these served only a small percentage of the children formerly employed on the plantations.[47] Coca-Cola's first response was also disappointing. When Human Rights Watch brought its findings to the company, Coca-Cola did not dispute that children were working on the sugarcane plantations, but said that it was in compliance with its code of conduct, which prohibited child labor by its direct suppliers (the sugar mills) but not its indirect suppliers (the plantations that supplied sugar to the mills).[48]

Despite these initial problems, over time the government and sugar industry developed a comprehensive approach, working together on several fronts: raising awareness about child labor among rural families, sugar mills, the sugar cooperatives, and local leaders; increasing services, including educational opportunities, for rural families; and stepping up enforcement efforts. The ILO was a key supporting partner; between 2001 and 2007, it received nearly $8 million from the US Department of Labor to support El Salvador's efforts to eliminate the worst forms of child labor and strengthen educational opportunities for children.[49]

The Ministry of Education, together with FUNDAZUCAR, developed informal education, such as "leveling classes," to allow child workers to catch up with their peers and reenter the formal educational system. Literacy circles helped illiterate adults and youth learn to read and write. By helping adults, particularly mothers, increase their educational level, parents also learned the importance of education for their children.

Awareness-raising activities were organized at local schools and community meetings, targeting principals, teachers, and other local leaders to highlight the legal prohibitions on child labor in sugarcane and its health risks. Meetings were held with the sugarcane cooperatives and at sugar mill facilities, stressing the importance of eliminating child labor to ensure the profitability of the industry and meet the requirements of trade agreements.

The industry developed a code of conduct, pledging that children under age 18 would not be allowed to participate in hazardous activities or work at sugar mills. In 2007, zero-tolerance clauses regarding child labor were introduced into sales contracts with sugar producers. Under the contracts, all sugar mills in El Salvador committed not to tolerate child labor in their supply chains and reserved the right to reject sugarcane from any producer that used children in its harvest.[50] Because all sugar mills participated, plantations had no choice but to comply with the clause to sell their sugar.

Although Coca-Cola initially denied responsibility for child labor in its supply chain, it ultimately played a positive role. According to Benjamin Smith, senior officer for corporate social responsibility at the ILO, "After the Human Rights Watch report, Coca-Cola started coming down to find out what was going on, and asking the ILO for data and numbers. It had an important role in influencing the sugar association and government, using their leverage (and they had quite a bit) to promote a stepped up response."[51] The company chose to continue to source sugar from El Salvador and initiated a project to keep children in school while they earned income through a greenhouse project where they learned to cultivate eggplant, corn, cucumbers, tomatoes, and other vegetables.[52]

Monitoring was set up through several channels. The Ministry of Labor stepped up inspections, changing the schedules of labor inspectors during the sugarcane harvest to more closely match workers' hours and coordinating with sugar mills to identify the times and places where sugar was being harvested. The sugar association set up forty local monitoring committees to help with awareness raising and enforcement of the zero-tolerance policy. Sugar mills monitored their suppliers through unannounced visits. Suppliers found to be using children were sent a written notice, and if child labor was found a second time, the mill refused sugarcane from that plantation until it received a letter of commitment from the producer agreeing not to use child labor. A third violation resulted in permanent suspension of the plantation. The sugar association also contracted with an outside auditor, UL, which conducted daily visits to 10 percent of all plantations in the country to track child labor.[53]

The collective efforts had a significant impact. According to data from the Ministry of Education, the number of child laborers in sugarcane dropped from 12,380 children in 2004 to 1,559 in 2009, a decline of nearly 88 percent in five years.[54] An external assessment concluded that several factors accelerated this dramatic progress, including a change in government in El Salvador (with the new government exhibiting stronger political will to address child labor); external pressure created by the Human Rights Watch report (including its focus on the "paradigmatic" case of Coca-Cola); and the sugar industry's adoption of a clear code of conduct.[55] The assessment also highlighted the importance of trade agreements binding on El Salvador. In 2004, the United States reached a free-trade agreement with five Central American countries and the Dominican Republic. Known as DR-CAFTA, the agreement boosted El Salvador's sugar economy by providing the industry with an export quota, and it committed El Salvador to uphold ILO labor standards, including the elimination of the worst forms of child labor. The need to comply with CAFTA forced the business sector to substantially step up its response to child labor.[56]

Child Labor and Chocolate

In the 1990s, filmmakers Brian Wood and Kate Blewett traveled to West Africa to interview young men and boys working on cocoa plantations. They found that some of the workers had been trafficked from Mali to Côte d'Ivoire and had worked for as long as five years with no pay. Their bodies were covered with scars from beatings, and some described being locked in sheds at night to prevent their escape. When Wood and Blewett's documentary aired on the BBC in 2000, it brought global attention to child slavery in the cocoa industry.[57] The former slaves in the film had never tasted chocolate, but when asked what they would say to consumers of chocolate in other parts of the world, one said, "They enjoy something I suffered to make; I worked hard for them, but saw no benefit. They are eating my flesh."[58]

On a typical day, an estimated 1 billion people eat chocolate. In 2014, the chocolate industry earned an estimated $117 billion in global revenue, an increase of 6 percent over the previous year.[59] Up to 90 percent of the world's cocoa is produced on small, independent farms, with Côte d'Ivoire and Ghana providing 60 percent of the cocoa beans for the industry.[60] Despite the industry's huge profits, the International Labor Rights Forum estimated in 2014 that most cocoa-farming families in Ghana and Côte d'Ivoire survived on incomes of only 40 cents per dependent per day.[61]

An estimated 2 million children work in cocoa production in Ghana and Côte d'Ivoire.[62] Children working on a cocoa plantation typically climb cocoa trees to cut bean pods with a heavy, sharp machete. They then pack the bean pods into sacks that can weigh more than 100 pounds when full, and drag them through the forest. To open the pods and extract the cocoa beans, they hold a pod in one hand and strike it with a machete in the other. Cuts are common, and many child cocoa workers have scars on their hands, arms, legs, and shoulders from the machetes.

The BBC documentary and a series of Knight Ridder articles put pressure on major chocolate companies to verify that their chocolate was not made with slave or child labor. Their fears that the media reports would deter consumers from buying chocolate seemed well founded: in 2001, the year after the broadcast of the BBC documentary, the chocolate market in the United Kingdom shrank by 2 percent after years of consistent growth.[63]

The reports of child slavery also gained the attention of US members of Congress. In July 2001, the US House of Representatives adopted a provision requiring chocolate companies to label their products and classify cocoa as "slave free" if it could be documented that its production had not involved the exploitation of children. The chocolate industry feared that if the Senate passed a similar bill, they would be subject to a costly and onerous mandatory certification program. Seeking an alternative, the chocolate industry engaged in negotiations with Senator Tom Harkin and Congressman Eliot Engel. The result was the Harkin-Engel Protocol, signed in September 2001 by the Chocolate Manufacturers Association and the World Cocoa Foundation, organizations that represent nearly all the world's largest chocolate brands.[64] Under the protocol, companies agreed to eliminate the worst forms of child labor and slave labor throughout their supply chains. They pledged to implement an industry-wide certification system by 2005 to give a public accounting of labor practices in cocoa-growing countries and establish a joint foundation (the International Cocoa Initiative) to implement measures to address child labor.[65] Compared to the proposed legislation, the protocol gave the company more time to address the problem and created a voluntary certification system rather than a mandatory one.

Despite high expectations after the agreement was signed, the industry made little progress in implementing the protocol and repeatedly missed its deadlines. The International Cocoa Initiative was established in 2002 to develop projects to address the worst forms of child labor, but it became clear that the goal of implementing an industry-wide certification system by 2005 would not be met. In 2005, Harkin and Engel publicly expressed their frustration in the *Los Angeles Times*, complaining that the chocolate industry's plans to initiate a small pilot program in Ghana fell "woefully short of the robust action" that the protocol had promised.[66] The industry signed new declarations in 2005, 2008, and 2010, each extending previously agreed deadlines. The 2005 declaration pledged that a certification system would be in place in 50 percent of cocoa-producing communities by July 2008. When that deadline was not met, a 2008 declaration committed to reaching 100 percent of cocoa-producing communities by 2010. That goal was also missed. In 2010, a new declaration and framework of action set a different goal: to reduce the worst forms of child labor in cocoa by 70 percent by 2020.

By 2011, the International Cocoa Initiative had set up remediation programs focused on expanding children's educational opportunities in 133 communities in Côte d'Ivoire and 157 in Ghana, but these benefited only a small portion of cocoa-producing communities. An assessment by Tulane University in 2011 acknowledged some advances but criticized the chocolate industry for "insufficient" investments in addressing child labor and said that activities needed to be "drastically expanded" to achieve the goal of eliminating the worst forms of child labor in the cocoa sector.[67] Between 2002 and 2015, the chocolate industry committed $25 million for the International Cocoa Initiative and its activities (in addition to more than $10 million from the US Department of Labor), but Tulane estimated that $75 million was necessary to reach all cocoa-producing communities in Ghana and Côte d'Ivoire with remediation activities.[68]

From the beginning, child labor advocates believed the Harkin-Engel Protocol was profoundly flawed. According to Bama Athreya, director of the International Labor Rights Forum (IRLF) at the time, "There hadn't really been good consultations with people who were child rights or child labor advocates. There seemed to be a quick but non-inclusive process to develop the protocol and then ask for NGOs' endorsement. We saw it had no teeth but there was little anyone could do to hold them accountable, apart from a name and shame strategy."[69]

The protocol had no enforcement mechanism and no clear commitment for the remediation of children who were involved in the worst forms of child labor. Under the protocol, companies committed to develop and implement "credible, mutually-acceptable, voluntary, industry-wide standards of public certification" that their cocoa was not produced with the worst forms of child labor, but it became clear over time that the industry's concept of certification bore little resemblance to a true certification program.

Simply put, certification creates a set of standards against which a product can be measured and verifies through a third party that those standards are being met. Many certification systems also confer a label on products to communicate to consumers that the product was produced under certain conditions. For agricultural products like cocoa, certification should ensure that labor standards prohibiting the use of child labor are met at every stage of the supply chain, down to the individual farm where the cocoa is produced. Although no certification system can completely guarantee that standards are met, it can give consumers greater confidence that products are produced under decent conditions. Fairtrade International, UTZ Certified, and the Rainforest Alliance are three major organizations that work with companies to help ensure that agricultural products are made ethically and sustainably, and meet ILO standards prohibiting forced and child labor.[70]

In several meetings with the US-based Child Labor Coalition in 2004, 2005, and 2007, chocolate industry representatives said that they were not willing to commit to a certification system that involved verification at an individual farm level.[71] Instead, their proposal was simply to verify the results of national surveys on child labor. In a 2008 letter to Senator Harkin, nongovernmental organizations (NGOs) pointed out that the likely outcome of the industry's proposed cocoa "certification" would be to simply confirm that child labor was still being used.[72] In a critique of the protocol, IRLF asserted that consumers had no more assurance in 2008 than they did in 2001 that their chocolate bars were not made with child labor.[73]

As NGOs' impatience grew, some decided that it was time to campaign more actively. In early 2008, Stop the Traffik, a global network based in London, began a campaign to end child trafficking in the chocolate industry. In its statement launching the campaign, it said, "We are tired of hearing excuses, how long it takes, how impossible it is but every minute the industry makes profit and the children are trafficked."[74] It called on chocolate companies to set a deadline for true certification of all their products, report annually on their efforts, provide a fair income for cocoa farmers, and set up independent, third-party auditing.

Ruth Dearnley, a British lawyer by training, helped establish Stop the Traffik in 2005 and became its CEO in 2008. She was inspired by William Wilberforce's efforts two hundred years earlier to abolish the Atlantic slave trade:

> Wilberforce struggled to make the slave trade relevant for people. A break-through was when he linked the issue of transatlantic slavery to the issue of sugar. It was a genius move. He didn't go about talking about the supply chain, but he made it clear for everyone who put sugar in their tea that they were linked to the crime that had taken place. The person who was drinking that tea had power in their hands to act, even if they never had the opportunity to meet the slaves being walked in chains portside.
>
> We are seeing the same issue today. The chocolate we eat is our connection to a supply chain where young boys are being trafficked from surrounding areas into the Ivory Coast. Guilt doesn't change anything, but the ability to take action can empower. Our passion was how to enable ordinary people to feel they could do something, because we knew that consumers have power. And in our world today, we can spread the word much faster than in Wilberforce's day.[75]

Stop the Traffik conducted its campaign almost entirely through the Internet, posting information, ideas, and resources and inviting people to participate. Tens of thousands of consumers wrote letters, sent e-mails and text messages, posted on social media, and committed to buy only certified chocolate. Stop the Traffik posted scripts and phone numbers, encouraging consumers to contact major chocolate brands to ask, "When will my chocolate be traffic free?" Activists held Fairtrade chocolate fondue parties to raise awareness and engaged in creative actions such as a Great Easter Egg Hunt in the run-up to Easter. Thousands of people visited shops in their area, searching for Fairtrade chocolate eggs, commending managers of shops that carried Fairtrade products, and sending letters of complaint to those who didn't.[76] The campaign partnered with an advertising agency that created hard-hitting images to run in media outlets near Christmas and Easter, when sales of chocolate soar. A regular blog shared action suggestions and stories from campaign supporters about their activities. Dearnley said, "When we put our materials up, people took them up in countries all over the world, translated them and made them even better."[77]

The campaign's first victory happened quickly. Stop the Traffik (STT) Netherlands and Fairfood, a local NGO, ran a full-page advertisement linking Royal Verkade, a Dutch company, with the worst forms of child labor in Ivory Coast. "Within a day we had a phone call from Fairtrade, saying that Verkade had just called them to talk about the possibility of Fairtrade sourcing for their cocoa," reported STT.[78] A few months later, Verkade announced that beginning in late 2008, it would be using 100 percent Fairtrade cocoa and sugar in its products.[79]

The next victory involved Cadbury, famous for its Dairy Milk chocolate bars. Stop the Traffik had met with Cadbury in 2006 to urge it to certify its products but was told certification was "impossible and impracticable."[80] But in late 2008, Cadbury announced that its Dairy Milk bar would be Fairtrade certified by late 2009. Stop the Traffik welcomed the decision, saying it "demonstrates the power of ordinary consumers to bring about change and freedom. . . . This is a victory for every person who has complained, campaigned and spread the message."[81]

Stop the Traffik then launched a March on Mars campaign, targeting the world's largest candy company, Mars Inc. Just six weeks later, Mars became the first major company to announce that it would certify 100 percent of its cocoa products as sustainably produced by 2020.[82] Mars partnered with Fairtrade, Rainforest Alliance, and UTZ Certified to verify that its certification standards would be met. Stop the Traffik saw the announcement as "proof that the tide is turning" and that the chocolate industry was beginning to take consumers' concerns seriously.[83] The campaign then turned its attention to another chocolate giant, Nestlé, which soon announced that its popular Kit Kat bar would be certified beginning in January 2010. In 2011, it announced that other products would also be certified by 2014. Other companies followed suit: Unilever committed in 2010 to certify 100 percent of its products by 2020, and Ferrero did the same in 2012. Dearnley reflected, "We've learned how fast change can happen. Sometimes you think that nothing is happening but you have to keep going and not feel demoralized. Then other times, you see a cascade of action."[84]

By 2010, Hershey, the largest US chocolate company, was the only major chocolate company that had made no commitment to third-party certification that its products were made without child labor. That September, three US-based organizations—Green America, IRLF, and Global Exchange—launched its Raise the Bar, Hershey! campaign, calling on Hershey to commit to sourcing

100 percent fair trade–certified cocoa beans for at least one of its top-five selling chocolate bars within two years, and certify all five of its top-selling bars within ten years.[85] The campaign pointed out that while Hershey held 42 percent of the US market share of chocolate sales, it lagged other companies in addressing child labor in its supply chain. The day that Hershey issued its first official report on corporate social responsibility, the campaign published its own alternative report, *Time to Raise the Bar: The Real Corporate Social Responsibility Report for the Hershey Company*.[86] The report discussed child labor in the cocoa industry and outlined the steps that Hershey should take to be a leader on the issue.

Over 150,000 consumers took action during the campaign, contacting Hershey through e-mails, phone calls, and petitions to urge it to commit to fair trade certification. The campaign organized Facebook "rallies" to blanket the Hershey Facebook wall with messages. A Brand Jamming Contest solicited mock commercials, advertisements, and taglines to lampoon Hershey marketing messages.[87] For every chocolate "holiday," especially Halloween and Valentine's Day, the campaign issued press releases and organized actions. On Valentine's Day 2011, hundreds of young people sent handmade Valentine cards to Hershey's CEO, calling on him to "have a heart" and take action. Initially Hershey did not respond. "For a long time, they ignored our work," said Elizabeth O'Connell, campaigns director for Green America. "They maintained that child labor wasn't Hershey's problem, it was a sector problem and an African problem, and not their problem on farms that they didn't own."[88]

In June 2011, the campaign worked with teachers' unions to organize a protest at the Hershey store in New York City's Times Square, coinciding with the World Day against Child Labor. Hundreds of teachers, students, and other consumers participated. Hershey finally agreed to a meeting, but organizers who participated in the meeting were disappointed in the company's refusal to make concrete commitments.

Campaign activists looked for ways to escalate the campaign. They went to Hershey's annual meeting of shareholders, where they asked the CEO to address child labor. They teamed up with a filmmaker, U. Robin Romano, to make his documentary about the exploitation of children, *The Dark Side of Chocolate*, available as a public education tool, together with a home screening kit. Over the course of the campaign, the film was screened hundreds of times. The campaign also worked with the American Federation of Teachers to develop a curriculum and suggested activities for teachers to use in their classrooms. In October, the campaign delivered 100,000 petition signatures to Hershey's corporate headquarters and sent copies to Hershey's board members.[89]

In early 2012, the campaign began to see progress. A donor had approached the campaign, offering to sponsor an ad during the Super Bowl about Hershey's use of child labor in cocoa production. The campaign put out a press release in advance and told Hershey what they were planning. "That got them mobilized," said O'Connell.[90] Less than a week later, Hershey announced that it would use Rainforest Alliance to certify all of its "Bliss" chocolate products beginning later that year. The announcement was Hersey's first commitment to using an independent, third-party certification system to ensure that its cocoa products were grown sustainably, without the use of forced or child labor.[91]

Organizers decided not to run the Super Bowl ad but continued the campaign. They expanded outreach to constituencies that they believed Hershey would see as mainstream consumers, such as the United Methodist Women, an 800,000-member faith-based organization. Methodist Women joined in campaign activities, and the group's executive director sent letters to the editor of the *New York Times* and *USA Today* on the tenth anniversary of the Harkin-Engel Protocol, noting that Hershey's failure to verify the source of its chocolate undermined its brand image. In advance of a regional United Methodist Women conference in Hershey, Pennsylvania, its leaders initiated a postcard campaign, urging Hershey to adopt fair trade certification for all of its chocolate products. Hershey responded by agreeing to meet with representatives of the group during the conference.[92]

The campaign decided it needed to expand its target audience further, to include Hershey's business partners. It began to contact natural food stores and food co-ops, inviting them to sign an open letter urging Hershey to fully commit to ethically sourced cocoa produced under fair labor standards. Forty-one co-ops and retailers signed the letter.[93] Campaign organizers then approached Whole Foods, a natural foods supermarket chain with 425 stores across North America and the United Kingdom. Initially Whole Foods did not respond, but less than three days after Green America set up an online petition targeting the company and urging it to sign the letter, Whole Foods announced that it was removing Hershey's artisanal Scharffen Berger chocolate line from its shelves until Hershey took steps to address child labor in its supply chain.[94]

Within a week of the Whole Foods announcement, Hershey announced that it would certify 100 percent of its cocoa by 2020.[95] "Consistent with Hershey's values, we are directly addressing the economic and social issues that impact West Africa's two million cocoa farmers and families," the company's CEO said in a public statement.[96] The company noted that certified cocoa accounted for less than 5 percent of the world's cocoa supply and that as the largest chocolate manufacturer in North America, Hershey's new commitment would significantly expand the global supply of certified cocoa.[97]

"Initially, I thought the campaign was taking forever," said O'Connell. "But when we finally saw progress, it happened really fast."[98] The campaign welcomed Hershey's announcement and urged the company to provide details of how it would reach its goal.[99] A few months later, Hershey stated publicly that it would work with three independent certifiers—UTZ, Fair Trade USA, and Rainforest Alliance—to certify 10 percent of its products by the end of 2013 and 40 to 50 percent by 2016.[100] In June 2016, the company announced that it was sourcing 50 percent of its cocoa from certified sustainable sources and was on track to reach its 2020 goal.[101]

Challenges

Child labor is inextricably linked with poverty. When families are poor, basic survival needs frequently push children into the workforce. Some argue that in these situations, limiting children's work will leave these families worse off and that allowing children to work is better than destitute children and families. While virtually all child rights advocates agree that children should be protected from the worst forms of child labor, some argue that international standards regarding the minimum age of employment are too restrictive and prohibit children from work that may not be harmful and may even be beneficial for a child's development. Bourdillon et al., for example, argue that "a 'workless' childhood free of all responsibilities may not be good preparation for adult life for children in any society and any social class."[102]

In some countries, working children have formed unions or associations to advocate for better working conditions, not for an end to child labor. In Bolivia, for example, working children formed the Union of Child and Adolescent Workers of Bolivia, which advocated on behalf of a controversial law adopted in 2014 that set the lowest legal age for employment in the world. The law allows children as young as 12 to work with parental permission for up to six hours a day as long as the work does not interfere with their education and is not harmful. Self-employed children can work from age 10.[103] Critics of the law argue that it legitimizes child labor and may encourage even more children to enter the workforce at a young age, while others argue that many children have no choice but to work and that the law protects them by regulating their work and guaranteeing a minimum wage.

Eliminating child labor in some sectors is easier than in others. In El Salvador's sugar industry, for example, individual farms belong to a limited number of sugarcane cooperatives. This structure allowed government and industry leaders to easily communicate with the leadership of the cooperatives and facilitated monitoring and awareness-raising activities on child labor. In contrast, cocoa production is extremely diffuse, relying on thousands of small-scale cocoa farms that are rarely organized into larger collectives. In this context, establishing effective interventions and monitoring is much more difficult. According to the ILO's Benjamin Smith, "It's more complex in cocoa, though that doesn't mean that cocoa plantations can't get more organized. The Sugar Association knew who to talk to, and had the structure to carry out monitoring and awareness raising. That was critical, and that's where cocoa needs to go."[104]

Despite the many commitments of the chocolate industry to address child labor, results have been disappointing. A 2015 Tulane University report, based on over a thousand household surveys in Ghana and Côte d'Ivoire, found that the number of children engaged in hazardous work in cocoa in Ghana had declined only slightly over the previous five years and had increased in Côte d'Ivoire.[105] Several factors may help explain the lack of progress, including a significant increase in cocoa production in both countries during the period, political violence in Côte d'Ivoire that disrupted child labor programs and education in cocoa-producing areas, insufficient investment by both national governments and the industry in addressing the issue, and the time required to implement certification programs to meet the 2020 goals set by major chocolate companies.

In reflecting on their campaign efforts, advocates also felt that inadequate attention had been given to the compensation of cocoa-producing families. To meet the growing international demand for chocolate, companies worked with cocoa farmers to increase the quantity and quality of their cocoa; however, salaries did not increase accordingly. These low wages fuel child labor, as farmers are unable to pay hired laborers the legally required minimum wage.[106] Elizabeth O'Connell said, "The demands of the campaign didn't go far enough to address farmers' concerns. If we get farmers more sustainable wages, it will lead to the need for less child labor."[107]

The Way Forward

At the policy level, the ILO has identified several successful interventions to reduce rates of child labor, including strong legislative frameworks, initiatives to increase children's enrollment in school, and programs to alleviate economic stress for poor families, such as cash transfer programs that provide poor families with monthly stipends. Action by the corporate sector is also required, including due diligence throughout supply chains to identify, prevent, and remedy child labor and other human rights abuses.

Advocates have found that public pressure is often necessary to prompt government and corporate action on child labor. "You have to campaign to get control of the discourse," reflected Bama Athreya.[108] The Global March against Child Labour and its high-profile 50,000-mile march through 103 countries was instrumental in the adoption of the Worst Forms of Child Labor Convention in 1999, one of the key international instruments in combating dangerous and exploitative child labor. Broad-based consumer-oriented campaigns based in Europe and the United States persuaded the world's largest chocolate companies to commit to certify their chocolate products as child labor free by 2020, and international exposure of child labor in El Salvador's sugar industry also prompted significant reforms.

To curb child labor, the right actors need to be involved. In India, BBA found that it often took a year of dialogue in local villages, involving village leaders, village assemblies, women's groups, and children themselves, to win a commitment from all stakeholders to prohibit child labor and ensure that every child attended school. In El Salvador, collaborative efforts by the country's sugar industry, government, and multinational corporations such as Coca-Cola helped spur progress in eliminating child labor in the industry. In contrast, observers believed that the Harkin-Engel Protocol on child labor and cocoa was negotiated too quickly, without the right people at the table. "The best multistakeholder initiatives emerge from negotiations and buy-in from a representative set of civil society actors and a representative set from the industry," said Bama Athreya.[109] In particular, cocoa farmers were left out of the Harkin-Engel process, with little attention to their need for sustainable income.

Commitments to end child labor also need to be enforceable. When India failed to enforce its own laws, BBA successfully used legal complaints against employers to win the freedom of children caught in bonded child labor. In El Salvador, the sugar industry adopted a clear code of conduct on child labor that applied to all sugar mills and included a zero-tolerance child labor clause in all sales contracts with sugar producers. It also introduced rigorous third-party monitoring of these commitments. Binding free-trade agreements between El Salvador and the United States, which required compliance with ILO standards, including the elimination of the worst forms of child labor, also prompted the business sector to substantially step up its response to child labor. In contrast, the Harkin-Engel Protocol to eliminate the worst forms of child labor in cocoa production in West Africa was voluntary and had no enforcement mechanisms. Ten years after the protocol was signed, Tulane University concluded that the protocol's self-regulation of the industry had yielded "mixed results" and that a "legal framework" might have been more effective in holding companies accountable.[110]

Athreya believed that "the real work on child labor in the cocoa sector was done despite the protocol, not because of it," and credited the consumer campaigns that pushed for meaningful certification with achieving real progress.[111] Elizabeth O'Connell, campaigns director for Green America, believed that one of the reasons the Raise the Bar, Hershey! campaign was successful was that it mobilized a broad group of partners.[112] Engaging not just consumers but Hershey's business partners, notably Whole Foods, was a clear tipping point for the campaign, prompting Hershey's announcement that it would certify 100 percent of its chocolate products by 2020.

Dearnley felt a significant strength of Stop the Traffik's campaign was the ability to continuously generate new resources and creative tools to keep individuals engaged with the campaign and pull new people in. She also believed that recognizing progress was essential to maintaining the campaign's momentum. "It felt like quite a long time to get our first big win," she said, referring to Cadbury's announcement that it would certify its Dairy Milk bars. "When you get moments like that and congratulate them, everyone who was part of the action learned that they were listened to."[113]

6   Corporal Punishment

HILLARY ADAMS was a 16-year-old Texas girl with a passion for technology. One day, her father discovered that she had illegally downloaded music and games from the Internet. In punishment, he removed his belt, told her to lie down on a bed, and proceeded to beat her repeatedly while she screamed and pleaded with him to stop. He yelled at her, "Are you happy? Disobeying your parents? You don't deserve to f—ing be in this house."[1] Later, her legs covered in bruises, she told him that it hurt to walk. She said his reply was, "Good."[2]

Hillary's father was an elected family court judge, and when she had previously tried to tell people that he beat her, no one would listen. She finally resorted to setting up a camera in her room that caught the beating, which took place in 2004, on tape. Several years later, she decided to make it public on the Internet. "I wanted him to be shocked and wanted other people to see it to try and get him to change," she said. "I thought this was a way to get through to him."[3] The video quickly went viral, accumulating nearly 8 million views. When confronted by the media about the beating, her father said, "In my mind, I haven't done anything wrong other than discipline my child."

Local police investigated the incident but filed no charges because of the time that had elapsed.[4] The judge was suspended with full pay but then reinstated a year later by the Texas Supreme Court. He continued serving as a judge for two more years, until he finally lost his bid for reelection in 2014.

After making the video public, Hillary said, "I've gotten messages from literally all over the world, Germany, Costa Rica, Netherlands, Australia, France, Mexico, the UK. . . . I had no idea it was such a global issue, that so many people were being hurt in their own homes. I guess nobody really knows how to talk about it."[5]

Children are subjected to violent "discipline" with alarming frequency. According to a 2014 survey, four of every five children between the ages of 2 and 14, an estimated 1 billion globally, experience physical punishment in their home on a regular basis.[6] Such punishment most often takes the form of spanking or hitting a child with a bare hand or an object such as a belt, shoe, cane, or stick, but it can also include kicking, shaking, scratching, biting, pulling hair, boxing ears, forcing children to stay in uncomfortable positions, burning, or scalding a child.[7]

Corporal (or physical) punishment is any punishment in which physical force is used and intended to cause some degree of pain or discomfort, however light.[8] It is used in schools, care institutions, and penal institutions but is most common in the home. In some countries, such as Yemen, 95 percent of children experience violent punishment by their parents or caregivers at least once a month, but even in "low-incidence" countries, like Panama, nearly half of children are subjected regularly to physical punishment.[9]

Although hitting an adult is considered assault in most countries, hitting children is commonly accepted as "discipline." Parents often hit their children because it is socially accepted and because they themselves were hit when growing up. A growing body of research, however, shows that the use of corporal punishment can cause enormous harm. Children who experience corporal punishment are more aggressive toward others and more likely to resort to violence to respond to conflict.[10] They are more likely to engage in delinquent or antisocial behavior, including bullying, lying, cheating, truancy, and criminal activity. Corporal punishment damages children's mental health, leading to greater anxiety, depression, low self-esteem, and hopelessness. It is also linked to lower IQ scores and poor school performance.[11]

The harmful impacts of corporal punishment extend well into adulthood. Adults who experienced corporal punishment as a child are more likely to engage in aggression, criminal behavior, or domestic violence toward an intimate partner or child, and they experience higher rates of depression, alcoholism, and suicidal tendencies.[12] Economists have estimated that severe physical punishment of children—taking into account short- and long-term costs for medical and other treatment, child welfare costs, and lower future earnings—costs the global economy a staggering *US$3.6 trillion* a year. This figure is twenty times higher than the estimated cost, US$170 billion, of civil wars each year.[13]

In the most extreme cases, corporal punishment can lead to injury and death. When parents physically punish their children, they are often angry, making it easy for the level of punishment to escalate beyond what was intended. Thousands of children are killed by their parents or caregivers every year.[14]

In addition, corporal punishment doesn't work as a disciplinary measure. Although it may result in short-term submission, studies have found that it does not contribute to compliance over the long term; instead, children learn the lesson that it is important not to get caught in misbehavior. Corporal punishment also damages parent-child relationships; children report that after being physically punished, they feel hurt, angry, and frightened of their parents. Of more than 250 published studies examining corporal punishment and its impacts, not a single one found any benefits to the practice.[15]

Regardless of the scientific evidence of harm, any corporal punishment violates the human rights of children. Children, like adults, have a right to respect for their dignity and physical integrity and to equal protection of the law. The Convention on the Rights of the Child obliges governments to take all appropriate measures "to protect the child from all forms of physical or mental violence, injury or abuse ... while in the care of parent(s), legal guardian(s) or any other person who has the care of that child."[16] The Committee on the Rights of the Child, which monitors compliance with the convention, has stated that this obligation "does not leave room for any level of legalized violence against children. Corporal punishment and other cruel or degrading forms of punishment are forms of violence and States must take all appropriate legislative, administrative, social and educational measures to eliminate them."[17]

In 1979, Sweden became the first country to explicitly prohibit all forms of corporal punishment of children, including in the home. During the following decade, only three others—Finland, Norway, and Austria—followed suit, and by 2001, only eleven countries had legally prohibited all corporal punishment of children.[18] That year, Peter Newell and Thomas Hammarberg launched the Global Initiative to End All Corporal Punishment of Children. This chapter explores the initiative's campaign to protect children from corporal punishment and its remarkable success, as well as a contentious national campaign in New Zealand. With the Global Initiative as a catalyst, the number of states prohibiting all corporal punishment of children quadrupled, from eleven in 2001 to fifty-two in 2017. An additional fifty-four have pledged to achieve a legal ban.[19]

The Campaign

A child rights advocate and former journalist from England, Peter Newell, began focusing his attention on corporal punishment in the 1980s. "It's a highly symbolic issue in society," he says. "The fact that it's legal to hit children reflects a concept of ownership of children. Once they're apparent, you can't leave issues like that until you have won them."[20] He helped lobby successfully for a ban on school corporal punishment in the United Kingdom and in 1989 launched EPOCH: End Physical Punishment of Children, a campaign to prohibit corporal punishment in the home and all other settings in the United Kingdom. In 1994, he took a landmark case, *A v. UK*, to the European Court of Human Rights, charging the government of the United Kingdom with violating the rights of a boy who had been beaten by his stepparent. Newell hoped that the court case would prompt a change in UK law, but the 1998 judgment forced the United Kingdom only to prohibit "severe" cases of corporal punishment; parents in the United Kingdom today can still defend violent measures as "reasonable punishment."

Newell found that activists in other countries were interested in the campaign, and in the 1990s, he began to collaborate with Thomas Hammarberg, a Swede who served as one of the first members of the UN Committee on the Rights of the Child.[21] Previously Hammarberg had served as the secretary-general of both Amnesty International and Save the Children Sweden. In 2001, the two men decided to launch the Global Initiative to End All Corporal Punishment of Children as a global campaign.

Hammarberg explained his motivation for focusing on corporal punishment:

> It goes to the very dignity of children. If this right is violated, it creates a chain reaction and violates other rights. If you are beaten up because of your opinion, you have no freedom of expression. Instead of encouraging development and the freedom to speak out and negotiate different opinions from parents and teachers, the use of violence legitimizes repressive attitudes.[22]

The Global Initiative's intention was not to put parents and other caregivers in prison for hitting children, but to use the law primarily as an educational tool to decrease its use. It argued that children should have at least the same legal protections as adults, including in the home, and that as long as corporal punishment was legal, parents and other caregivers were more likely to believe it was okay to hit children in their care. Prohibiting corporal punishment by law would motivate parents and others to look into alternative forms of discipline that did not involve physical punishment.

This was the approach Sweden took. When its parliament began to debate prohibition, members called it a "signal law," that is, a law that signaled an approach and was used primarily for public education. Before the law was enacted, parliamentarians consulted with pediatricians and lawyers about the way the law could be used to influence public opinion and create momentum to reduce the use of corporal punishment. The strategy worked. Studies found that until the 1960s, nine out of ten Swedish preschool children were spanked at home, but by the 1980s, after Sweden enacted its ban, the proportion of children spanked at home dropped to one-third, and by the 1990s, to one-fifth.[23]

Newell and Hammarberg met with the UN Committee on the Rights of the Child in May 2000 to discuss their planned campaign and launched the Global Initiative in April 2001 in Geneva. Mary Robinson, then the UN high commissioner for human rights, spoke at the event, calling for a ban on any act of violence against children. To build support, the Global Initiative secured endorsements from hundreds of national and international organizations and prominent individuals, including Desmond Tutu, the Dalai Lama and other religious leaders, and national ombudsmen and commissioners for children from around the globe.[24]

As the basis for its advocacy, the Global Initiative tracked the status of national legislation and court cases regarding corporal punishment in every country worldwide. This mapping examined all relevant national legislation, including the settings where corporal punishment might already be illegal and what further changes were necessary to achieve a comprehensive ban. It also tracked relevant court decisions, recommendations from relevant UN bodies, any commitments that countries had made to ban corporal punishment, and new laws under consideration that could be used to prohibit the practice.

The Global Initiative uses this information to systematically brief UN treaty bodies. It began with the Committee on the Rights of the Child—the committee of UN experts appointed to monitor states' compliance with the Convention on the Rights of the Child. The Global Initiative submitted information for every country coming for review before the committee; by 2015, it had submitted 258 briefings.[25] Based on the Global Initiative's information, the committee made recommendations to 188 states urging the complete prohibition of corporal punishment of children. In over a hundred of these cases, the committee made the recommendation more than once, as states came under subsequent reviews. Every few years, representatives of the Global Initiative met with the full committee to update its members regarding progress toward global prohibition and highlight key issues.[26]

Encouraged by the Committee on the Rights of the Child's willingness to take up the issue, the Global Initiative widened its focus and began making regular submissions to committees monitoring compliance with other human rights treaties, which also began recommending that states prohibit all corporal punishment of children.[27] In the case of the Committee against Torture, recommendations to prohibit corporal punishment increased sixfold after the Global Initiative started submitting its briefings.[28]

In 2006, the United Nations established the Human Rights Council to replace the Commission on Human Rights. The new Human Rights Council had an entirely new feature, the universal periodic review (UPR), under which members assess the human rights record of every UN member state every four years. The Global Initiative saw the UPR as another important opportunity to urge states to ban corporal punishment and began submitting briefings on every state, beginning with the first UPR session in 2008. During the first four-year cycle, the Global Initiative submitted briefings on 175 states; 96 of these (or 55 percent) received recommendations on corporal punishment. The Global Initiative also began meeting individually with UN missions in Geneva to discuss corporal punishment and to encourage them to recommend prohibition during states' reviews. Some missions also agreed to host briefings on the issue for other interested states. Slovenia became the most active country to raise the issue of corporal punishment during the UPR, posing questions or recommendations to more than fifty states between 2008 and 2015. Sweden and Uruguay raised the issue with more than two dozen states; over seventy countries raised the issue at least once.[29]

The UPR requires states under review to respond to the recommendations they have received by indicating whether they accept, reject, or take note of them. Between 2008 and 2015, 129 states received at least one recommendation regarding corporal punishment. By 2015, nineteen of these had banned all corporal punishment of children, and an additional thirty-eight had publicly committed to legal reform.[30]

Newell found that the UPR process was extremely useful. "It gave a new path for advocacy and helped speed things up," he said. "Slightly to my surprise, states are taking UPR recommendations more seriously than recommendations from treaty bodies."[31] Of the fifty-four states that had committed themselves publicly to prohibition by early 2017, the majority did so in the context of the UPR. Newell speculated that this might be because the UPR typically involves ministers and other high-level government representatives and is very public, whereas treaty body reviews often involve lower-level diplomats.[32]

The Global Initiative systematically follows up the recommendations from these UN processes, writing to national governments, national human rights commissions, and national nongovernmental organizations to urge them to pursue legal reform and offering technical assistance. Finding national organizations that were interested in the issue was a challenge initially. The activists found that in many countries, not a single organization was addressing corporal punishment. But as the treaty bodies and UPR began generating more recommendations and as more countries began prohibiting corporal punishment, it became easier to find organizations to follow up. The Global Initiative monitored new opportunities for legal reform, supported national organizations in their advocacy, and commented on bills and draft laws in nearly three dozen countries. In collaboration with Save the Children Sweden, the Global Initiative conducted law reform workshops in several regions and published a series of briefing papers on how to campaign for changes in law.

The Global Initiative discovered that some of the strongest opposition to eliminating corporal punishment came from religious communities. Leaders from various faiths often cited biblical texts and other scriptures that appear to condone physical punishment of children.[33] Faith-based schools and madrasas routinely practice corporal punishment, and sharia, or Islamic law, often relies on corporal punishment as part of its justice system. Religious groups opposing corporal punishment were not necessarily large but were often very well organized. When corporal punishment was raised in parliament in Wales, for example, members were flooded with e-mails from religious groups claiming their "biblical right" to use physical punishment with their children.[34]

Chris Dodd coordinates faith-based advocacy with the Global Initiative and previously helped found the Churches' Network for Non-Violence. For years, she worked in public health and early childhood development and saw violence against children as a crucial issue affecting families. "When children have their physical and mental integrity violated by corporal punishment, it opens the way for other forms of violence," she said. "It's about respect for the child, and it's about recognizing the child as a person in his or her own right."[35]

Dodd seeks to find ways of challenging those who use their scriptures and religious faith to justify corporal punishment and broadening support of religious leaders who support abolition and are willing to speak out and take action. She works with religious communities, develops resources, and conducts trainings and workshops. "It's very important to create a culture in religious communities that says corporal punishment of children is incompatible with religious values and teachings and to encourage religious communities to take action to end violent punishment of children and lead on the issue," she says.[36] She has helped develop handbooks that examine the teachings of major faiths on nonviolence. A key message is that corporal punishment is contrary to universal religious values of compassion, justice, equality, and nonviolence.

One of the most influential religious figures to take up the issue was Desmond Tutu, the Nobel Peace Prize winner and archbishop emeritus in South Africa. He issued a statement in 2006 that became widely cited:

> Progress towards abolishing corporal punishment is being made, but millions of the world's children still suffer from humiliating acts of violence and these violations of their rights as human beings can have serious lifelong effects. Violence begets violence and we shall reap a whirlwind. Children can be disciplined without violence that instils fear and misery. . . . If we really want a peaceful and compassionate world, we need to build communities of trust where children are respected, where home and school are safe places to be and where discipline is taught by example.[37]

In 2006, Dodd and Sharon Owen, the research and information coordinator for the Global Initiative, participated in a high-level meeting of religious leaders in Toledo, Spain, to discuss faith-based perspectives on corporal punishment. The meeting led to "A Multi-Religious Commitment to Confront Violence against Children" that they helped to draft and was endorsed later that year by eight hundred religious leaders from all faiths at the Eighth Assembly of Religions for Peace in Kyoto, Japan. The Kyoto Declaration addressed the role of religious communities in prohibiting and eliminating corporal punishment and called on governments to adopt legislation to prohibit all forms of violence against children.[38] "It has been hugely influential in engaging with people of all faiths on the issue," said Dodd, who uses the declaration as a basis for workshops, discussion, and as a guide for action.[39]

Although most of the organized religious opposition to banning corporal punishment has come from Christian organizations, the Global Initiative has also promoted statements from other faith leaders and groups that favor banning the practice. For example, in 2009, a group of imams in Mauritania met to determine whether Islam allowed corporal punishment of children and concluded that it was in clear contradiction to the teachings of the Quran. They issued a fatwa (religious edict) calling for an immediate end to corporal punishment, regardless of pretext.[40]

New Zealand

One of the most contentious national campaigns to prohibit corporal punishment of children took place in New Zealand. Supporters and opponents of corporal punishment engaged in nearly two years of fierce and acrimonious public debate before a law permitting parents to physically punish their children finally was overturned in 2007. The campaign was marked by intense media attention, public demonstrations, weeks of parliamentary debate, and even threats against advocates.

Initially the voices advocating for prohibition of all corporal punishment of children were few and isolated. In the 1970s, two psychologists proposed repeal of the law known as section 59 that explicitly permitted New Zealand parents to physically punish their children.[41] In the 1980s, targeted lobbying led to a prohibition on corporal punishment in child care centers, institutions, and schools, but there was little headway in banning it in the home. In 1989, New Zealand appointed its first commissioner for children, Ian Hassall, who began to advocate actively for repeal of section 59 and a full prohibition on all corporal punishment of children.

Beth Wood, a leading advocate behind New Zealand's campaign, worked for Hassall in the office of the Commissioner for Children in the early 1990s. "As a social worker, I had seen a lot of smacking, and it seemed very damaging to me," she said. "Working with Ian, I got very enthusiastic about the topic. Legislative reform felt like something that was both tangible and manageable."[42]

In 1997, the Committee on the Rights of the Child conducted its first review of New Zealand's compliance with the Convention on the Rights of the Child. It recommended that New Zealand review its law and prohibit all corporal punishment of children. That same year, Wood and a small group of women from Wellington founded EPOCH (End Physical Punishment of Children) New Zealand. They began to develop public education campaigns and resources and, most important, build a network of supportive organizations. "Over that period, EPOCH worked and worked and worked to engage other organizations," Wood recalled. "I can't tell you how many conferences I attended to present the issue. We tried to engage advocacy organizations and major social service providers, violence prevention agencies, the Pediatric society, and early childhood education associations."[43] In general, however, the campaign was fairly low level, marked by sporadic lobbying of politicians, some media and public education work, and opportunistic presentations at conferences.[44]

In response to the Committee on the Rights of the Child's initial recommendations, New Zealand's cabinet instructed government officials to report on how other countries approached the issue of corporal punishment. The Ministry of Justice conducted research on public opinions regarding the law and found that a strong majority—80 percent—of parents believed that it was acceptable to smack a child, though only 9 percent believed that it was an "effective" strategy in guiding a child toward better behavior. The ministry said publicly that it supported alternative forms of discipline but that the government had no plans to repeal section 59.[45]

In late 2003, the convergence of three events brought increased attention to the issue of corporal punishment. In September, a 6-year-old girl, Coral Burrows, was brutally beaten and killed by her mother's boyfriend. He had driven her to school, and when she refused to get out of the car in the pouring rain, he flew into a rage and punched her repeatedly, breaking her jaw in two places. He drove her, unconscious, into the countryside, and when he realized she was still alive, he beat her head with a tree branch, fracturing her skull.[46] The case generated huge media attention. Just weeks after her murder, UNICEF published a new report that placed New Zealand third among the world's richest countries in its rate of child deaths from maltreatment. The report found that children in New Zealand were six times more likely to die from physical abuse as in the other countries surveyed.[47] That same month, the Committee on the Rights of the Child concluded its second review of New Zealand, criticizing its failure to repeal section 59 and again recommending that the country prohibit corporal punishment of children.

That year, Sue Bradford, a member of parliament from the Green Party, introduced a bill to repeal section 59. Wood had spoken with her about corporal punishment over the years, and Bradford said she was influenced to introduce the bill by the Committee on the Rights of the Child's recommendations, New Zealand's high rates of family violence, the urging of advocates on the issue, and her own experience as a mother. "Physical punishment harms children and is unnecessary," she said. "It also affronts my personal values about how human beings ought to treat each other."[48]

In 2005, Bradford's bill was placed on the parliamentary agenda, which catapulted the issue onto the public agenda. The topic was now on the front page of newspapers, the lead story on evening television news, and the focus of radio talk shows. Groups opposing the repeal of section 59 began organizing aggressively, buying full-page ads in newspapers and launching a petition campaign that garnered over 200,000 signatures. Their opposition to Bradford's bill focused on three primary concerns: that physical punishment was a necessary and positive aspect of parental discipline, that the proposed law unnecessarily intruded into family life, and that the repeal of section 59 would result in criminal prosecution of parents for even minor cases of physical punishment.

The selection of Bradford's bill was unexpected, but when it happened, advocates for the prohibition of corporal punishment were ready to take advantage of the opportunity. "It was a matter of luck that it was drawn then," said Wood, "but we had worked for years and years to build a base of support."[49] Advocates had gathered a wealth of research supporting abolition, established relationships with key politicians and other prominent leaders, and developed a wide network of supporters.[50] When Bradford's bill was selected, 140 organizations already supported prohibition, an impressive number for a small country like New Zealand.

Once Bradford's bill was drawn, organizations supporting repeal began meeting regularly to strategize and coordinate campaign activities. The main goals were to increase public support for repeal, counter misinformation, and lobby politicians to gain support for the bill's passage. To do this, advocates maintained regular contact with politicians in Wellington, providing them with briefing sheets and other arguments in support of repeal, and ensured a significant presence in the gallery every time parliament debated the bill. Wood believed that the direct contact with politicians was essential in gaining their support. "It was the personal conversations, backed up with information, research, and UN comments," she said.[51] The children's commissioner's office continued to support repeal of the law.

The campaign developed media kits addressing myths and misunderstandings around the proposed law, produced media releases, and presented spokespeople supporting prohibition to newspapers, radio, and television. "In a small country, there are relatively few tv stations and newspapers," said Wood, "so we tried to get to know journalists and get them onside. It was contact, contact, contact."[52]

Save the Children New Zealand commissioned and published research focusing on children's experiences of corporal punishment, finding that 40 percent of 5- to 7-year-olds reported being smacked or hit around the face or head, and 25 percent had been hit with objects including belts, canes, tennis rackets, and spatulas.[53] The study also found that many children believed that their parents beat them not to provide guidance but out of anger.[54]

The campaign reached out to celebrities and religious organizations to secure their support and provided avenues for religious leaders to speak out on the issue. They also established a website that provided information for supporters, including an easy mechanism to send e-mails to members of parliament in support of repeal. This mechanism proved extremely useful; politicians reported that before it was set up, the majority of the e-mails they received on the issue opposed the bill; after the mechanism was established, the majority of e-mails were in support.[55] When the public was invited to comment on the bill, the campaign's network responded; 185 organizations made well-informed and referenced submissions.

As interest in the issue grew, several city councils voted to support repeal of section 59. Ngongotaha, a Maori community of four thousand on New Zealand's North Island, declared its intention to become the "first smack-free community in New Zealand and the safest place in the world to bring up children."[56] However, opponents also intensified their efforts, organizing rallies in several locations around the country, coordinating an extensive lobbying campaign, and bringing international experts to New Zealand to advocate in favor of physical punishment.

As the bill worked its way through the political process, a recurring concern was possible prosecution of parents for relatively minor acts of physical punishment or for restraining a child to protect him or her from danger. It became clear that for the law to pass, amendments would need to be made to address the public's anxiety.

May 2, 2007, turned out to be a watershed. The debate over the bill had consumed parliament for a month, and tensions were running high. Hundreds of the bill's supporters packed the capital's cathedral for an ecumenical prayer vigil with religious leaders, while outside, over a thousand noisy protesters gathered in front of parliament, waving banners and chanting slogans opposing the controversial "antismacking law."

That morning, Prime Minister Helen Clark and the leader of the opposition, John Key, held a surprise press conference to announce their joint support for an amended bill. The new amendment explicitly stated that the police had the discretion not to prosecute cases considered "inconsequential" to the public interest. Following the press conference, the prime minister and several dozen other politicians left the parliament building, walked past the angry protesters, and filed into the cathedral to join the prayer vigil, where they received a standing ovation from the supporters assembled there. Wood recalled, "It was one of the most amazing experiences of my life, seeing those politicians enter the cathedral."[57]

That evening, a large majority of members of parliament voted in favor of the pending bill. Two weeks later, New Zealand became the first English-speaking country and the seventeenth in the world to prohibit all corporal punishment of children.

Several years after the law was adopted, Wood reflected, "We were lucky that there were politicians in 2007 that were prepared to stick their necks out about it. There were enough of them that believed that it was the right thing to do, from both a legal point of view and child's best interest point of view."[58] Key to the law's passage were Sue Bradford and Prime Minister Clark. Just after the law's adoption, Clark stated:

> In all conscience there is no way I could have led a party that didn't support a change. The change was about trying to stop the appalling toll of death and injury for children in homes in our country. When you have the opportunity to do something about it you can either take that opportunity or curse yourself for the rest of your life that you didn't act.[59]

The change in the law changed public attitudes. Before legal reform, surveys had found consistently that approximately 80 percent of the public supported the legal use of corporal punishment. The year after the law was adopted, 62 percent of New Zealand parents surveyed believed it was okay to use physical punishment, and by 2013, that figure had dropped to 37 percent.[60]

Growing Momentum

By the end of 2007, twenty-four states had prohibited all corporal punishment of children. Over the next decade, that number would more than double, as more and more countries acted on recommendations from the UPR, treaty bodies, and national campaigns. As the number grew, it became easier to use peer pressure with states as leverage. Hammarberg, who became the Council of Europe's commissioner for human rights in 2006, continued to raise the issue in his country visits. With countries that had not yet abolished corporal punishment, he would ask, "Will you be in the minority? Other countries have done it, why is it so difficult for you to do it?" He reflected, "The comparative approach had some impact, especially as we approached 50 percent in Europe."[61]

In 2013, Newell brought complaints against seven European countries before the European Committee of Social Rights, alleging that Belgium, Cyprus, the Czech Republic, France, Ireland, Italy, and Slovenia were in violation of the European Social Charter, which specifically prohibits violence against children.[62] The complaints claimed that none of the countries had laws that adequately protected children from physical punishment. Each of the seven countries had ratified an additional protocol to the charter, which allows organizations recognized by the Council of Europe to bring complaints against them. The Global Initiative explained, "The strategy was a simple one really. We looked at each of the countries [which had not yet prohibited corporal punishment] that had ratified the additional protocol that lets us bring a collective complaint and then targeted them. We thought—if you can do seven, then why not, rather than just doing one?"[63]

In responding to the complaint, the government of Cyprus wrote that it was working on law reform to complete prohibition of corporal punishment of children. In 2015, the committee issued its findings on the remaining countries, finding that five of the six—Ireland, Slovenia, Belgium, the Czech Republic, and France—were in breach of the charter.[64] The committee further noted a "wide consensus" at both the European and international levels that the corporal punishment of children should be "expressly and comprehensively" prohibited in law.[65] By 2017, both Ireland and Slovenia had changed their laws and banned corporal punishment.[66] The French parliament adopted a law prohibiting corporal violence in late 2016, but the provision was later removed by the Constitutional Council.[67]

Challenges

Ending the violent punishment of children is not easy. Many people, including policymakers, do not perceive corporal punishment as violence or a violation of children's rights. Because corporal punishment is so ingrained in many cultures, it is often seen as a normal and reasonable form of discipline. Most people who spank their children were themselves spanked, and in many countries, strong majorities of people still support the practice. In the United States, for example, a 2013 survey of over two thousand adults found that 81 percent believed it was sometimes appropriate to spank their children. This figure had changed little from nearly twenty years previously, when 87 percent of respondents said it was sometimes appropriate.[68]

Policymakers may resist attempts to legislate on the issue out of a belief that the government should keep its hand out of family affairs or that change in legislation should only follow changes in attitudes. Hammarberg recalled that while many government officials he met agreed personally that corporal punishment should be abolished, they rationalized that "the public is not ready for it yet," citing public opinion polls that favored corporal punishment.[69] Some also argued that attitudes change more readily by promoting positive discipline through education campaigns, supporting parenting classes, and positive discipline manuals. Newell found that such efforts generally fell short:

> You can't achieve children's rights without changing the law, and anyway, law is a very powerful tool for changing social norms. Of course you won't achieve a big change in attitudes and practice by just changing the law: you need to accompany it with widespread dissemination of the law and children's right to protection, awareness-raising of the harm that corporal punishment does,

and education on positive discipline. But in the absence of legal reform, educational strategies have little impact. The UK has tried this, but with little effect.[70]

The examples of Sweden and New Zealand show the impact of legal reform on public attitudes. In both countries, support for corporal punishment fell significantly following changes in the law.

Well-organized religious groups actively oppose law reform, often defending corporal punishment as a "biblical right" based in scripture. At the same time, the world's major religions all embrace universal religious values of compassion, justice, equality, and nonviolence. Prominent religious figures who do not support corporal punishment have played an important role in the campaign for prohibition.

The Way Forward

Over a decade and a half, the Global Initiative built a systematic and highly effective campaign to bring attention to corporal punishment as a fundamental violation of children's rights and, more important, to persuade governments to take concrete action by banning it in law.

The foundation of the campaign was creating a detailed global map of the legality of corporal punishment in every country and keeping it up to date. Newell credits Sharon Owen, the Global Initiative's research and information coordinator, for this significant contribution. "Both of us find it extraordinary that other campaigns on children's rights issues do not see such mapping as the necessary basis for advocacy," he says. The Global Initiative used the information systematically with treaty bodies and the UPR to generate recommendations to states, and for national level advocacy. Hammarberg also relied heavily on the Global Initiative's legislative mapping in his advocacy: "Every time I went to a country I knew exactly where they were on this issue because of the Global Initiative's constantly updated analysis. It has been very skillful in giving information that's been relevant for every situation."[71]

Another critical component of the campaign was the systematic use of UN human rights mechanisms. The Global Initiative used its information to methodically brief relevant UN treaty bodies, submit information for the UPR, and encourage allied states to regularly raise the issue with countries undergoing the UPR. An independent assessment of the Global Initiative concluded in 2015 that this strategy had been particularly influential and found a clear correlation between the interventions of the Global Initiative and the countries that have prohibited corporal punishment.[72]

Another key to the campaign has been careful messaging. One of the Global Initiative's most compelling arguments was that children should receive the same protection under the law from violence as adults. It reasoned, "If the law prohibits you from beating an adult, why should you be able to beat a child?" Hammarberg reflected, "This is a lesson for other campaigns. Be very focused and develop the messaging very carefully. Stick with that argumentation and follow through with information."[73]

Many of the Global Initiative's activities were behind the scenes, quietly prodding policymakers, providing resources and drafting statements for others to use, and helping to facilitate reform. "The whole aim always is to get other people to own the issue and take credit," said Newell. "The focus should be for governments and MPs [members of parliament] to take up the issue and pursue it to success. It's remarkable how much you can achieve if you don't feel any need to take credit for it. It's not just a false form of modesty, it's an advocacy strategy."[74]

For both policymakers and advocates, a key lesson of the campaign is that legal reform should not wait for a change in public attitudes and that prohibiting corporal punishment can, in fact, prompt significant shifts in both behavior and public opinion. Advocates can build on the growing momentum against corporal punishment by using the growing body of research on its costs and harms; fully using the UN human rights architecture (including opportunities for formal recommendations through treaty bodies and the UPR); and strengthening alliances among organizations, with the religious community, and with legislators.

Newell said that when he and Hammarberg established the Global Initiative, their goal was to accelerate the trend toward prohibition across the world. "I'm a very impatient person," he reflected, "but the progress is definitely accelerating."[75] When asked what others could learn from the New Zealand campaign to prohibit corporal punishment, Beth Wood replied, "Persistence. Leadership and persistence. Just persisting and growing a movement about it."[76]

7 Child Sex Tourism

JOHN WRENSHALL, a balding man with gray hair and wire-rim glasses, was a former Boy Scout leader from Calgary, Canada. He also exploited children for sex. He served time in a Canadian prison for sexual abuse of boys in a church choir and then moved to Bangkok, Thailand, in 2000. There, he taught English at an international school for nearly ten years while simultaneously running a "travel service" for men seeking sex with young Thai boys. In e-mails to potential customers, he gave prices for sex acts on children and encouraged travelers to bring bubble bath and other items that were hard to find in Thailand. Wrenshall allowed his customers to videotape and photograph their abuse of young victims. He also victimized boys, some as young as 4 years old, to "train" them for his paying customers.[1]

One of Wrenshall's customers was Wayne Nelson Corliss, an actor and children's entertainer from New Jersey who was known for playing Santa Claus at Christmas events. With Wrenshall's help, Corliss traveled to Thailand three times to have sex with two boys, ages 6 and 9. Interpol identified him by releasing a sanitized photo of Corliss sexually abusing a Thai boy and requesting help to identify the man. Within forty-eight hours, police arrested Corliss. The police found over a thousand images of child pornography on his computers, including photos of him personally abusing young boys.[2] Corliss was prosecuted and sentenced to twenty years in prison. Wrenshall himself was arrested at London's Heathrow Airport in 2008 and extradited to the United States, where he was sentenced to twenty-five years in prison.[3]

The commercial sexual exploitation of children, including child prostitution and child pornography, is a multibillion-dollar industry affecting millions of children each year.[4] The rapid expansion of global tourism has fueled the sexual exploitation of children in travel and tourism (often referred to as "child sex tourism"), with increasing numbers of people traveling locally or internationally to engage in sexual activities with children. Perpetrators often believe that by traveling overseas, they can escape detection and that lax local laws or corrupt law enforcement offer protection. The proliferation of Internet travel sites offers tourists anonymity, allowing them to book travel and accommodations and find other services, including sex, online. According to End Child Prostitution, Child Pornography and Trafficking of Children for Sexual Purposes (ECPAT), the leading organization combating child sex tourism, it is a crime "fuelled by a toxic mix of power, impunity and anonymity."[5]

Sex tourism became common in Southeast Asia as a legacy of the Vietnam War. US soldiers on leave traveled to Thailand and other countries in the region, often seeking sex during their time off. During the height of the war, tens of thousands flew to Thailand every week.[6] Increased demand for sex produced middlemen who found it profitable to secure women and girls for the foreign soldiers. Some tour operators began promoting Thailand as "the sex capital of the world."[7] The spread of HIV and AIDS in the 1980s fueled demand for sex with underage girls because perpetrators believed they would be less likely to become infected.

The Internet became a boon for sex tourism. Organized prostitution tours from the United States started appearing on the web in 1995. One of the first sex tour websites, PIMPS 'R' US, offered four-day/three-night group prostitution tours to the Dominican Republic, promising a "wonderful setting" including "many female prostitutes." Ads for "erotic vacations" to Costa Rica informed potential clients that a "companion" would meet them at their hotel and offered multiple "companions" for longer tours. As travelers returned from these trips, they posted information on Internet newsgroups, providing advice on locations where others could go to buy sex.[8]

As more and more developing countries build thriving tourism industries, criminals see the demand for sex by outside visitors as an opportunity for profit. Recruiters, traffickers, and even family members draw vulnerable children into commercial sexual exploitation, often through deception, violence, or drugs. Children from poor families and those with little education, opportunity, or family support are most likely to be pulled into the sex trade.

A "preferential" child sex tourist travels specifically with the aim of abusing children. Most perpetrators, however, are "situational child sex tourists," who take advantage of the underage sex market in tourist destinations but do not sexually abuse children at home. Some justify their behavior on the belief that it is acceptable in the culture of the place they are visiting or that they are "help-ing" a local child economically.[9] One offender rationalized, "They are different here, do you get what I mean? People do not have the same prejudices here as at home. Here they are truly free. . . . As they live in a poor country, the majority of these children have had a difficult time and this gives them a little taste of the good life."[10] Despite the term *child sex tourist*, perpetrators may travel for leisure or business, with most coming from Europe, North America, Russia, Japan, Australia, and New Zealand.[11]

The consequences for child victims can include serious and long-lasting emotional, psychological, and physical damage, including physical injury, sex-ually transmitted infections, guilt, low self-esteem, depression, and, in some cases, suicide.[12] Most children never report the abuse out of fear, shame, a sense of obligation to their intermediary, or, in some situations, concern that they will be prosecuted.

The Convention on the Rights of the Child obliges states parties to pro-tect children from all forms of sexual exploitation and sexual abuse, includ-ing their use for prostitution or pornography.[13] An optional protocol to the convention was adopted in 2000, specifically addressing the sale of children, child prostitution, and child pornography, and setting out specific measures for states to take to prevent sexual exploitation of children and hold perpetra-tors accountable. Yet the scale of sexual exploitation indicates that most gov-ernments have failed to uphold these obligations. This chapter explores civil society efforts to engage not only governments but also the tourism industry to better protect children.

ECPAT

Amihan Abueva, a long-time Filipina activist, first became aware of the sex-ual exploitation of children during the Vietnam War in the 1970s. The United States maintained large military bases in the Philippines, and Abueva observed women and girls working in bars that catered to US soldiers. Through groups working with street children, she discovered clear links between tourism and the sexual exploitation of children, particularly involving US soldiers on leave.

Abueva became involved in one of the first studies of child sex tourism, conducted in the 1980s by a church-based organization in Thailand.[14] The study documented child sexual abuse by foreign tourists in several Asian coun-tries, including Sri Lanka, the Philippines, and Thailand. In 1990, activists from the region met in Thailand to discuss the results. "We were appalled," recalled Abueva.[15] It was clear that child sex tourism was a big problem and that none of their countries had clear laws to protect children. They decided to initiate a three-year campaign to end child sex tourism in Asia.[16]

The campaign, End Child Prostitution in Asian Tourism (ECPAT), started with just a few thousand dollars. Organizers set up an international office in Bangkok and national offices in the Philippines, Taiwan, and Sri Lanka. In the Philippines, Abueva approached senators and other prominent individuals to endorse the campaign, and when a new government was elected in 1992, she set up a group to work for a law to protect children from sexual exploitation, including sex tourism. The law, passed that same year, was one of the group's earliest successes.

"We realized that child sex tourism couldn't be solved only in the countries that children came from, but needed work in the countries where tourists came from," said Abueva. She and another ECPAT founder, Ron O'Grady, traveled to European countries to speak about the issue. By late 1991, ten solidarity groups had formed in Western countries.[17] A group of German parliamentarians came to Thailand to learn about the issue and then worked to get a law passed in Germany to make it possible to prosecute Germans who sexually abused children in other countries. Over the next two years, similar extraterritorial legislation was adopted in Australia, Belgium, France, New Zealand, Sri Lanka, Taiwan, and the United States.[18]

In 1994, ECPAT organized a global conference to mobilize action on the commercial sexual exploitation of children. The activists believed that governments needed to be involved and that they would be most likely to attend if another government hosted the conference. Helena Karlén, ECPAT's first vice chair and a former Swedish diplomat, recalled, "We looked at a world map and asked ourselves, 'what sympathetic countries do we have?'"[19] They decided to focus on Sweden. Karlén was initially skeptical that Sweden was the right choice because of upcoming elections. But the timing turned out to be fortuitous. Karlén contacted government officials she believed would become ministers or have influence in a new government. "Once the elections happened, it turned out I guessed pretty well," she said.

Immediately after the Swedish election, Karlén asked for a meeting with the new prime minister. To her amazement, he agreed to see her and O'Grady. After two hours, Karlén and O'Grady left the meeting with a promise that Sweden would host the first World Congress against the Commercial Sexual Exploitation of Children. UNICEF and the NGO Group for the Rights of the Child (now known as Child Rights Connect) agreed to help organize the conference. ECPAT representatives traveled to different regions to encourage organizations that might be interested in participating.

Just two weeks before the conference, an arrest in Belgium made the sexual abuse of children world news. Marc Dutroux was arrested for kidnapping, torturing, and sexually abusing six girls and young women, ranging in age from 8 to 19. He held two of the girls, both 8 years old, in a basement for over a year, where he sexually abused them repeatedly and made pornographic videos of the abuse. The girls eventually starved to death.

Europe was shaken by the Dutroux case, said Karlén. "The governments believed that these abuses happened in other parts of the world, but not in 'civilized' Europe."[20] Interest in the Stockholm Congress soared. The Swedish prime minister had initially predicted that about 50 governments might attend. But when the congress convened in Stockholm in August 1996, 122 governments were present. In total, more than thirteen hundred delegates participated, including nongovernmental and UN representatives from around the world, and a delegation of forty-seven young people. Participants adopted the Stockholm Agenda for Action, committing themselves to combat the commercial sexual exploitation of children, including mobilization of the business sector and tourism industry, the development and implementation of extrajudicial jurisdiction to prosecute child sex abusers, increased use of extradition, and the seizure of assets and other sanctions against perpetrators committing crimes against children in destination countries.[21]

Bolstered by the support for the World Congress, ECPAT decided to pursue a global campaign. It changed its name to ECPAT: End Child Prostitution, Child Pornography and Trafficking of Children for Sexual Purposes, and grew into an international network working to eliminate all forms of commercial sexual exploitation of children.[22] By 2017, it had ninety member organizations in eighty-two countries.

The Code of Conduct for the Protection of Children from Sexual Exploitation in Travel and Tourism

In 1994, Helena Karlén attended one of ECPAT's first global meetings, held in Bangkok. She said that what she learned about child sex tourism in Asia "shocked me to the bones."[23] She began to think about how to engage the tourism industry in addressing the issue and realized that the environmental movement's outreach to businesses provided a useful example. "These companies realized that being environmentally friendly would get them great credit," she said. "I thought that the next step, to protect children, was not so big."[24] Her initial efforts, however, were discouraging. In her first discussions with representatives of the tourism industry, they denied they had clients who engaged in sexual abuse of children. Companies were afraid that being linked to child sex tourism would drive customers away. "The topic is so sensitive," Karlén says. "It's so hard, so difficult for any normal human being to accept that it exists. That goes for politicians, NGOs, people with companies, any human being. You don't want to accept that this happens."[25]

Karlén persevered and identified allies at both the World Tourism Organization and the Universal Federation of Travel Agents Association. At her kitchen table, she began drafting criteria for what became the Code of Conduct for the Protection of Children from Sexual Exploitation in Travel and Tourism. The idea behind the code was that tourism-related companies would commit to create a zero-tolerance environment for potential child sex tourists by taking specific, concrete actions. As she drafted provisions for the code, she sent them for feedback to her allies at the World Trade Organization and the Travel Agents Association. One weekend, Marina Diotallevi, from World Trade Organization, flew to Stockholm to work with Karlén on the code at Karlén's home.

The final code included six steps for companies that committed to it: adopt corporate policies against sexual exploitation of children, educate and train their personnel, provide information to travelers, secure commitments against child sexual exploitation in contracts with suppliers, engage with key stakeholders in tourism destinations, and report annually on their compliance with the code.[26]

Once the code was ready, Karlén approached Fritidsresor (Free Time Travel), a Swedish tour company that was known for its environmentally friendly policies. "I was fortunate to get a very sympathetic person on the line," she recalled. "They said, 'We don't have clients like that.' I said, 'Of course not, but you don't want them to come.'"[27] In 1998, Fritidsresor became the first company to commit to the code. Other tour operators in Sweden and Scandinavia began to sign up as well. ECPAT began promoting the code in other countries, telling businesses that the code was not only a way to help keep children safe but also provided the companies with a competitive edge by being seen as a leader in the tourism sector and developing a reputation as a responsible brand. They also argued that the code offered businesses the opportunity to mitigate potential risks of being implicated in child sexual exploitation and provided connections with other leaders in the tourism industry.[28]

By 2014, more than thirteen hundred companies from sixty-six countries had joined the code, including leading hotel chains such as Accor, travel agencies such as Carlson, tour operators, airlines, and rental car companies. In 2003, British Airways gave the code the Tourism for Tomorrow award, and Europe's Organization for Security and Cooperation recognized the code as "the primary international tool for preventing and combatting child sex tourism in the travel and tourism sector."[29]

As part of the code, Air France aired videos on its long-haul flights, warning passengers that they could be criminally prosecuted for engaging in child sex tourism. One of the code's largest members, the Accor hotel chain, trains over thirty thousand employees every year to be alert for child sex tourism and how to report it. According to ECPAT leaders, the biggest impact of the code has been in raising awareness and changing attitudes. "It's now internalized in the industry that the commercial sexual exploitation of children should not be part of tourism," says Theo Noten of ECPAT Netherlands. "Employees are not only looking for it in their workplace, but go home with the awareness and talk about it in their communities."[30]

A 2012 evaluation of the code by UNICEF's Innocenti Research Center found that despite limited resources, the code achieved significant success in a short period of time in raising awareness of child sexual exploitation in travel and tourism, achieving international recognition and respect, and securing a large number of members, including some major players in the travel industry. The assessment also noted that the code was one of the first instances where the private sector acknowledged responsibility to protect human rights in the context of its business practices. It took another thirteen years after the code was launched before the United Nations Human Rights Council established global standards of practice with regard to business and human rights, by endorsing the Guiding Principles for Business and Human Rights (also known as the Ruggie Principles).[31]

The Code in Costa Rica

"When tourists arrive from other countries and get into my taxi, the first question they ask is, 'Where are the girls? Where are the little girls?'"
—**Taxi driver in Costa Rica, 2004**[32]

A lawyer by training, Milena Grillo has run Fundacion Paniamor, a Costa Rican NGO, for more than twenty-five years. She attended the Stockholm Congress in 1996, where she was shocked to learn that Interpol had identified Costa Rica as a destination for sex tourism. Once back home, she pulled together six or seven organizations to look at the issue. "We started doing our own research and found it was true," she said. "We could see it at hotels. We realized the issue was present in the country but that no one was addressing it."[33]

Previously Paniamor had been working with the health and education sector to address children's issues, but it realized that to combat the impunity of sexual offenders, it needed allies in the police and judicial system. The group began to look at Costa Rica's legislative framework and helped to revise its criminal laws.

Grillo learned of the code in 2001 at the Yokohama Congress on Commercial Sexual Exploitation of Children, a follow-up to the Stockholm Congress. She saw the code as a way of addressing the demand side of child sex tourism by focusing on the perpetrators, particularly foreign tourists, and their intermediaries. She explained:

> It wasn't that we thought foreign tourists created the main demand. We know that the main demand is from the local guys. But foreign tourism brings so much money to the market that it becomes attractive to children, families, and organized crime. With drugs or arms, criminal networks can only sell their goods once. But with girls, criminal networks can provide some clothes and jewels and then sell them as many times as they want. The rate of profit is immense.[34]

Grillo knew that she needed allies in the tourism industry. She approached the National Chamber of Tourism, Chamber of Hotels, and the National Association of Professionals in Tourism. "We needed to partner with groups that had the muscle to mobilize," she said. "When they understood the problem, they said, 'We're in.'"[35] In contrast, the government reacted negatively, denying that child sex tourism was happening. It was concerned that raising the issue would tarnish Costa Rica's reputation and draw more sex tourists to the country.

With a small grant from the International Labour Organization, Paniamor undertook a viability study with the industry. Staff surveyed managers and human resources staff at hotels and tour operators regarding their awareness of child sex tourism, the role of the tourism sector, and what kind of support and training they would need to address it. Paniamor concluded that the code could be a useful tool for organizing in Costa Rica. It developed an advisory council with representatives from the tourism industry and organized a public education campaign that followed the path of tourists from the time they arrived at the airport, to when they rented a car, to their hotel. At the airport baggage carousel, for example, signs informed visitors that sex with a child under the age of 18 was a crime punishable by jail time. "At every step, we ensured there was some message, and training for the persons involved," said Grillo.[36]

When promoting the code with companies, organizers adopted the tourism industry's discourse about sustainability and argued that addressing child sex tourism was essential to present Costa Rica as a sustainable tourism destination. They presented the code's benefits as reducing criminal activity, enhancing Costa Rica's reputation, and building ethical tourism. A 2012 assessment also found that implementation of the code increased employee morale and staff retention and that employees believed that code training contributed to a safer workplace.[37]

By 2015, more than four hundred Costa Rican hotels, tour operators, and other companies had signed the code, and Paniamor staff had trained more than six thousand workers in the industry to recognize and report child sex tourism. Initially companies were required only to train two staff members in the code, but as interest in the initiative grew, companies were expected to train 100 percent of their staff before they were allowed to join and display the code's logo.

As they implemented the code, hotels and other businesses put systems into place to deter child sexual exploitation. For example, the Radisson Hotel in San José developed a system with taxi drivers. If drivers believed they were transporting a client with an underage girl, they would flash their lights when they arrived at the hotel. The arrangement allowed the taxi driver to receive the fare, and hotel staff then blocked the client's access to the hotel. Some tour operators shared with Paniamor e-mail queries that they received from prospective visitors to Costa Rica, asking about access to underage girls. The tour operators responded that they did not handle that kind of business and that such activity is illegal in Costa Rica.[38]

In 2008, the Costa Rican Tourism Institute made affiliation with the code a prerequisite to receive the Certificate of Sustainable Tourism. By 2009, the government integrated implementation of the code into its national policy for sustainable tourism.

Grillo believes that the code has mobilized Costa Rica's tourism sector to adopt a zero-tolerance approach to child sex tourism and has had a substantial impact. At least eleven foreign tourists have been criminally prosecuted for engaging in child sex tourism in Costa Rica, including nine perpetrators from the United States. "From our perspective, the goal is not to have jails full of foreigners," says Grillo. "We want to deter these crimes, and ensure fewer children are victimized."[39]

Challenges

ECPAT believes that the sexual exploitation of children in travel and tourism has outpaced the response and that more children are affected than ever before. Tourism continues to grow: the number of people crossing international borders doubled from 527 million in 1995 to 1.3 billion in 2014.[40] New regions of the world have become popular destinations, and the profile of child sex offenders has changed, with fewer coming from Western countries and more from India, China, and Japan.[41] According to ECPAT:

> Twenty years ago, it might have been possible to sketch a rough global map showing where international travelling sex offenders were from, and where they were going. Today, the distinctions between countries of origin and countries of destination are blurring. Terms such as country of "origin," "destination" or "transit" are rapidly becoming outdated—countries can be any of these, or even all three, at different times.[42]

The nature of travel and tourism has evolved. More tourists are using AirBnB and other booking sites that access private homes rather than established hotels. So-called voluntourism is on the rise, with foreign travelers volunteering at orphanages and other programs that give them access to underage children. Offenders also have become more sophisticated at using new technologies to exploit children. For example, in some communities, intermediaries pay parents to use webcams to stream images of their children performing sexual acts to offenders in other countries.[43]

The code has acknowledged shortcomings in addressing child sexual exploitation. The lack of any baseline data makes it impossible to measure whether the code has been successful in preventing child sexual exploitation. Reporting abuses under the code is voluntary, while some critics believe it should be mandatory. The code may also deter sexual exploitation in some locations but simply shift it to others, where it is harder to detect and laws are weak or unenforced. Grillo, for example, acknowledges that as Costa Rica has become known for combating child sex tourism, some perpetrators are simply changing their destination, traveling to the Dominican Republic or Cuba instead.

While a large number of companies have signed the code, ECPAT estimated in 2015 that only 250 to 300 were actively implementing it. The Innocenti assessment found that while most signatories have adopted a policy on child sex tourism and have conducted some training, only a few provide information to tourists or report on their code-related activities.[44]

Activists who work with the code caution that it is limited in what it can accomplish. "It's a wonderful self-regulating mechanism to organize participation of the tourism sector to close their doors to the sexual exploitation of children and educate their clients that this is not allowed," says Grillo. "But the Code can't do more than that."[45]

The Way Forward

A 2016 global study by ECPAT concluded that a complex and multifaceted issue such as the sexual exploitation of children in travel and tourism cannot be addressed effectively through ad hoc and siloed approaches. A key finding, it found, is that effective responses are always cross-sectoral, ensuring effective laws, strong enforcement, better protection of child victims, and an end to impunity for offenders.[46] Such efforts must engage key stakeholders, including government authorities, NGOs, the travel and tourism sector, the information and communications technology industry, and companies with traveling staff.[47]

ECPAT also urged a new understanding of the sexual exploitation of children in travel and tourism, reflecting the reality that offenders are not just Western tourists but also local and regional travelers, people traveling for business, as well as expatriates, voluntourists, or "caregivers" living abroad. It argues for a broader framing of the issue as "acts of sexual exploitation of children embedded in the context of travel, tourism, or both."[48]

A comprehensive 2012 UN report on the sexual exploitation of children in travel and tourism recommended several key steps to address the problem, including stronger legal frameworks; making the code a legal obligation for all concerned businesses; regular monitoring of tourist areas by law enforcement; better information-gathering systems on offenders; child-sensitive complaints, justice, and support systems; ongoing awareness raising and training; and better cooperation between law enforcement systems.[49]

"You need to put in place different pieces to protect children," says Grillo. "Each actor needs to play a different role. A role for the tourism industry, a role for the police, a role for families. . . . The more complex problems can be addressed if you study it in detail, identify the different elements that allow it to happen and then look for those in a position of power to tackle those elements. It's not a short-term intervention. You have to keep going."[50]

Criminal prosecution of perpetrators is vital for deterrence and ultimately rests with law enforcement. But even when law enforcement is committed to addressing the issue, bringing perpetrators to justice is difficult because victims are often reluctant to testify, evidence is difficult to obtain, and investigations often involve international travel. ECPAT's executive director, Dorothy Rozga, believes that some forces have done a good job but that the investigation and prosecution of child sex tourism is severely underresourced. She noted that in some countries, the police don't even have computers and called it a "scandal" that Interpol had only five people assigned to cover commercial sexual exploitation of children in 2014.[51]

Prosecutions for child sex tourism have taken place largely in the United States, Australia, the United Kingdom, and Canada. In 2012, sixty-four UK nationals were convicted for committing sexual crimes against children in other countries.[52] In Australia, approximately thirty people were charged with child sex tourism offenses between 1994 and 2011; 70 percent were convicted.[53] By June 2012, US law enforcement had arrested and convicted ninety-nine individuals for child sex tourism under the 2003 PROTECT Act. Under the law, Americans who travel abroad to engage in illicit sexual activity with children may face thirty years in prison.[54]

A particularly useful tool is Interpol's Green Notice, which is issued when known child sex offenders travel to other countries. The notice allows law enforcement in the destination country to monitor the person's activities. Interpol also coordinates joint operations with other countries to track down offenders, and it maintains the International Child Sexual Exploitation image database. By January 2017, that database project had identified more than ten thousand victims from around the world.[55] Despite efforts to date, however, prosecutions and convictions are still quite rare given the scope of the problem.

In September 2015, 193 governments adopted the 2030 Agenda for Sustainable Development, outlining a series of goals to be reached by the year 2030. The agenda puts forward a vision of a world free of violence, with just and inclusive societies. One specific target is to "eliminate all forms of violence against all women and girls in the public and private spheres, including trafficking and sexual and other types of exploitation."[56]

The experience of recent decades, where the scale of sexual exploitation of children in travel and tourism has grown, suggests that this goal may be wildly unrealistic. At the same time, previous efforts and research suggest what must be done. Given the unconscionable nature of the crime, we cannot afford not to try.

8 Child Soldiers

ARUNA GREW UP on the eastern coast of Sri Lanka, near sandy beaches, shallow lagoons, and palm trees. She was a Tamil, an ethnic group that had experienced decades of discrimination by Sri Lanka's majority Sinhalese. When Aruna was 15 and in grade 10, her family received a letter from the Liberation Tigers of Tamil Eelam (LTTE, or Tamil Tigers), a rebel group fighting for an independent state for Sri Lanka's Tamils. The letter instructed the family to send one of their children to join the Tamil Tigers and help fight against the government. The Tamil Tigers were conducting a massive recruitment drive in the area, visiting families house to house, convening community meetings, making radio announcements, and sending letters saying that every Tamil family had to give a child for the cause. Aruna's parents ignored the letter, but one day, Tamil Tigers came to Aruna's house and told them, "Each house has to turn over one child. If you don't agree, we will take a child anyway."[1]

Aruna didn't want to join. She knew that the Tamil Tigers regularly used children at the front lines of fighting and that many children had already been killed in the long-running armed conflict. The Tamil Tigers gave each new recruit a cyanide capsule with instructions that if they were captured, they were to take the capsule or blow themselves up rather than let themselves be captured by the Sri Lankan Army. Aruna knew that female soldiers, including girls, were often used to carry out suicide bomb attacks, in part because they were less likely to undergo rigorous checks at government checkpoints.[2]

Not long after the Tamil Tigers' visit to her house, the Tamil Tigers abducted Aruna and fifteen other girls as they walked to school. They took them to a training camp, where Aruna spent six months in physical and weapons training. "It was very difficult," she said. "If you get too tired and can't continue, they beat you. Once [during training], I was dizzy. I couldn't continue and asked for a rest. They hit me and said, 'This is the LTTE. You can't rest.'"[3] Aruna learned later that soon after her abduction, her parents had come to the camp looking for her, but the Tamil Tigers denied that she was there.

Some of the other girls at the training camp tried to escape, but if they returned to their home, the Tamil Tigers recaptured them, brought them back to the camp, and beat them. "I thought about trying to escape, but I saw others being beaten, so I changed my mind," she said. She ended up spending two and a half years with the Tamil Tigers before being captured during a battle and then released.

Both government armies and opposition forces have long used children as soldiers. In 2016, the United Nations reported that more than fifty parties to armed conflict were using child soldiers in seventeen countries around the globe.[4] Children serve as informants, guards, porters, cooks, and, often, armed combatants. Some military commanders simply want able-bodied recruits, regardless of age, while others specifically recruit children because they can be easier to control than adults and more easily indoctrinated. A senior officer in Chad's army explained to a human rights investigator, "Child soldiers are ideal because they don't complain, they don't expect to be paid, and if you tell them to kill, they kill."[5]

Child soldiers are often depicted as passive victims recruited through coercion or force, but the reality is far more complex. Many children join armed groups because they are offered money or other incentives, believe in the group's cause, want revenge for abuses committed by opposing forces, or believe that joining provides them their best chance for survival.[6]

In Colombia's long-running civil war, children made up an estimated one in four combatants in the guerrilla forces, or paramilitaries.[7] The paramilitaries often gained child recruits by offering salaries, funded by drug trafficking and extortion. Other children joined the guerrillas because they had few employment opportunities, had left school, were influenced by friends, or were victims of abuse or neglect by their families. Severo, for example, joined the guerrillas to escape a difficult home environment: "My father was always fighting with my mother and with us, too. That's why I went off with the guerrillas, to get away from the fighting. It was mainly because I was fed up at home. I was studying and they didn't want to pay for my studies."[8] Severo attended a community meeting that the guerrillas held near his home. When the deputy commander invited Severo to join and told him he would be paid, Severo agreed.[9]

Colombian guerrilla and paramilitaries recruited children as young as 8 years old to carry supplies or information, act as early-warning guards, or carry explosives. By the time they were 13, most child soldiers were trained in the use of automatic weapons, mortars, grenades, and explosives. Children participated in battles and were often expected to torture or execute captured enemies. Many children who joined had little idea of what their lives would be like as soldiers until it was too late to back out. Those who tried to desert were often shot.[10]

In some conflicts, girls make up 30 percent or more of children recruited into armed groups or forces.[11] They often receive weapons training and participate in combat, but they may also be subjected to sexual exploitation or forced to "marry" their commanders. They face not only the risks of warfare, but also rape, sexually transmitted diseases, and early childbirth. For girl soldiers, return to their home communities is particularly difficult because they suffer additional stigma due to presumed sexual exploitation and may have young children to support. "Christine," for example, was abducted by the Lord's Resistance Army in northern Uganda at age 10, and at age 16 she was forced to become a "wife" to one of the rebel commanders. She had two babies, and after her release, she said, "They ruined me. I had to cut short my studies. I have no hope that I will one day be somebody. I gave birth to two children and was not prepared. I have two children and no means of survival."[12]

Child soldiers who are released, escape, or apprehended face numerous challenges on reentering civilian society. If they escaped, they may be unable to return home for fear of punishment or re-recruitment. Their families and home communities may be unwilling to accept them, particularly if they committed atrocities. Some suffer trauma from exposure to extreme violence. Many have missed years of schooling and have few job skills with which to support themselves. UNICEF and NGOs have established rehabilitation programs in many countries to provide former child soldiers with medical care and counseling, assist them in locating their families, and provide education or vocational training, but many former child soldiers never benefit from this assistance, and others need more help than the programs are able to provide.

Until the year 2000, it was legal under international law to recruit children as young as age 15 and to send them into battle. The 1977 Additional Protocols to the 1949 Geneva Conventions prohibited armed forces or groups from recruiting children under age 15 or using them to take part in hostilities.[13] The Convention on the Rights of the Child, adopted in 1989, also set the age of 15 as the minimum for recruitment or use in armed forces, even though the convention extended a wide range of other protections to children under the age of 18, including protection from sexual exploitation, harmful child labor, and

violence.[14] By the late 1990s, the minimum age of 15 was considered customary international law, and governments negotiating the 1998 Rome Statute for
the International Criminal Court included the conscription, enlistment, or use
of children under the age of 15 as a war crime under the court's jurisdiction.[15]

Many NGOs and governments believed that the minimum age of 15 was
unacceptably low. In 1999, governments negotiating the International Labour
Organization's Worst Forms of Child Labour Convention agreed that the forced
recruitment of children under age 18 for use in armed conflict should be prohibited as one of the worst forms of child labor.[16] In 2000, after several years of
negotiations and a global campaign led by the Coalition to Stop the Use of Child
Soldiers, the United Nations adopted an optional protocol to the Convention on
the Rights of the Child on the involvement of children in armed conflict, raising
the minimum age for all direct participation in hostilities to age 18.[17] The protocol prohibited government forces from conscripting or forcibly recruiting children under the age of 18 but allowed voluntary recruitment from the age of 16
with certain safeguards, provided the child did not take part in hostilities. The
protocol stated that nonstate armed groups should not recruit children under
the age of 18 for any purpose, whether "voluntarily" or otherwise.[18]

Although optional protocols are usually open for ratification only by states
parties to the parent convention, in this case, the United States requested—and
other governments agreed—to open it to states that had signed but not ratified
the Convention on the Rights of the Child. This allowed the United States, at
the time one of the few nonstates parties to the convention, to ratify the instrument in 2002. By early 2017, 166 states had ratified the optional protocol, committing themselves not to use children as soldiers in armed conflict. Two-thirds
of states parties went even further, depositing voluntary declarations stating
that they would not recruit children under age 18 into their armed forces, even
on a voluntary basis.

International courts began to prosecute individuals for using child soldiers.
Between 2005 and 2008, the International Criminal Court issued arrest warrants against six individuals from the Congo and Uganda for the enlistment or
conscription of children under the age of 15.[19] In March 2012, the International
Criminal Court found the Congolese warlord Thomas Lubanga guilty of recruiting and using child soldiers in the armed conflict in that country, making
him the court's first convicted war criminal.[20] The statute for the Special Court
for Sierra Leone also treated the recruitment and use of children under the age
of 15 as a war crime. The court convicted nine individuals for recruiting and
using child soldiers, including Liberia's former president, Charles Taylor. These

convictions may have a deterrent effect on other commanders. Child Soldiers International, for example, reported that following Lubanga's conviction, other commanders in the Congo expressed fear of possible criminal prosecution and began releasing children from their ranks more systematically.[21]

As conflicts ended and some governments and armed groups acknowledged their use of child soldiers, thousands of children were released or demobilized in countries such as Afghanistan, Angola, the Democratic Republic of Congo, Liberia, Nepal, and Sierra Leone. The release of children from armed groups raised questions regarding their level of accountability for violations they may have committed. Some organizations have argued that child soldiers are primarily victims and should not be prosecuted for illegal acts, while others take the position that criminal prosecution of children could be appropriate in some cases if conducted in accordance with international juvenile justice standards. Many advocate for alternative forms of accountability, for example, transitional justice approaches that encourage children to recount their actions and engage in community service as reparation.

The number of countries known to have children participating in armed conflicts dropped from thirty in the mid-1990s to seventeen in 2015.[22] Despite progress, however, the practice persisted, particularly among nonstate armed groups. In some countries, such as the Central African Republic, Iraq, Nigeria, South Sudan, and Syria, the recruitment and use of child soldiers increased as conflicts escalated and extremist groups like ISIS and Boko Haram gained influence. Some countries that ratified the optional protocol continued to use child soldiers contrary to international law. In 2016, eight of the eleven governments known to use child soldiers or support allied militias using child soldiers in 2015 were parties to the optional protocol.[23]

Clearly international standards alone were not enough to end the use of child soldiers. This chapter looks at efforts to achieve compliance with international law, particularly through action by the UN Security Council, and a groundbreaking US law, the Child Soldiers Prevention Act.

Security Council

The fifteen-member UN Security Council is the most powerful organ of the United Nations: it can respond to threats to international peace and security with the use of military force and a range of sanctions, including arms embargoes, travel bans, and asset freezes. In 1998, the Special Representative to the Secretary General (SRSG) on Children and Armed Conflict, then Olara Otunnu, persuaded members of the council that the widespread effects of

armed conflict on children and the increasing use of children as soldiers consti-
tuted a threat to international peace and security and belonged on the Security
Council's agenda. The Security Council began to hold annual debates on the
issue, adopted a series of resolutions calling on parties to armed conflict to end
their use of child soldiers, and created mechanisms designed to protect children
and hold perpetrators accountable. Over time, it created a system for addressing violations against children that was unlike any other in the UN.

A network of human rights and humanitarian organizations, known as
the Watchlist on Children and Armed Conflict, helped influence the Security Council's approach to children and armed conflict.[24] Formed in 2001, the
Watchlist met regularly with Security Council members, briefed them on de-
velopments related to children in conflict situations, developed policy papers
recommending actions the Security Council should take, and worked closely
with the SRSG on children and armed conflict. The founding director, Julia
Freedson, observed that the composition of the network was a huge asset:
"Having the big humanitarian agencies allowed us to draw expertise from the
field and get information and ideas from affected communities, and the human
rights organizations gave us advocacy skills that we needed. That network was
a real linchpin in our success."[25]

One of the first, and most significant, actions by the Security Council was
its request in November 2001 that the secretary-general compile a public list
of parties to armed conflict that were using children as soldiers in violation of
international standards. The result was a name-and-shame technique that the
council had rarely used.[26] The first such "list of shame," issued in 2002, identified
twenty-three parties in five countries: Afghanistan, Burundi, the Democratic
Republic of the Congo, Liberia, and Somalia. The list of countries was small
because the Security Council considered only a limited number of armed conflicts on its official agenda. Nongovernmental organizations pushed strongly
to expand the list to include parties using child soldiers in other countries,
such as Colombia and the Philippines. One of Watchlist's members, Human
Rights Watch, enlisted the support of US senators to expand the list, prompting US diplomats at the UN to make it a priority. The council agreed, and the
secretary-general's 2003 list was expanded to include governments and armed
groups in fourteen countries.[27] In 2004, the Security Council called on the parties that had been listed to collaborate with the United Nations to create action
plans within three months to end their use of child soldiers and threatened to
impose targeted sanctions, such as arms embargoes, against those that refused
or did not implement such plans.[28]

The Watchlist worked diligently to build credibility and crucial relationships with individual Security Council members. "We would have coffee and lunches with the diplomats," said Freedson. "After those meetings, they would call us and solicit advice and information. Building those relationships is what allowed the doors to open."[29] She found that putting together talking points for diplomats in advance of the Security Council's open debates or negotiations on resolutions was particularly helpful. "Understanding the way the UN system works and then preempting what they need was incredibly effective," said Freedson. "They need to produce a resolution or make an intervention at an open debate, but they are not experts on these issues. They were just so grateful for an organization that knows the issues inside out and can give them a crib sheet."[30]

In 2004, the Security Council asked the secretary-general to devise an action plan for the systematic and comprehensive monitoring and reporting on children and armed conflict to provide the Security Council with "timely, objective, accurate and reliable" information on the recruitment and use of child soldiers and other grave violations against children.[31] The Watchlist produced detailed recommendations for how such a monitoring and reporting mechanism could be developed[32] and maintained close contact with many Security Council members as they negotiated a new resolution. "There were a lot of phone calls and emails," recalled Freedson. "The diplomats were really looking to us for advice on which way to go."[33]

In July 2015, the Security Council adopted resolution 1612, later described by the French ambassador to the United Nations as "the centerpiece" of the Security Council's work on children and armed conflict.[34] The resolution instructed the secretary-general to set up a monitoring and reporting mechanism in the countries where parties to armed conflict were included on the secretary-general's list of shame. It also established a Security Council working group on children and armed conflict to consider the information produced by the mechanism and recommend action in cases of ongoing violations.

As part of the monitoring and reporting mechanism, UN country teams and civil society groups on the ground collect reports of violations, and after verification by the United Nations, funnel the information to the SRSG on children and armed conflict for inclusion in the secretary-general's reports to the Security Council. The Security Council working group then considers the reports and negotiates conclusions for each situation, including recommendations for the parties concerned, the secretary-general, and other actors. Watchlist worked closely with the French, the first country to chair the working group, to develop a tool kit of twenty-six actions the working group could take, including public statements and démarches, emergency meetings, field trips to countries where violations were taking place, referral of information to international tribunals, and recommendations for sanctions.[35]

In 2007, the Security Council working group considered Sri Lanka for the first time. It expressed grave concern over the Tamil Tigers' continued recruitment of child soldiers and requested a follow-up report from the secretary-general in six months. The working group made it clear that if it did not see significant progress during that time, it would consider additional measures, implying the possibility of sanctions.[36] The threat had impact: over the following six months, Tamil Tiger child recruitment rates dropped by 50 percent.

Advocates were eager for the Security Council to impose sanctions on armed forces and groups that continued to use child soldiers, believing such measures would have a powerful deterrent effect on perpetrators. However, they found members reluctant to do so. Some members, like China and Russia, were disinclined to impose sanctions for any reason, and others, like the United Kingdom, believed that the threat of sanctions was often more effective than actually imposing them. In repeated resolutions, the Security Council expressed its willingness to impose sanctions on perpetrators, but in practice, it took action against only a small number of individuals, imposing travel bans or asset freezes on two commanders from Côte d'Ivoire and fourteen from the Democratic Republic of Congo.[37]

The SRSG plays a critical role in following up the working group's recommendations, making frequent field trips to conflict countries, meeting with both governments and nonstate armed groups to discuss their use of child soldiers and other violations against children, and urging them to enter into action plans—formal signed agreements—with the United Nations to end their violations.[38] In 2007, the secretary-general made clear that the only way that governments or armed groups would be removed from his list of shame was to sign and implement such an agreement.[39] For many perpetrators, the naming-and-shaming technique worked: they did not want the public stigma of being included in the secretary-general's list, particularly with such pariah groups as al-Qaeda, Boko Haram, and the Taliban. By early 2017, twenty-six parties to armed conflict had signed action plans with the United Nations, including eleven governments and fifteen nonstate armed groups. Nine of the twenty-six had successfully implemented their plan and were "delisted" by the secretary-general, including the government armed forces of Chad, Côte d'Ivoire, and Uganda; the Unified Communist Party of Nepal Maoist; and several nonstate armed groups in Côte d'Ivoire. However, other listed parties either ignored the Security Council or calculated that the benefits of using child soldiers outweighed possible negative repercussions.

Ambassador Jean-Marc de la Sablière of France, the first chair of the Security Council's working group, felt that the Security Council was able to achieve remarkable progress in part because members saw themselves as being "in the vanguard" of an innovative council approach.[40] Another Security Council member remarked that he had never seen an agenda move so far so quickly in the Security Council as the agenda on children and armed conflict.[41] Nonetheless, neither diplomats nor civil society were satisfied with the results. "Ten years ago, we didn't even dream these tools would exist," said Freedson. "I don't want to lose sight of what's been established, but it's not enough. These tools are not being used sufficiently the way they were meant to be used, and the results fall short."[42]

A Success Story: Chad

Chad experienced decades of civil war and violence following its independence from France in 1960, including rebel insurgencies, interethnic conflicts, and a proxy war with neighboring Sudan. The participation of children in armed forces and groups was a common feature and widely accepted by Chadian society.

Although children had long participated in Chad's conflicts, Chad first appeared on the secretary-general's list of shame in 2006. His 2007 report listed multiple perpetrators for recruiting child soldiers, including the government armed forces, rebel forces, village-based self-defense groups, the Sudan-supported Janjaweed, and Sudanese armed groups backed by the Chadian government. Children as young as 8 served as fighters, guards, cooks, and lookouts on the front lines of the conflict. One 12-year-old fighter explained why he joined a rebel group: "The village is not safe; it is better to go to war," the boy said. "If I go to war and I am killed, it is finished for me. If I kill my enemy, it is finished for him. I won't wait in the village to die. I'm a man. I want to participate."[43] Another boy joined the rebels after an attack on his village. "The Tama were always being attacked, and we have to defend ourselves," the boy said. "In order to get a rifle I had to join the FUC [a rebel group]. If security returns, I'll leave the FUC and go back to school."[44]

The government of France, which chaired the Security Council's working group on children and armed conflict, began raising the issue of child soldiers with Chad's government as early as 2006. France had a military assistance agreement with Chad and had over a thousand French troops stationed in the country. That year, French troops discovered children among Chadian armed forces that were receiving transport on French military aircraft. The French defense minister wrote to Chadian President Idriss Déby Itno to raise concerns about the issue but was reportedly ignored. France subsequently threatened to withdraw its military forces from Chad unless the government took concrete steps to demobilize children from its forces. This pressure contributed to Chad's signing an agreement with UNICEF in 2007 for the demobilization of child soldiers.[45]

In early 2008, the secretary-general appointed Rima Salah as his deputy special representative for the UN mission in Chad. Salah was Jordanian and had worked for UNICEF for nearly twenty years. She had a particular concern for children in armed conflict and made the issue a high priority. After both UN and State Department reports highlighted Chad's use of child soldiers, she went to Chad's foreign minister and told him, "This is not good for your image."[46]

Soon after, Radhika Coomeraswamy, the new SRSG on children and armed conflict, traveled to Chad to assess the situation. She met with Chad's prime minister and the ministers of defense, justice, and social affairs, and secured a commitment from the government to cooperate with a UN verification process to identify child soldiers in its detention centers, training camps, and military facilities; to release child soldiers from rebel forces that were held in its detention facilities; and to form a joint task force with UNICEF to ensure effective reintegration of former child soldiers.

Salah made sure that the UN mission in Chad kept child soldiers high on its agenda. Many children were being recruited from refugee camps, so she ensured UN teams visited the camps every day. In 2009, UNICEF and the UN mission went through all of the military camps in the country to identify child soldiers. Salah met regularly with the Chadian government and on several occasions took Chad's minister for human rights to the eastern part of the country, where child recruitment was most acute, so that he could see the situation for himself. Every month, she held briefings with NGOs and with the five permanent members of the Security Council—France, the United States, the United Kingdom, China, and Russia—known as the "P5."[47] France in particular played an important role; it hosted meetings for the other P5 members and repeatedly raised the issue with the Chadian government.

Verification visits continued through 2009. Although 240 children were released from armed groups, new cases of child recruitment by both the government armed forces and armed groups continued to be reported.[48] With Salah's encouragement, the government organized a regional conference in June 2010 on ending the recruitment and use of child soldiers, with government representatives from several countries in the region and over two hundred other participants, including former child soldiers from Chad, Sierra Leone, Liberia, and the Sudan. Participants discussed the factors that facilitate the recruitment and use of child soldiers, ways to prevent child recruitment, and good practices for demobilization and reintegration of former child soldiers. The conference culminated in the signing of the N'Djaména Declaration, where participants committed to end the recruitment and use of child soldiers. Later that year, the SRSG met again with Chadian government officials and secured a commitment that Chad would prepare a formal action plan with the UN to end its use of child soldiers.

In June 2011, SRSG Coomaraswamy traveled to Chad again to witness the signing of a formal action plan by the Chadian government with the United Nations. The plan set out specific steps that the government would take to ensure its national forces and armed groups that had recently integrated into the army would be free of child soldiers, including continued verification visits to military bases by the United Nations, legislative reform to prohibit the use of child soldiers, and punitive measures against child recruiters. In a meeting with the SRSG, President Déby gave his personal commitment to ensure the plan would be implemented.[49]

In 2012, the United Nations reported significant progress. The army had apparently stopped recruiting children and only a very small number of children were believed to remain in the government's forces.[50] But this progress reversed in 2013, when the United Nations found several dozen children in army training centers who had been swept up in a new government recruitment drive. In response, the government appointed new focal points in the Ministries of Defense and Social Welfare to ensure implementation of the action plans, and the army issued a series of military directives prohibiting the recruitment of children.[51]

In 2013, a controversy emerged as Chadian troops were to be deployed to a new UN peacekeeping mission in Mali. NGOs warned publicly that allowing a government that was still on the secretary-general's list of shame to participate in a UN peacekeeping mission sent the wrong message.[52] The Watchlist stated that it would be a "harmful, precedent-setting action" that could discredit the United Nations.[53] Reporters raised the issue with senior UN officials, and the controversy became a catalyst to accelerate implementation of Chad's action plan. The SRSG traveled again to Chad and negotiated a ten-point road map with the government, outlining specific and time-bound actions to achieve compliance with the action plan. The president issued a directive confirming 18 as the minimum age for all recruitment and a presidential decree criminalizing child recruitment. Over eight hundred soldiers who were to be deployed to Mali were trained in child protection. The government set up child protection units in all eight of its security zones, and between August and October, it helped the UN screen thirty-eight hundred troops.[54]

In mid-2014, the secretary-general reported that Chad had fully implemented its plan, no new cases of child recruitment by Chad's army were reported the previous year, and Chad was being removed from his list of shame. Although the delisting signified an apparent success story, NGOs warned that Chad's progress was fragile and that sustained attention and resources were needed to fully implement its commitments.[55] The Chadian government itself recognized at a Security Council open debate that year that the measures it had taken "need to be consolidated daily in order to be sustainable and to avoid backsliding."[56]

Citing the success in Chad, the Watchlist pushed for a comprehensive UN policy linking eligibility for UN peacekeeping forces to effective measures to end the use of child soldiers and other violations against children. It published a policy brief and raised the issue with Security Council members, the UN Department of Peacekeeping Operations, and a high-level panel evaluating UN peace operations. In September 2015, the secretary-general announced a new policy banning countries repeatedly included in his list of shame from contributing troops to UN peacekeeping operations.[57]

The Child Soldiers Prevention Act

In the 1990s, the United States strongly opposed raising the minimum age for participation in armed conflict to age 18. It had a long history of deploying 17-year-old soldiers to combat situations and saw little reason to change its practices. Over time, however, its policy changed significantly in response to civil society pressure, an evolving international consensus that the use of children under the age of 18 in hostilities was unacceptable, and internal advocacy from officials at both the State Department and Defense Department.[58] In December 2002, the United States ratified the optional protocol and immediately issued new regulations for all branches of the armed services, instructing them that soldiers below the age of 18 should not be deployed into hostilities.

Four US-based organizations—Amnesty International USA, the Center for Defense Information, Human Rights Watch, and World Vision USA—had led advocacy efforts to secure US support for the optional protocol. After ratification and changes in US deployment policy, the advocates began searching for additional ways that the United States could use its considerable diplomatic and military weight to influence other countries to comply with the new international standards. Rachel Stohl, who worked for the Center for Defense Information, reflected,

> Inherently, everyone thinks the use of child soldiers is bad. No one thinks it's a great idea to use children. We had already won the hearts and minds campaign and convinced people it was a terrible practice. But how could it be transferred into meaningful action? We were trying to think of how to make practical impact.[59]

In conversations with US Congressional staff, the advocates realized that it was important for the US government itself to be documenting the problem. Many lawmakers had a suspicion of documentation from either the United Nations or from NGOs and saw US government data as the only credible basis for policy action. Encouraged by the advocates, staffers in Congress developed new provisions for a foreign policy bill, requiring the State Department to include information in its annual country human rights reports on the "nature and extent of the compulsory recruitment and conscription of individuals under the age of 18 by all armed groups in every country." Enacted in 2002, the law also required the State Department to describe the steps taken by governments to eliminate such practices.[60] The first such report, issued in early 2004, highlighted over twenty countries where child soldiers were participating in armed conflict.[61]

The advocates next turned their attention to the issue of US military assistance. They knew that as the world's largest arms exporter, the United States had enormous leverage with countries that received arms and other military assistance. Their research revealed that of the ten countries known at the time to be using child soldiers in their national armed forces or government-supported militias, nine were receiving US military assistance. They began discussing the possibility of a US law to prohibit military assistance to governments using child soldiers. "It was an innovative and pragmatic approach to stopping something that people agree is a horrific practice," said Stohl. "Countries want US military assistance and training. The law would be a mechanism to help states stop a practice and reward them when they do."[62]

The advocates knew that enacting such a law could be a difficult task. Although nearly all policymakers agreed that the use of child soldiers was a serious problem, arms sales and military assistance were perceived as powerful foreign policy tools for the United States. They were used to cultivate allies and ensure that other countries were equipped to help pursue US military objectives. Particularly in the post-9/11 "war on terror," assistance to US allies engaged in counterterrorism was considered essential.

The group assembled data showing the levels of US assistance that countries using child soldiers received and the continuing scope of child soldier use around the world, and they began to approach members of Congress to discuss the issue. One of the first members they approached was Senator Richard Durbin, a Democrat from Illinois. Durbin had a strong human rights record, and as a member of the Judiciary Committee, he had initiated a subcommittee on human rights and the law. Senator Durbin and his staff were immediately drawn to the issue and agreed to champion it.

For the legislation to have a chance, it needed to be bipartisan, with support from both Democrats and Republicans. One of the organizations that had long been active on the child soldiers issue, World Vision, had worked on human trafficking issues with Senator Sam Brownback, a conservative Republican. "That relationship was really important," said Joe Mettimano, who headed up the child soldiers work for World Vision. "It was built on experience and trust."[63] When Mettimano presented Brownback's staff with the idea of teaming up with Senator Durbin to combat the recruitment and use of child soldiers, they agreed. "Senator Brownback had a real heart for humanitarian and children's issues," said Mettimano. "This struck a personal note for him, despite the political aspects that could make it complicated."[64]

Over the next three years, activists worked to build support for the legislation. They met repeatedly with Durbin's and Brownback's staffs to discuss the language of the bill and debate the forms of US military assistance that should be prohibited for countries using child soldiers. Ultimately they agreed that five military aid programs should be restricted: foreign military sales, direct commercial sales, excess defense articles, international military education and training, and foreign military financing. Under the agreed text of the bill, countries that the State Department identified as recruiting or using child soldiers in government armed forces or government-supported paramilitaries or militias in violation of international standards would be eligible only for military assistance designed to address the issue of child soldiers or otherwise professionalize their armed forces until the problem was remedied.

One difficult issue was whether to include a national interest waiver in the text of the legislation. Such a provision would allow the US president to waive the sanctions in the bill, allowing countries using child soldiers to continue receiving military assistance, if he or she deemed it in the national interest for military or political reasons. The advocates were reluctant to include such a provision, since it gave the White House significant latitude to circumvent the bill's goal, but they were eventually convinced that such a provision would be necessary to gain the bill's passage.

After Senators Durbin and Brownback introduced the bill, the Child Soldier Prevention Act, in April 2007,[65] NGO supporters began to mobilize broader support.[66] They developed fact sheets on the use of child soldiers and the goal of the bill, met with dozens of congressional offices to discuss the bill, and enlisted endorsements from other NGOs and commitments to mobilize their constituencies. They wrote sample letters, organized a national call-in day for supporters to contact their representatives in Congress, sent out regular updates to interested organizations, and produced a four-minute video. They worked with Senator Durbin to organize a Senate hearing on child soldiers. One of the speakers was Ishmael Beah, who had written a best-selling memoir about his experiences as a child soldier in Sierra Leone.[67] After hearing Beah speak, Republican Senator Tom Coburn immediately pledged his support to the bill.

One of the messages that resonated with both members of Congress and activist partners was that US taxpayer money should not be used to support the recruitment and use of child soldiers. Nevertheless, some members of Congress were concerned that even with the national interest waiver, the proposed law could inhibit the US counterterrorism agenda. Others agreed that the issue was important but didn't believe it was a priority for their constituents. For example, one aide to a Florida senator tried for two months to get the senator's support, but said she was told "no way." "It had nothing to do with the state, and [at the time], we weren't being pushed by constituents to co-sponsor," she said.[68] But the advocates' broad mobilization paid off. Later, the aide told advocates that her boss had decided to cosponsor the bill. She explained:

> Over the last month or so, we started to receive a steady stream of mail. Two weeks ago it picked up momentum, and we started to receive lots of phone calls as well. I don't know about other offices, but we really pay attention to the constituent campaigns and getting multiple packets of letters from middle and high school classrooms is really what did the trick.[69]

By November 2007, thirty members of the Senate, both Republican and Democrat, had cosponsored the bill. Despite the strong bipartisan support, however, the bill didn't move forward for a vote. Mettimano recalled, "One of the challenges was trying to get the leadership in the House and Senate to prioritize this among the thousands of other worthy issues we were competing with."[70] For almost a year, little happened, but in 2008, the expected congressional reauthorization of a trafficking bill presented an opportunity. Supporters of the Child Soldiers Prevention Act introduced it as an amendment to the trafficking measure. It was adopted in December 2008.[71] Less than two weeks later, President George W. Bush signed the legislation, and it became law.

The law was groundbreaking. At the time, only one other country had any similar legislation: the Belgian parliament had adopted a law in 2003 barring arms transfers to forces using child soldiers. When the law came into force in 2010, the State Department identified six countries for using children in their national armed forces or supporting allied militias that used child soldiers—Burma, Chad, Democratic Republic of the Congo (DRC), Somalia, Sudan, and Yemen. Four of the countries—Chad, DRC, Sudan, and Yemen—received US aid that would be prohibited under the Child Soldiers Prevention Act.[72] Advocates were hopeful that the sanctions in the bill would put pressure on the countries to take action to end their use of child soldiers. Instead, they were shocked when President Obama issued waivers for all four of the affected countries, allowing them to continue receiving military aid despite their use of child soldiers. "We were blindsided by the waivers, and really disappointed," said Stohl. "I think we were a little naïve after the legislation was passed. We thought that was the victory and that the administration would abide by the intent of the law."[73]

An online blogger named Josh Rogin first became aware of the president's decision and contacted Human Rights Watch for background on the issue. After he wrote about it for ForeignPolicy.com, the mainstream media picked up the story. The *New York Times* and *Washington Post* quoted activists who accused President Obama of giving countries using child soldiers "a pass" and undercutting the law and its intent.[74] The White House defended its decision, saying, "We put these four countries on notice by naming them as having child soldiers. . . . Our intention is to work with them over the next year to try to solve this problem."[75] Within just a few days, nearly thirty NGOs signed a letter to the president, saying that the president's decision sent an unfortunate message that the administration was not seriously committed to ending the use of child soldiers and that by giving blanket waivers, the administration had given up the significant leverage that the law provided to influence other countries' child soldier use.[76] Members of Congress also sharply criticized the administration. Congressman Jeff Fortenberry called the waivers "an assault on human dignity" and said that national security "must not be an excuse to allow us to be complicit with countries using child soldiers."[77]

In response to the initial criticism of the waivers, the White House quickly organized a conference call between the president's human rights advisor, Samantha Power, and NGOs that were involved in the issue. The White House let the waivers stand but initiated a more consultative process with NGOs, meeting at least twice a year to discuss which countries should be on the State Department's list and how the Child Soldiers Prevention Act's sanctions should be applied.

In subsequent years, between six and ten countries a year appeared on the State Department's list. Despite continued NGO criticism, the administration continued to issue waivers for many of the countries, particularly for allies in counterterrorism operations. However, it began to make better use of the leverage the law provided, and in 2012, the potential of the law for impact became evident. The Obama administration announced it would withhold foreign military financing and training from a Congolese battalion until Congo signed an action plan with the United Nations to end its use of child soldiers. At the height of Congo's war, UNICEF estimated that as many as thirty thousand children fought on all sides of the conflict. The UN had tried for seven years to get the Congolese government to sign an action plan, but the government had been dragging its feet. Five days after the US announcement, Congo signed the plan. The United States maintained partial sanctions on the Congo to keep pressure on the government to implement the action plan. By 2015, government forces had ended its recruitment of children, a significant change from years of child soldier use.[78]

Rwanda provided another positive example of how the law could be used. In 2013, the State Department placed Rwanda on its Child Soldiers Prevention Act list due to its support for the M23, an armed group operating in eastern Congo. With Rwandan backing, the M23 had forcibly recruited large numbers of child soldiers and carried out brutal abuses against civilians.[79] That September, the administration applied full sanctions on Rwanda under the Child Soldiers Prevention Act, withholding foreign military financing and military training. A few weeks later, the M23 admitted defeat and laid down its weapons. Although part of the M23's defeat was due to Congolese military operations and support from a UN peacekeeping force, mounting pressure on Rwanda to stop supporting the M23 played a crucial role. After aid suspensions from the United States and most other major donors to Rwanda and phone calls to Rwandan president Paul Kagame from Secretary of State John Kerry, the Rwandan government may have concluded that its support of M23 had become too damaging to its public image.

The United States also used the law to help pressure Chad to end its use of child soldiers. Although the United States gave Chad waivers to allow military assistance, it applied diplomatic pressure, with the threat of sanctions, to persuade Chad to sign and implement an action plan with the United Nations. After the United Nations reported that Chad had ended its use of child soldiers, Chad was removed from both the State Department's and secretary-general's list of perpetrators in 2014.

Challenges

Despite the evolution of clear international law prohibiting the use of children as soldiers, widespread ratification of relevant treaties, and some successes in ending the practice, in early 2017 the use of child soldiers persisted in approximately 17 countries. For both governments and armed groups, the utility of using children often outweighs the risk of criminal prosecution, Security Council sanctions, or international criticism. While some perpetrators have explicit policies prohibiting the practice, they fail to effectively implement them, lacking either political will or sufficient control over their chain of command. The convictions of Thomas Lubanga, Charles Taylor, and other commanders for recruiting and using child soldiers by international tribunals has brought additional stigma to the practice, but many individual commanders rightly believe the chance that they will be prosecuted is slim. Disciplinary action or criminal prosecution at the country level remains relatively rare.

Some countries make considerable progress in ending the use of child soldiers as conflicts die down, only to resume child recruitment when conflicts flare up again. In South Sudan, for example, the government set up a system to screen its forces to identify and release children and had made tangible progress when a new conflict erupted in December 2013.[80] Over the course of the next two years, this progress completely unraveled. As the new conflict raged, UNICEF estimated that government and opposition forces recruited as many as sixteen thousand children to fight.[81]

By 2016, the secretary-general had included thirty-two armed forces or groups on his list of shame for at least five consecutive years, designating them as "persistent perpetrators."[82] Eleven governments and armed groups had been on the list every year since its inception in 2002. Although the Security Council repeatedly expressed its intention to impose sanctions on armed forces and groups that continued to use child soldiers, it generally failed to do so. "The Security Council is so politicized," said Freedson. "It's not just about kids, it's about high-stakes politics between these powerful countries. International politics ends up trumping again and again these tools that have so much potential."[83]

In the case of the United States, the administration frequently gave its military alliances and national security concerns priority over using the Child Soldiers Prevention Act to maximum effect. Progress was also limited when UN country teams failed to make the issue a priority, had limited access to perpetrators, or were constrained in their activity because of the dangers posed by the conflict.

The Way Forward

Despite the obstacles, some efforts have achieved significant results. Between 2005 and 2017, twenty-six governments and armed groups signed action plans with the United Nations, committing to end their use of child soldiers, and at least nine parties to armed conflict were removed from the secretary-general's list of shame after successfully implementing their plans. Between 2000 and 2017, over 115,000 children were released from armed forces and armed groups, with 8,000 released in 2015 alone.[84] Of the seven governments still on the secretary-general's list for child soldier use in 2016, all had signed action plans, and some, like Congo, had made significant progress in ending the practice.

In 2013, the Watchlist conducted research to determine the factors that contributed to the successful signing and implementation of action plans. After interviewing nearly fifty individual stakeholders and examining six country examples,[85] it concluded that three critical factors facilitated the signing of an action plan: (1) political interest by the signatory party; (2) sustained and high-level UN advocacy, supported by bilateral démarches from third-party governments; and (3) a UN mission structure that facilitates senior-level engagement.[86]

Chad was one of the apparent success stories, delisted in 2014 following years of child soldier use by all parties to the armed conflict. Each of the factors Watchlist identified was present. The government expressed a strong interest in ending its use of child soldiers, particularly after its listing by the secretary-general emerged as an obstacle to the inclusion of Chad's troops in the UN peacekeeping mission in Mali. The controversy over Chad's inclusion in the mission put both Chad's and the United Nations's reputation on the line, providing both with an incentive to accelerate implementation of the action plan. High-level UN advocacy by the UN's deputy special representative in Chad, Rima Salah, elevated children and armed conflict in the engagement with the Chadian government and the UN mission's work. She raised the issue frequently with high-level government officials, personally traveled with government ministers to areas where child recruitment took place to ensure they saw the situation for themselves, and regularly briefed permanent members of the Security Council and NGOs so that they could raise the issue with the government as well. She made sure that UN police were trained to monitor for child recruitment in refugee camps and worked with both the government and UNICEF to set up verification visits at military camps.

Senior UN officials from New York and influential members of the Security Council reinforced Salah's efforts. The SRSG on children and armed conflict made multiple visits to Chad between 2008 and 2013 to secure concrete commitments from the government to address the issue, including signed action plans and road maps for implementation. France in particular pressured the Chadian government on the issue over several years, threatening withdrawal of French troops if action was not taken. Similarly, the United States raised the issue at senior levels, citing the possibility of military sanctions under the Child Soldiers Prevention Act if progress was not achieved. Ultimately the combination of sustained pressure from the United Nations both on the ground and from headquarters, engagement from powerful countries such as France and the United States, and Chad's willing to take action on the issue appear to have prompted the action needed to end Chad's use of child soldiers and win its removal from the SG's list of shame.

The Child Soldiers Prevention Act illustrates the potential of bilateral state action and using military assistance as leverage with governments using child soldiers. The law was instrumental in securing commitments from Chad and Congo to end the use of child soldiers and persuading Rwanda to end its support for the M23. Although the enactment of the law opened a promising avenue to end child soldier use, advocates quickly discovered that the US administration was likely to prioritize other national interests and waive the law's provisions. Sharp NGO criticism, including through the media, prompted the administration to begin to withhold military assistance from some countries.

Ending the use of child soldiers demands a multifaceted approach, incorporating clear legal prohibitions against the use of child soldiers, effective screening of recruits, and punitive action against commanders who use children. It also requires action on the ground to provide children with schooling and viable alternatives to recruitment and ensure adequate rehabilitation and reintegration programs for former child soldiers to prevent their re-recruitment and ensure their successful reintegration into civilian life.

For policymakers, the examples explored in this chapter suggest some important ways forward in cases where perpetrators have failed to take action. In particular, sustained engagement by the United Nations and third-party governments with governments and groups using child soldiers, linked with tangible consequences for continued child soldiers use, such as a reduction in military assistance or exclusion from UN peacekeeping missions, have had demonstrable results and should be pursued consistently.

For civil society advocates working to end the use of child soldiers, progress depends on building personal relationships with policymakers, developing concrete recommendations for action backed by solid information, and, perhaps most important, applying continuous pressure to ensure that available points of leverage are used.

In particular, advocates have learned they need to stay engaged for the long haul. Mettimano reflected on the period of time when the Child Soldiers Prevention Act languished in Congress, "Looking back on that time, I'm proud of the fact that we didn't give up. During that lull, it would have been easy to go onto something else. But we didn't, and when the window opened again, we got right back on it and saw it through. Getting people to do the right thing can really take time and perseverance. It's not something that happens easily or quickly."[87] Stohl similarly reflected on efforts to ensure effective implementation of the law: "We've had to be proactive and keep the pressure on. The work wasn't done once we got the legislation. Sometimes people see the legislation as the end, but in many ways, it was just the beginning."[88]

9 Access to Education

TEN-YEAR-OLD BARA'A sets a chalkboard against a tree and gathers a group of children. They are all Syrians, living in an informal refugee camp made up of shacks and tents among hills and olive groves in Ketermaya, Lebanon. She directs the younger children to sit on a row of rocks in front of her and the older children to sit in the back. Then she begins to teach what she can remember from the first grade, her last year of school in Syria.

Bara'a wistfully recalled her days at school: "School meant so much to me. I loved school so much."[1] She lived near Damascus, where her family had a garden and three cows. But the Syrian war made it too dangerous to stay. A missile hit their home, injuring Bara'a's sister, and Bara'a's school was destroyed in another air attack. In 2013, the family fled to Lebanon.

In the refugee camp where they settled, there was no school, and the schools in nearby towns demanded money that the family did not have. Bara'a decided that even if she couldn't go to school, she could help other children and began to organize daily classes. "They should be studying so when they grow up they can be whatever they want," she said. "If one of them wants to be a teacher or a doctor she needs to know how to read and write."[2]

After two years in the camp, Bara'a was finally able to enroll in a special evening shift for Syrian students at a public school, but she continued teaching other children at the refugee camp. "I also help my friends and explain lessons to them," she said. "Knowledge is the light, and ignorance is the darkness."[3]

Around the world, 263 million children between ages 6 and 17 are out of school.[4] Nearly a quarter of these children, like Bara'a, are from conflict-affected countries, where war has decimated the education system or made it too dangerous for children to attend school. In other cases, children are too poor to pay school-related expenses; face discrimination based on gender, race, or disability; have no school near their home; or drop out because of violent discipline or harassment.

Education is arguably the most powerful catalyst for improving children's lives. Children who are in school enjoy better health, better job prospects, and higher earnings as adults, and they are less likely to end up in child labor, child marriage, or as child soldiers. According to UNESCO, each year of schooling can increase a child's potential earnings as an adult by 10 percent. If all children in low-income countries left school with basic reading skills, global poverty could be reduced by 12 percent.[5] UNESCO's director-general, Irina Bokova, says, "There is simply no more powerful or longer-lasting investment in human rights and dignity, in social inclusion and sustainable development."[6]

The Convention on the Rights of the Child guarantees children free and compulsory primary education and secondary education that is available and accessible to every child. It specifies that the aim of education should be to develop the child's "personality, talents and mental and physical abilities to their fullest potential," his or her respect for human rights and fundamental freedoms, and to "prepare the child for responsible life in a free society."[7] The International Covenant on Economic, Social and Cultural Rights also recognizes the right of everyone to education,[8] and the Convention on the Rights of Persons with Disabilities recognizes the right to education without discrimination for children with disabilities.[9]

In the year 2000, 164 governments gathered in Dakar, Senegal, and agreed on an ambitious Education for All agenda. They pledged to reach six education goals by the year 2015, including gender equality in education, improving the quality of education, and ensuring that all children complete primary education.[10] At the time, 374 million children and adolescents were not in school, including 100 million children of primary school age. Only 92 girls were enrolled in primary school for every 100 boys. Girls were least likely to attend primary school in South and West Asia, where only 83 girls were enrolled for every 100 boys.[11]

Fifteen years after Dakar, none of the Education for All goals had been met. Barely half of countries were expected to meet the 2015 target of universal primary education, and more than 61 million primary-aged children worldwide were still out of school. Nearly a third of countries with data still had gender disparities.[12] Nevertheless, countries had made remarkable progress. Between 2000 and 2014, the overall number of children out of school had fallen by more than 110 million, and the number of countries with severe gender disparities dropped from thirty-three to sixteen.[13]

Some individual countries had made astounding gains. Burundi, for example, increased its primary school enrollment from less than 41 percent to 94 percent in just a decade. Burkino Faso and Mozambique both increased their primary enrollment by over 66 percent in twelve years.[14] Afghanistan made astonishing progress toward gender parity: in 1999, less than 4 percent of girls were enrolled in primary school, but by 2012 the proportion had risen to 87 percent.[15]

Several key strategies have proven effective in increasing the number of children in school: abolishing school fees; increasing the demand for education through incentives such as school meals and cash transfers to poor families; and increasing the supply of schools and classrooms.

During the 1980s, structural adjustment policies forced many poor countries to impose user fees on public services such as education and health care as a condition for receiving World Bank or International Monetary Fund loans. These school fees often made education prohibitively expensive for poor families. Many families could not afford education for any of their children, and others, forced to choose among their children, often gave preference to boys.

In the 1990s, many countries began abolishing these school fees, resulting in dramatic increases in enrollment. Malawi, for example, abolished primary school fees in 1994; within a year, 1 million new students signed up, increasing enrollment by 50 percent.[16] Kenya abolished primary school fees in 2003, and within weeks, 1.3 million new children enrolled.[17] The sudden influx of new students, however, often resulted in overcrowded classrooms, a lack of textbooks, and shortages of trained teachers. To avoid such strains on the system, some countries took a more gradual approach. Benin, for example, abolished fees for girls in rural areas in the 1990s and eliminated fees nationwide in 2006.[18] By 2015, over 135 countries had laws guaranteeing free primary education, with some enshrining the right in their constitutions.[19] Others adopted free education through nonlegislative policy measures.

Even when education is free, children often must pay for uniforms, books, transportation, or informal fees introduced by local schools. For some families, these costs still put school beyond reach. Some countries have addressed these barriers by providing free uniforms and books or waiving informal fees for poor students. The Philippines' constitution, for example, provides for scholarships, student loans, subsidies, and other incentives to support the education of low-income children.[20]

Another effective strategy, sometimes called "the development revolution from the Global South," is to provide poor families with cash transfers.[21] These programs, pioneered in Latin America through programs such as Bolsa Família in Brazil and Opportunidades in Mexico, provide monthly cash stipends for poor families, often targeting those in rural areas in particular. Conditional cash transfers link the stipends to school attendance or accessing health services, or both. Unconditional cash transfers have no such requirements but are cheaper to implement, and they assume that if poor families have more available income, they will direct it toward their children's education. A meta-analysis of twenty-five studies found that both programs improve enrollment. In families receiving conditional cash transfers, a child is 41 percent more likely to be enrolled in school; in families receiving unconditional cash transfers, a child is 23 percent more likely to be enrolled.[22] In Morocco, for example, the Tayssir cash transfer program decreased annual dropout rates by 68 percent in just three years and also helped reduce child labor.[23] (The link between cash transfers and reductions in child labor is further discussed in chapter 5). By 2010, cash transfer programs covered nearly 20 percent of populations across Latin America, and other regions had begun to implement similar programs.[24] In sub-Saharan Africa, for example, the number of countries with some form of cash transfer program nearly doubled in just three years, increasing from twenty-one in 2010 to thirty-seven in 2013.[25]

Providing free school meals is another effective way to boost school enrollment and attendance generally and increase girls' enrollment in particular. A meta-analysis of thirty-two countries in sub-Saharan Africa found that providing free meals at school increased the enrollment of boys by 22 percent and of girls by 28 percent.[26] By 2015, school feeding programs reached 368 million children in 169 countries.[27]

Not surprisingly, another way to boost school attendance is to increase the number of schools and classrooms. If schools are too far away or transportation is unavailable, families are much less likely to send their children—girls in particular. In Afghanistan, for example, where many families believe that girls are more vulnerable to security risks than boys, girls' attendance fell by 19 percentage points for every additional mile she needed to travel to school.[28]

Investing in more schools and infrastructure, such as building roads to make them more accessible, has had some of the largest impact on education indicators.[29] Between 1992 and 2010, for example, Mozambique tripled the number of primary and secondary schools in the country. Coupled with the abolition of school fees, this increased its net enrollment by nearly 35 percent.[30]

Girls face particular challenges in accessing schooling. Families often prioritize their sons' schooling over their daughters', particularly when costs are involved. Families may keep their girls home from school because of security threats or to help with household chores, including caring for younger siblings. Girls are more likely to drop out due to early marriage or pregnancy or if their schools lack facilities where they can manage their menstruation.[31]

Many countries have made substantial progress in closing the gender gap and boosting girls' enrollment by providing targeted incentives for girls (including free textbooks, scholarships, fee waivers, and cash stipends), increasing the number of schools, recruiting more female teachers, improving sanitation facilities, and conducting community education about the value of educating girls. Cambodia, for example, which had only 66 girls attending school for every 100 boys in 2000, achieved gender parity just ten years later.[32]

The long-term benefits of education are clear, but the most effective strategies to get more children into school require resources. In many cases, organizing by civil society has been the essential catalyst to push governments to adopt the policies and allocate the resources necessary to expand children's access to education. This chapter examines organizing by children to achieve free education in postwar Sierra Leone and worldwide mobilization by the Global Campaign for Education.

Sierra Leone

Chernor Bah was twelve years old when the war in Sierra Leone came to his city, Freetown. Suddenly soldiers were everywhere, and he no longer went to the beach to play in the sea. After his home was burned to the ground, he and his family fled. For three years, they lived in camps for displaced persons and refugees. Both of Bah's parents were teachers, and they made sure he continued his education during the war. He attended classes that his father taught in the refugee camp, and his mother made him read so that he wouldn't fall behind. "That's my luck," Bah says, "Having parents that really made education a priority. Surviving *is* going to school."[33]

In 2001, the war ended. Bah was fifteen and returned to Freetown with his family. Over fifty thousand people had lost their lives, and the educational system was in shambles. Many schools were destroyed, teachers were displaced, and schools in safer areas were severely overcrowded. Nevertheless, the peace process was underway, and Bah started talking with his friends about how they could be part of it. He recalled thinking, "It would be great if our voices mattered." He and his friends arranged a meeting with the minister of social welfare, gender, and children to propose the creation of a children's parliament. "I think she was more amused than interested," he said. She proposed a Children's Forum instead and invited them to create a plan.

With the support of UNICEF and Plan International, Bah and his friends put together a three-day planning workshop with fifty children from around the country. The children decided to create the Children's Forum Network and elected Bah as president. Over the next year, Bah visited more than forty schools across the country. With a letter from the minister, he was permitted to address school assemblies and explain the Children's Forum. Eventually nearly every school had a children's club. The network organized district, regional, and national executive groups.

When the network started, it had two primary goals: to be a voice in the peace process and to enshrine children's rights, including the right to education, in Sierra Leone's law. Bah and other leaders from the Children's Forum Network traveled around the country to gather stories from children about what had happened to them during the war and what they wanted for the future to present to Sierra Leone's Truth and Reconciliation Commission. Across the country, children said they wanted education. "Education was our major platform," Bah said. "We wanted to go to school. We wanted the government to make education a right."[34]

The Children's Forum began a Voice of Children radio project to allow children to air their views and engage directly with the country's leaders. Over two hundred children became broadcasters, and Bah hosted a weekly program, inviting the vice president, minister for social welfare, and other policymakers to discuss children's issues in front of a live audience. "This was unprecedented," said Bah. "Public servants rarely answered to anyone before, let alone to a group of children. These forums undoubtedly helped mainstream children's rights issues in the country and sunk into the national consciousness that children have a right to air their voices too."[35]

At the time, primary education in Sierra Leone was not free. Children who hadn't paid their fees would be called to the front of their classroom, beaten, and sent home. Bah recalled that when he was young, his parents were separated, and his mother wasn't always able to pay the fees on time. Several times he was sent home from school until his mother could take out a loan to cover his fees.

In advance of national elections in 2002, the Children's Forum created a Children's Manifesto, based on the views the forum had collected through their surveys and radio programs. One of its main demands was eliminating school fees and enshrining the right to free education in the law. The forum organized a program inviting national party leaders to sign the manifesto and commit to its implementation.

Sierra Leone introduced a free education policy in 2002–2003, and in 2004, it adopted the Education Act, guaranteeing free primary and junior secondary education for every child. Primary school enrollment quickly doubled,[36] and studies found that once children were enrolled, they tended to remain in school. By 2010, the primary completion rate was 76 percent. Even more impressive, junior secondary enrollment increased fourfold between 2000 and 2010, and senior secondary enrollment increased by a factor of five.[37] By 2011, education accounted for 29 percent of public expenditures, well above the international benchmark of 20 percent.[38]

Sierra Leone nevertheless continues to face significant challenges. In 2010, 23 percent of primary-aged children were still out of school. Surveys found that although fees had officially been lifted, the cost of uniforms and related expenses remained the biggest barrier for families whose children had never been to school.[39] Many teachers were not adequately trained, and for many families, schools were too far away. While Sierra Leone designates a significant amount of its budget for education and its economy has been growing steadily since the end of the war, budgetary resources remain small.

Nevertheless, Sierra Leone has made significant progress, and its children have played a central role in shaping the country's policies and practices. The Children's Forum Network continued to use its manifesto as a scorecard in every election to grade the commitment of the country's leaders. The network helped draft a comprehensive Child Rights Act and campaigned for it in speeches, marches, and meetings with parliamentarians and other government officials. The law was adopted in 2007.

Bah credits the Children's Forum Network with socializing the concept of children's rights in Sierra Leone. "When we started, the idea was scandalous and we got a lot of pushback. People thought we were trying to take away the rights of parents. But now, people believe that children do have a voice."[40]

Bah attended university in Sierra Leone. After he graduated, he began working with the United Nations and eventually attended graduate school in the United States. He continued to advocate for the right to education and worked with youth in Liberia, the Philippines, Ethiopia, and other countries. In 2012, the UN secretary-general launched the Global Education First Initiative, appointing Bah as the youth representative on its High Level Steering Committee. Bah says that his own experiences shaped his decision to advocate for education: "Education made such a difference in my life. I look at my friends who didn't have the same opportunities and what happened to them. Every single child I talk to, the one thing everyone says they want is education."[41]

Global Campaign for Education

In 1999, six months before governments from around the world would gather in Dakar, Senegal, for the World Education Forum, a group of education activists met in Brussels. They were dismayed at governments' poor progress in ensuring children's right to education and decided to launch a short-term Global Campaign for Education. Their aim was to pressure governments to make concrete commitments in Dakar to ensure universal enrollment in and completion of free primary education by 2015.[42]

The initial meeting was organized by ActionAid, Oxfam, Education International, and the Global March against Child Labor and included representatives from Ghana, Brazil, India, Kenya, Peru, Bolivia, Bangladesh, Mozambique, and Tanzania. Within six months, the campaign grew to include thirty-eight national coalitions, as well as eight regional networks and coalitions.

The campaign undertook an ambitious agenda in advance of the Dakar forum. It sent a Millennium Appeal for education for all to all heads of state, prepared policy demands, organized joint media and public actions around regional meetings leading up to the Dakar summit, and launched a Week of Action in early April, engaging nongovernmental organizations (NGOs), teachers, and community groups from around the world in events to draw attention to the situation of education in their country. During the Week of Action, the campaign held press conferences with heads of state and finance ministers in Tokyo, Washington, the Netherlands, the United Kingdom, and Belgium.

Over one thousand people participated in the Dakar summit in April 2000. As it was underway, the campaign lobbied delegates and met with the UN secretary-general and the heads of UNICEF, UNESCO, and the World Bank. NGOs served on key drafting committees and participated in the final press conference. The campaigners influenced key aspects of the forum's Framework for Action, including acceptance of free and compulsory education, recognition of the role of civil society, and commitments to clear, time-bound national follow-up and action plans. Under the Dakar Framework for Action, governments pledged to meet six education goals by 2015, including free and compulsory primary education for all, gender equality in education, and a 50 percent reduction in illiteracy.

Energized by the Dakar forum, campaign members agreed to continue their efforts. They felt that bringing NGOs and trade unions together from both the North and South to work together on a unified platform had established the campaign as a powerful, effective, and legitimate voice. Anne

Jellema, an American who had spent several years working for Action Aid, became its first coordinator. Early the next year, the Global Campaign for Education (GCE) held its first World Assembly in Delhi, where it committed itself to "the building of an international movement, one with minimal bureaucracy and with a long-term commitment to monitor the achievement of the Education for All goals."[43] Members agreed that the campaign would continue its advocacy until at least 2016.

For the campaign, its diversity was both an asset and a challenge. Jellema recalled that initially, "There was a lot of uncertainty and tension between southern civil society groups and big northern NGOs. A lot of work had to be done to build trust on both sides before we decided to continue."[44] Among the campaign's members, some organizations were comfortable with a hierarchical top-down approach, while others embraced bottom-up organizing. To accommodate these differences, the campaign developed clear governance structures and decision-making processes, and it formalized procedures for membership. It also tried to use the respective strengths of its members. At the international level, some, like Oxfam, were very skilled with policy and lobbying work, while others, like the Global March against Child Labor and Action Aid, were strong on mobilization and engaging partners. Both skill sets contributed to the campaign's impact.

Developing a strategy for the campaign was challenging. "Other than the demand for more aid for education, there was no single obvious international target for the campaign, since the impactful stuff needed to happen at a national level," said Jellema.[45] The campaign began to organize Global Action Weeks every April. These weeks became vehicles for national coalitions to raise public awareness about the need for education, build the GCE network, and mobilize pressure on policymakers to meet their Education for All commitments. "It was a week when we all came together under the same banner and made a big noise," said Jellema.[46]

Each year, the Global Action Week focused on a specific theme, such as girls' education, the need for more teachers, quality education, disability, and early childhood education. "People saw that being focused and being simple really worked," said Jellema. In 2005, for example, the theme of the week was Send my Friend to School. Over 5 million people in ninety countries took part, making 3.5 million cut-outs of "friends" or "buddies" representing children who were out of school. These "buddies" were used in marches, exhibitions, rallies, and meetings with Nelson Mandela, Tony Blair, and other officials. Three thousand parliamentarians and twenty-five heads of state "went back to school" where students presented them with the cut-out figures. At least thirteen national leaders pledged specific policy changes, including education budget increases in the Ivory Coast, Democratic Republic of the Congo, and Niger, and assurances that school fees would be abolished in Cameroon, Sierra Leone, Sudan, and Burundi.

The 2009 week focused on adult literacy with the theme the Big Read. Prominent figures including Paulo Coelho, Alice Walker, Desmond Tutu, Natalie Portman, and Chimamanda Ngozi Adichie wrote stories for a Big Read Story Book. Many of the authors participated in special events to read their stories, and Queen Rania of Jordan led events in Johannesburg and Washington, DC. Over 14 million people participated in reading stories and signed their names to an appeal to be delivered to world leaders. In the Democratic Republic of the Congo, over one thousand schools in eleven provinces participated in the Big Read, and government ministers attended a Big Read held at the Ministry of Foreign Affairs. In Latvia, more than ten thousand students, teachers, parents, and others took part in the largest street demonstration since the country's independence.

Beginning in 2003, the GCE began publishing annual reports assessing the world's wealthiest countries' performance in providing aid to basic education. The report simulated school report cards with grades from A to F and included typical teacher remarks on report cards such as "needs improvement," or "at the back of the class." For example, in 2003, the United States was ranked 20 out of 22, and the teacher's remarks said, "Disappointing. George [George W. Bush] says that no child should be left behind, but the US continues to be the least generous aid giver as a share of national income, and the least generous donor to education." A former UK official said the school reports were "clever, effective, and very helpful." He pointed out that "Tony Blair was only getting a C to begin with, but over two years the UK increased spending [to become] the second biggest funder."[47]

By 2015, the campaign had members in nearly one hundred countries. In dozens of low-income countries, it worked with the Global Partnership for Education to provide over $32 million to support national education coalitions. In the Dominican Republic, for example, a coalition of eight education organizations known as the Socio-Educational Forum (Foro Socioeducativo) began working in 2000 to highlight the negative impact of the country's low investment in education. The forum analyzed education plans and budgets and joined forces with other civil society groups to campaign for "4% for education." It achieved a major victory in 2012 when all of the country's presidential candidates signed commitments supporting the investment of 4 percent of the Dominican Republic's gross domestic product in pre-university education. The coordinator of the forum said,

> For the first time, candidates had to participate in public debates on their plans for education and undergo the scrutiny of experts in education, economics and social sciences in general. The general public was able to listen to the candidates, hear their proposals and consider their quality. These actions are unprecedented milestones in the country.[48]

Camilla Croso is a Brazilian education activist who cofounded the GCE and became its president in 2011. She, along with other members of the campaign, saw the negotiation of new global development goals for 2030 (the Sustainable Development Goals, SDGs) as a huge opportunity for the education movement. The GCE devoted three years of advocacy and lobbying to influence these goals, urging states to adopt concrete commitments that were both ambitious and rights based.

In September 2015, the UN General Assembly adopted the SDGs, committing to ensure that by 2030, all girls and boys complete free, equitable, and quality primary and secondary education. The goals also set commitments to ensure access to early childhood education, substantially increase the supply of qualified teachers, eliminate gender disparities, and ensure equal access for vulnerable populations, including children with disabilities.[49] Croso said, "Civil society needs a big round of applause for the SDGs. It's been spectacular. We've managed to gain a lot of ground. Three years ago, the education goals being discussed were from a much more reductionist perspective, looking at human capital development and jobs. Very far away from the concept of education as a fundamental human right."[50]

Challenges

Ensuring that all children complete both primary and secondary school by the year 2030 is a daunting and ambitious endeavor that will require significant resources. In 2015, the EFA Global Monitoring Report concluded that an additional US$39 billion in external revenue would be required each year to reach the new 2030 sustainable development goals.[51] But despite increases by some donor countries, overall financing for education has fallen. In 2013, total aid to education was 4 percent lower than in 2010, when it was at its peak.[52]

Although many countries have made progress by eliminating formal school fees, they have not always provided local schools with the resources they need.

As a consequence, many schools have imposed their own informal fees for registration, exams, certificates, and other expenses, creating insurmountable barriers for many children. Fees for secondary school are still common, and children of lower secondary school age (ages 12–15) are almost twice as likely to be out of school as primary-school-aged children.[53]

Displacement due to war and natural disasters has also created huge obstacles to schooling. The proportion of out-of-school children from countries in conflict has climbed as global displacement has hit historic highs. In 2016, for example, nearly 3 million Syrian children inside Syria and in neighboring countries were no longer in school.[54]

Other vulnerable groups also face formidable barriers to schooling. Children with disabilities, estimated at 93 to 150 million children worldwide, are among those most often left out. Schools may arbitrarily deny them access, lack accessible facilities or teachers with appropriate training, or charge special fees. One study found that disability was more likely than socioeconomic status, rural location, or gender in predicting that a child was not in school.[55]

The increasing privatization of education and explosive growth of private education providers also compromises access to education. As governments have struggled to boost enrollment, many have been attracted to private companies that promised cheaper and more effective education services, such as voucher programs, public-private partnerships, and "low-fee" private schools. Private companies, for their part, saw the potential for huge profits through the sale of textbooks, teacher training, and evaluation systems and by running private schools. These schemes, however, can undermine the universal right to education. The UN special rapporteur on the right to education has sharply criticized the privatization of education, finding that privatizing aggravates growing disparities in access to education and marginalizes the poor even more.[56]

Education campaigners and teachers have also faced increasing pressure to restrict their activities. Some governments have imposed restrictions on outside funding to national NGOs, limited or attacked public demonstrations and peaceful rallies led by teachers or students, and even criminalized activists' political activity. According to GCE, the restriction of space for civil society as political actors has became a major obstacle for effective citizen participation and influence.[57] "How contradictory is it to promote education as a human right, and then to criminalize and even kill the key actors in education, the teachers and the students?" asked Croso, GCE's president.[58]

The Way Forward

Although many countries were far from reaching the Education for All goals in 2015, several key policy shifts have helped governments dramatically increase primary school enrollment rates compared to 2000. One of the most important is to increase resource allocations for education, allow construction of additional schools, and increase the number of trained teachers. While some countries have been able to do this as their income levels rise or as they reassess spending priorities, others rely on financial assistance from donor countries to increase their investments in education. A second key strategy is to eliminate school fees and help eliminate other school-related expenses for poor children by providing free uniforms, books, and transportation. A third is to provide cash stipends to poor and vulnerable families and other incentives such as school meals. Nondiscrimination policies and action are also necessary, including monitoring and outreach to ensure that vulnerable groups, such as children with disabilities, are included. In combination, these strategies have helped dozens of countries make huge strides in expanding children's access to education.

Many of these actions would not have happened without dogged civil society campaigning. At the national and international levels, nongovernmental organizations have pushed governments to increase investments in education and adopt policies that have made education possible for millions of children who may otherwise have never gone to school.

The Children's Forum Network used school-based children's clubs to mobilize children across Sierra Leone and insert the views of children into their country's postwar policy agenda. It engaged policymakers at the highest level through radio shows and forums, and developed manifestos on children's rights to influence legislation guaranteeing free primary and junior secondary education. Other NGOs influenced the abolition of school fees in countries including Burundi, Cameroon, Kenya, Sudan, Tanzania, and Uganda and also helped to change the World Bank's policy on user fees.[59]

The GCE prompted significant increases in aid to education by international donors, such as the United Kingdom and the Netherlands. A Dutch official interviewed for a 2007 midterm review of the GCE said the campaign and its Dutch partners were responsible for the Dutch government's promise to dedicate 15 percent of its development budget to education.[60] A UK official described GCE as a "catalyst" and attributed an increase in UK aid to education to "a three-way coalition of political will, NGO advocacy, and technical expertise."[61]

Leaders within the GCE believed that several elements contributed to their campaign's impact. Among these were the ability to unify diverse members and national coalitions around common goals, effective strategizing and communication, and mechanisms to share knowledge and experience among the campaign's members.

Although differing national contexts and priorities could easily lead to a splintered campaign, the GCE used the Global Action Week to engage and unify its members, build visibility, and further its advocacy goals. "We needed to promote national diversity, but at the same time, have enough coherence so that the campaign was bigger than the sum of its parts," said Jellema. "The Week of Action was a way to tackle that problem." The Global Week of Action became extraordinarily successful, engaging as many as 20 million people a year in 120 countries. According to one board member, it was one of the most recognized campaign movements around the world.[62]

The campaign facilitated a new level of collaboration between NGOs and teachers' unions. "That proved to be something that was really important and eye-opening," said Jellema:

> For many years, NGOs and donors had been trying to fix education without talking to teachers. Breaking down those barriers turned out to be quite impactful. In some countries, teachers unions and NGOs had never gone together to parliament or to ministries to say what needed to happen. At the international level, with the World Bank and other key targets, bringing those groups together also made a much bigger impression.[63]

As a global network, collective communication and strategizing was essential. For example, during the negotiation of the post-2015 sustainable development goals, the campaign engaged its entire network in shaping its advocacy agenda, making sure that all members were informed and involved. "The process around defining the agenda was complex, with so many nuances and actors," said Croso. "We were doing advocacy at the global level, but ensured that it was anchored at the national and regional level." Croso also stressed that a fundamental value in the campaign was for members to learn from each other: "Sometimes within movements there is an assumption that the international knows more than the national. We work hard to break that pattern, so that we all learn from each other. We are a movement that seeks to be horizontal."[64] The campaign set up web platforms for members to upload experiences, wrote publications to document campaign successes, and organized seminars and other meetings to allow sharing and systematized reflection about what works and what doesn't work.

Anne Jellema, GCE's first coordinator, believes the campaign accomplished a fundamental attitude shift. In the wake of structural adjustment policies in the 1980s and 1990s, many policymakers regarded education as a service. "It was a radical thing to say that education was a right and no one should have to pay for it," she said. "I think GCE helped create a groundswell around education as a right."[65]

The 2030 goal of universal education is unquestionably ambitious. But for the GCE, it marks the beginning of a new phase of organizing to hold governments accountable for their commitments. "We are not naïve and we see the huge challenges ahead," said Croso. "But we believe that our renewed, shared vision for education is one which gives us all added vigour."[66]

10 Attacks on Education

When she accepted the Nobel Peace Prize in Oslo in December 2014, Malala Yousafzai said, "I tell my story, not because it is unique, but because it is not. It is the story of many girls."[1]

MALALA was barely ten years old when the Taliban began a violent campaign to gain control of the lush Swat river valley, her home in northwest Pakistan. The militants believed that educating females was contrary to Islam, and as they sought to impose their rigid interpretation of sharia (Islamic law), they damaged and destroyed hundreds of schools. When Malala was eleven, her father, a school principal, took her to speak at the local press club in Peshawar, where she described how she walked to school with her schoolbooks hidden under her clothes. She asked the audience, "How dare the Taliban take away my basic right to education?"[2]

In 2008, the Taliban took control of the Swat valley and announced a new edict, to take effect on January 15, 2009, banning all education for girls and prohibiting women from teaching. A local Taliban commander reportedly said over a radio broadcast that violators would be killed or attacked with acid and that schools that remained open would be bombed.[3]

With her father's encouragement, Malala began writing a blog for the BBC, "The Diary of a Pakistani Schoolgirl." She used the name of the heroine from a Pashtun folk tale, Gul Makai, as a pseudonym. The evening before the Taliban edict was to take effect, she blogged that her classmates were not excited about the upcoming winter holiday: "They knew if the Taliban implemented their edict they would not be able to come to school again."[4]

The Taliban enforced their edict with violence and forced nine hundred schools to close or stop accepting girls. They continued to carry out attacks on schools with bombs, grenades, guns, and mortars. According to the Human Rights Commission of Pakistan, the Taliban damaged or destroyed 505 schools in 2009 alone.[5] By May 2009, life in the Swat valley was too dangerous for Malala's family, and they fled. Her father went to Peshawar, while Malala lived with relatives in the countryside. When government forces regained control of the area a few months later, the family returned, but the Taliban continued its attacks. Many girls and teachers were too afraid to return to school.

Malala's identity as the BBC blogger was revealed in late 2009, but she continued to speak out about the right to education. She held a press conference to urge the government to restore education for children in the valley and gave interviews to newspapers and television. She became chair of the District Child Assembly of Swat, a child-only forum to protect children's rights in 2010, and the next year, she was awarded Pakistan's National Youth Peace Prize.

As Malala became better known, she began receiving death threats. They were slipped under her door, published in newspapers, and posted on Facebook. On October 9, 2012, a man boarded her school bus and shouted, "Which one of you is Malala?"[6] No one spoke, but when Malala's friends instinctively looked toward her, the gunman opened fire, shooting Malala in the head and injuring two other girls. The bullet that hit Malala traveled from the left side of her forehead down her neck and lodged near her spine. She was airlifted to a hospital in Peshwar and a few days later was transported to Birmingham, England. The attempted assassination attempt was covered by media worldwide, as was her remarkable recovery.

On her 16th birthday in 2013, Malala spoke at the United Nations General Assembly in New York:

> The terrorists thought they would change my aims and stop my ambitions, but nothing changed in my life except this: weakness, fear and hopelessness died. Strength, power and courage was born. . . . Let us pick up our books and pens. They are our most powerful weapons. One child, one teacher, one pen and one book can change the world. Education is the only solution.[7]

The following year, Malala became the youngest person in history to receive the Nobel Peace Prize.

Attacks on schools occur globally. Militants conducted at least 838 attacks on schools in Pakistan between 2009 and 2012, more than in any other country.[8] But during the same period, similar attacks took place in at least seventy countries worldwide.[9] Government forces and nonstate armed groups bombed and burned schools and kidnapped, injured, or killed schoolchildren and teachers.

In northern Nigeria, for example, the militant Islamist group known as Boko Haram has systematically attacked schools, killed teachers, and abducted students. Like the Taliban, Boko Haram (which means "Western education is a sin" in Hausa) seeks to impose a strict version of sharia law. Abubakar Shekau, the group's leader, declared in a 2013 video statement, "School teachers who are teaching Western education? We will kill them! We will kill them!" and claimed that non-Islamic schools should be burned down.[10] Between 2009 and 2015, Boko Haram destroyed more than nine hundred schools, and their attacks forced at least fifteen hundred more to close. The group deliberately killed more than six hundred teachers and abducted more than two thousand civilians, many of them schoolgirls.[11] The largest single such incident took place in April 2014, when Boko Haram abducted 276 girls from their school in Chibok, Borno state, prompting the global #BringBackOurGirls campaign for their return.[12]

In Syria, more than six thousand schools were destroyed, damaged, or no longer operating between 2011, when the country's war began, and 2016.[13] In Afghanistan, the Taliban and other armed opposition groups carried out more than eleven hundred attacks on education, according to the United Nations. These attacks included the use of improvised explosive devices, land mines and suicide bombings, grenades thrown into school buildings or playgrounds, rocket attacks, and setting schools on fire. In addition to attacking school buildings, armed groups killed, injured, abducted, and threatened teachers and students.

Armed forces and groups have a range of motives for targeting schools, teachers, and students. In some cases, armed opposition groups attack schools as symbols of government control. In many areas, schools represent the only government presence, and with little or no security, they present a perfect target for groups seeking to undermine government authority or instill fear in the local population. Some groups try to block education they perceive as contrary to their religious or cultural values, including the education of girls. In Colombia, teachers are targeted because of their trade union activity and in others, including Pakistan, Iraq, and Bangladesh, to inhibit academic freedom and freedom of speech.[14] Schools also provide easy access to students for abduction or recruitment as soldiers, sex slaves, or for ransom. Finally, both government and nonstate armed groups seize schools for use in their military operations, transforming them into barracks and military bases. Such use often provokes further attacks from opposing forces.

Attacks on education violate both international human rights law and international humanitarian law (also known as the laws of war). The laws of war prohibit direct attacks against "civilian objects," including schools, unless they are being used for military purposes.[15] Under the Rome Statute of the International Criminal Court, intentional direct attacks against schools when they are not legitimate military objectives constitutes a war crime.[16] Targeting schools, teachers, and students also impedes children's right to education, which is guaranteed at all times, during war and peace, by international human rights law.[17]

Attacks on schools, teachers, and students have been devastating. Apart from the thousands of schools attacked directly, thousands more have been shut down because of threats and insecurity. Even when schools remain open, parents are often afraid to send their children. Millions are deprived of their right to education and experience fear and trauma. According to UNESCO, 35 percent of the world's primary-aged children who were not in school in 2014—over 20 million—lived in conflict countries, an increase from 30 percent in 1999.[18] Children who attend primary school in conflict countries are 20 percent more likely to drop out than their counterparts in other countries.[19]

Despite the severity and prevalence of attacks on education, until 2010 they received little attention beyond the local communities where they took place. This chapter explores the evolution of a global coalition to mobilize international attention and action to stop attacks on education and an innovative initiative to end the use of schools for military purposes.

Global Coalition to Protect Education from Attack

In 2003, Zama Coursen-Neff, an American in her 30s, traveled to Afghanistan to investigate abuses by local militias for Human Rights Watch. It was just two years after the US ouster of the Taliban, and the return to school by many girls was perceived internationally as a success story. But as Coursen-Neff investigated abuses by the militias, including extortion and rape, people began telling her that their schools were being attacked. They described grenades left under teachers' chairs, schools and educational material being burned, and communities receiving written threats. "I started keeping a list in the back of my notebook," said Coursen-Neff. "When I went back to Kabul, I started asking groups what they were doing about it." She found that not only was no one tracking the issue, but no one wanted to admit it was a problem. A UNICEF representative told her, "We have not seen any evidence suggesting that these incidents comprise a concerted, anti-education effort."[20]

Coursen-Neff returned to Afghanistan in 2005 specifically to investigate attacks on education. She documented over two hundred attacks on teachers, students, and schools as part of resurgent activity by the Taliban and other armed groups. These groups were using suicide bombings and attacks against "soft targets" such as schools to provoke terror among ordinary Afghans and alienate civilians from the central government. She found entire districts in Afghanistan where all schools had closed and teachers had left in the face of continuing attacks and threats. Armed groups bombed and set fire to school buildings, assassinated teachers and principals, and in some cases went from village to village, calling meetings at local mosques where they announced that all schools should be closed.

The attacks had a chilling effect across the country. A mother of two daughters in Kandahar told Coursen-Neff that after public threats were posted in her community, families decided that it was not worth the risk to send their daughters to school. "My daughters are afraid," she said. "They are telling us 'we'll get killed and be lying on the streets and you won't even know.'"[21]

When Coursen-Neff again raised the attacks with the Afghan government and UN agencies, some admitted that they didn't want to bring attention to the problem because they were afraid that it would prompt donors to end desperately needed funding for Afghanistan's education system. Coursen-Neff was incredulous when the deputy minister of education told her that the ministry didn't track attacks on education because it would "have a negative effect on morale."[22] Human Rights Watch published Coursen-Neff's findings in 2006, urging the Afghan government and its supporters to monitor attacks on education; develop a prevention strategy focusing on the schools most at risk; and strengthen efforts to investigate, arrest, and prosecute those most responsible.

Later that year, two gunmen on a motorbike shot and killed an Afghan woman named Safia Ama Jan as she left her home in Kandahar for work. Ama Jan was the director of women's affairs in Kandahar province and had been a teacher for three decades. During Taliban rule, she risked her life running an underground school for girls from her home. The director-general of UNESCO, the UN's education, science, and culture agency, was outraged by the killing. "It was the brazenness of the event, that she was literally shot down outside her home," said Mark Richmond, who served as a director in UNESCO's education sector at the time. "It was such an outrageous thing, and somehow struck a strong nerve, especially in terms of girls' education."[23] The director-general wanted to issue a statement, and Richmond suggested that it should not only condemn the killing but also announce what UNESCO was going to do about attacks on teachers. Richmond had previously worked on education in sub-Saharan Africa and the Balkans, where attacks on schools, students, and teachers had also taken place, and he knew that no one had ever done a comprehensive or global study of the phenomenon. He proposed to the director-general that UNESCO undertake such a study and announce it as part of the statement about Ama Jan's murder.

UNESCO's *Education under Attack* was published in early 2007, drawing on research from Human Rights Watch and other nongovernmental organizations (NGOs), UN sources, and media accounts. It detailed attacks on schools, teachers, and students in more than thirteen countries and recommended concerted action to address the problem. That year, Richmond organized meetings around the report in April at UNESCO headquarters in Paris, in July in association with the meeting of ECOSOC in Geneva, and in the autumn to coincide with the UN General Assembly, reaching out to governments, media, NGOs, and the United Nations. But he realized that a stronger strategy for action was needed. "We were a little naïve about it," he said. "We thought we had a story that was obvious, but then realized that we hadn't thought through what would come after the study."[24]

With support from the Office of Sheikha Moza bint Nasser Al Missnad, the first lady of Qatar, UNESCO organized an expert seminar in Paris in late 2009, inviting a diverse group of seventy-five specialists from around the world, including Coursen-Neff, other NGO and UN representatives, and academics, to explore key gaps in data, research, policy, and advocacy on the issue. "It became clear that people were interested in doing more," said Coursen-Neff. The participants developed a set of recommendations for further research, advocacy, and policy development.[25] By the end of the seminar, they also agreed that a sustained campaign was needed to prevent and respond to attacks on education.

A few months later, UN agencies and NGOs met in New York around the launch of UNESCO's second edition of *Education under Attack* and agreed to create a new coalition. Eight NGOs and UN agencies stepped forward to form a steering committee for the fledgling entity, known as the Global Coalition to Protect Education from Attack (GCPEA).[26] With funding from donors, including Education above All (a Qatar-based foundation working to protect education in crisis), UNICEF, and an anonymous donor, GCPEA hired a coordinator and, later, additional staff who formed a secretariat based in New York. The steering committee agreed that GCPEA would work on four areas and established working groups for each: strengthening monitoring and reporting, promoting effective policies for protection and prevention, protecting schools and universities from military use during armed conflict, and protecting higher education from attack.[27]

One of the coalition's first major initiatives was to organize a workshop in Phuket, Thailand, to bring together practitioners to share practical measures that had already been developed by organizations and communities to respond to attacks on education. Participants shared how they had developed community protection teams to help guard local schools, negotiated with armed forces and armed groups, and developed alternative schools or remote learning to allow children in conflict areas to continue their education. In Colombia, where teachers are often under threat, escorts accompanied teachers to school. In Afghanistan, Save the Children worked with respected elders and religious leaders to promote education as a fundamental Islamic value. In the Democratic Republic of the Congo, an accelerated learning program allowed children who had missed out on school to condense six years of primary education into three years. In several countries, the United Nations or community organizations negotiated successfully with armed groups to rid schools of fighters or ban certain military activities from school grounds. In Côte d'Ivoire, for example, negotiations persuaded an armed group to vacate forty of forty-five occupied schools.[28]

After UNESCO published *Education under Attack* in 2010, some countries sharply criticized both the report and UNESCO. "Some of the member states felt that an accusatory finger was being pointed at them," said Richmond. "The study itself came under attack."[29] Meanwhile, UNESCO had a new director-general who sought to quickly take the heat out of the controversy. "It was a very difficult moment," said Richmond, who still stands by the findings of the 2010 study. Subsequently, UNESCO and GCPEA agreed that GCPEA would take on publication of future editions of *Education under Attack*.

The 2014 edition, for which Richmond was the chief editor, was the most comprehensive to date. It found that between 2009 and 2013, at least thirty countries experienced a significant pattern of attacks on education[30] and that some countries—Afghanistan, Colombia, Pakistan, Somalia, Sudan, and Syria—each experienced more than one thousand attacks during the time period.[31] The report also raised GCPEA's profile significantly. "Our ability to do advocacy increased exponentially after *Education Under Attack* came out," said Diya Nijhowne, GCPEA's director. "We need to have that data to make our arguments."[32]

GCPEA and its partners persuaded senior UN leaders to begin raising the issue publicly and began advocacy meetings with members of the UN Security

Council. An early advocacy success took place in July 2011, when the Security Council adopted a resolution strongly condemning attacks on schools and calling on parties to armed conflict to end all such attacks and refrain from actions that impede children's access to education. The resolution also asked the secretary-general to include parties to armed conflict that engage in such attacks in his annual list of perpetrators of grave violations against children.[33] By doing so, listed parties became subject to possible UN sanctions.

By 2017, GCPEA had made significant progress in raising global attention to attacks on education, placing it on the international agenda, securing commitments from governments and key bodies such as the Security Council, and developing a policy agenda to protect schools, teachers, and students. It also led a remarkable effort to end the military use of schools.

Ending the Military Use of Schools

In May 2009, Bede Sheppard traveled to central India to investigate attacks on schools by Maoist rebels. A New Zealander in his thirties, he was, like Coursen-Neff, a researcher for Human Rights Watch. As he entered the gates of a middle school in Kasma village, the first thing he saw was a pair of men's underpants hanging on a clothesline next to a pair of military camouflage pants. As he proceeded into the school courtyard, he saw beer bottles and a bottle of whiskey. "It wasn't what you'd expect to see in a school," he said.[34]

The school principal explained to Sheppard that several years before, some government security officers had begun using a couple of classrooms to sleep and spend time in when not carrying out operations against Maoists in the region. Sheppard said, "What struck me about the situation is that the school was in a very rural area where they already had a hard time keeping children in school, especially girls, because of pressures to work or get married."[35] The government had given the school over 1 million rupees to provide residential scholarships to help reenroll two hundred girls who had dropped out. But because of the presence of ten paramilitary police, parents wouldn't allow their daughters to return.[36] Sheppard found that security forces were using dozens of schools in the region, sometimes for short periods of time as temporary camps, but in other cases, they were there for months or even years, disrupting the education of thousands of students.[37]

Sheppard next traveled to southern Thailand to document attacks on teachers by separatist insurgents. After what he had found in India, he was curious if military forces were using schools in southern Thailand also. He found that they were. "It had a clear impact on children's education," he said, "and even more so on the safety of teachers and educational personnel. But no one out-side of Thailand seemed aware of it."[38]

Sheppard started looking for other examples and discovered that the mili-tary use of schools was common in conflict countries around the world. Sol-diers use schools as barracks, for military training, as operational headquarters, for weapons storage, as firing and observation positions, and for detention and interrogation centers. They often see schools as both convenient and advanta-geous for tactical reasons. For example, thick boundary walls can provide for-tification, and the height of a multistory building can be useful for surveillance or sniper positions. In some cases, soldiers take over an entire school, while in others, they use just a few classrooms or the school grounds.

A high school student in Somalia described how several of his classmates lost their lives after the militant group al-Shabaab set up military operations in his school:

> Al-Shabaab came into the compound of the school and told us to stay in class. It was noon and they set up a Hobiye [a surface-to-air rocket launcher] and they started launching from inside the school compound. . . . Some students tried to get out of the compound but they were turned back by al-Shabaab. We were trapped for two hours and they were firing. . . . There was incoming fire coming back at our direction. There were five rockets hit-ting around the school compound. One landed as we were released and it killed eight students who were walking home.[39]

The military use of schools not only threatens the lives and safety of stu-dents and teachers, but also violates children's right to education. Some children are forced to leave school entirely, while others may be crowded into whatever space is not being used by soldiers. In Bihar, India, for example, when police occupied eight classrooms at Tankuppa High School, seven hundred students were forced to share the remaining three.[40] Not surprisingly, under such condi-tions, performance suffers and dropout rates increase. Parents are understand-ably reluctant to send their children to schools where the military is present, and in particular, they fear their daughters may be at risk of sexual assault or harassment by male soldiers.

Soldiers may significantly damage school property, requiring allocation of precious resources for repairs. When government soldiers took over primary schools in the Democratic Republic of Congo, for example, they burned school desks and doors for fuel, used classrooms as toilets, and looted school materials. The United Nations in South Sudan estimated that on average, rehabilitating a single primary school after military occupation cost approximately US$67,000.[41] Soldiers may also leave behind razor wire, sandbags, and other signs of military use that could continue to draw attacks by opposition forces.

Under international humanitarian law, parties to armed conflict are prohibited from attacking civilian objects, including schools, as long as they are not being used for military purposes. They are also required to take "necessary precautions" to protect the civilian population from the dangers of military operations.[42] International humanitarian law, however, contains no specific ban on the use of schools for military purposes. Once a school is used for military activities, it can become a military objective and therefore a legitimate target of attack. If students and teachers are still present, their lives may be at grave risk.

Sheppard found that many people wrongly believed that the military use of schools was already prohibited by international law. "If you weren't talking to military lawyers," he said, "people generally assumed that this was something that was already illegal."[43] He examined the laws and practices regarding the military use of schools in fifty-six countries.[44] He found seven countries with laws or military policies that explicitly banned or restricted the use of education buildings by military forces: the Philippines, Colombia, Ireland, India, New Zealand, Ecuador, and the United Kingdom. Three of the countries—India, the Philippines, and Colombia—had experienced decades of conflict. Sheppard believed their example was very powerful, even if their rules were not always fully implemented. "Based on their experience with conflict," he said, "they had decided that this was a tactic that they wanted to take off the table, and in fact, *could* take off the table."[45]

GCPEA decided to make ending the military use of schools one of its first advocacy priorities. Sheppard agreed to lead a working group on the issue together with Courtney Erwin, who worked for Education above All. They decided that the first task was to undertake a global survey to demonstrate the scale of the problem.

The subsequent studies, published in 2012 and 2015, found that armed forces and armed groups used schools for military purposes in at least twenty-six countries between 2005 and 2015.[46] The most affected was Syria, where up to 1,000 schools were allegedly used by 2013 as temporary bases, military staging grounds, sniper posts, or detention or torture centers.[47] In Libya, armed groups reportedly used as many as 221 schools during the 2011 armed uprising. In India's military campaign against Maoist insurgents and other armed groups, government forces used at least 129 schools as barracks or bases, disrupting studies for over twenty thousand students.[48]

In some countries, UN peacekeeping forces used schools for their military operations. Sheppard met with the UN Department of Peacekeeping Operations in New York and shared some of the coalition's early research. "They instantly understood it was an issue," he said. The department subsequently developed a directive in the 2012 manual used to train all UN peacekeeper infantry, stating that schools should not be used by the military in their operations.[49] GCPEA highlighted the policy as a positive example in advocacy discussions with individual countries.

Sheppard also had discussions about the issue with Geneva Call, a Switzerland-based group that engages with nonstate armed groups around their conduct in war. Geneva Call was developing a "deed of commitment" on protecting children in armed conflict and included a provision committing signatories to "avoid using for military purposes schools or premises primarily used by children."[50] They launched the deed in 2009, and by 2017, nineteen nonstate armed groups from seven countries had signed on.[51]

In May 2012, Erwin and Sheppard organized an initial consultation hosted by the Geneva Academy for Humanitarian Law and Human Rights. Its purpose was to present the research to a broader group of stakeholders and discuss possible ways to end military use of schools. They invited a small group of states (Philippines, Netherlands, Qatar, and Switzerland), the International Committee of the Red Cross (ICRC), UNICEF, UNESCO, a few NGOs, and military experts. Most participants believed that it would be difficult to muster enough support for a new international treaty. "No one wanted a formal process that could take years and years," said Erwin. "There definitely was a feeling that a more formal convention or legal process would be too complicated and not as effective."[52]

The consultation's participants agreed that the best way forward would be to draft voluntary guidelines to help both government forces and nonstate armed groups avoid the military use of schools. GCPEA believed that someone with military expertise would bring credibility to the process and asked Steven Haines, a former commander in the UK armed forces, to help. Haines was a professor of international law, specializing in the conduct of military operations, and he had helped draft the United Kingdom's manual on the laws of war. He quickly agreed to help GCPEA put together draft guidelines.

In November 2012, GCPEA invited a larger group of government representatives and experts in human rights and humanitarian law to a picturesque thirteenth-century castle in Switzerland to discuss the draft guidelines.[53] Supporters of Human Rights Watch owned the castle and had donated its space for the meeting. "We weren't trying to make new international law, but we did want the guidelines to be taken seriously," said Sheppard. "We thought if we used a castle it would bring gravitas to the project."[54] The government representatives came from ministries of defense, education, and foreign affairs and included Liberia's education minister. Later, one of the participants admitted to Sheppard that the castle's appeal had persuaded him to attend.

Participants were enthusiastic about the guidelines' approach but had many comments about the initial draft. Haines worked with a small group to revise the guidelines, and the following June, GCPEA formally released them for comment at an event before the UN Committee on the Rights of the Child in Geneva. Named after the small Swiss village where the castle was located, the guidelines became known as the Draft Lucens Guidelines for Protecting Schools and Universities from Military Use during Armed Conflict.

The guidelines set out six key principles to encourage good practices by both government armed forces and nonstate armed groups during armed conflict. They urged parties to conflict to never use functioning schools for military purposes and to examine all possible alternatives before using abandoned schools. The guidelines acknowledged that certain uses of schools were not contrary to international humanitarian law, but urged that in such exceptional cases, armed forces should use schools only for the minimum amount of time necessary and remove all evidence of militarization before vacating the premises. Parties to armed conflict were expected to incorporate the guidelines into their military doctrine, rules of engagement, or operational orders to encourage good practices throughout their chain of command.[55]

As they launched the draft guidelines, GCPEA representatives met with government missions in New York and Geneva to explain their purpose, answer questions, and seek support. Over the summer and fall, Sheppard, Erwin, and Veronique Aubert of Save the Children traveled throughout Africa, Latin America, Europe, Asia, and the Middle East to meet with key decision makers in ministries of defense, foreign affairs, and education and to introduce the guidelines to civil society groups.

Erwin traveled to nearly twenty capitals and found that governments' reception to the guidelines varied a great deal. In Portugal, for example, "They were incredibly enthusiastic," she recalled. "They were very proud of their human rights record, especially in terms of education, and offered ideas that we hadn't even thought of, for example, how they could reach out to Portugal's former colonies about the guidelines." Liberia also showed strong interest. When Aubert and Steven Haines went to Monrovia, Liberia's capital, government representatives and fifty military officers met with them to discuss the guidelines. "There was a real appetite for the issue," Aubert said. "It was very relevant for them because of the history [in Liberia] of use of schools."[56] Other governments, however, were less enthusiastic, particularly when legal experts were brought in. "They [the legal experts] were against any protections that went beyond the law," said Erwin. "Even though the guidelines weren't binding, they said 'we have the law, we think its sufficient, and we don't want any more.'"[57]

A student task force affiliated with Human Rights Watch in California took a strong interest in the issue and decided to launch a youth-oriented campaign on the military use of schools.[58] They set up a website and invited students and teachers from around the world to submit photos of themselves, holding signs with a personal message about protecting schools from military use. Over seventeen hundred people from over thirty countries posted photos to the site, with messages in thirty languages. The student organizers used reprints of the photos for meetings with US congressional representatives and the consulate generals from Australia, Argentina, Canada, Finland, Mexico, New Zealand, and the Philippines, urging their governments to support the guidelines.[59]

GCPEA knew it would be helpful to identify one or more "champion" governments that would agree to promote the guidelines and sponsor a high-level event for government endorsements. Eventually they found interest from Norway and Argentina. Norway had a new government that had criticized the previous government for not doing enough on education. In meetings with Norwegian officials, GCPEA presented the guidelines as a way for the new government to deliver on its election promises.

The Norwegian ambassador to the United Nations in Geneva, Steffen Kongstad, became a key figure in the campaign. He had decades of diplomatic experience and had worked for nearly twenty years with other civil society groups to develop new norms to protect civilians, including the 1997 Mine Ban Treaty and 2008 Convention on Cluster Munitions. Sheppard and others in GCPEA felt that Kongstad was a huge asset to the initiative. Not only did he have considerable expertise leading similar initiatives, but he seemed deeply and genuinely committed to the idea of better protections for civilians in armed conflict.[60]

In March 2014, GCPEA invited Kongstad and Argentina's ambassador to participate on a panel at the United Nations in Geneva with Sheppard, Haines, and representatives from UNICEF and the UN Department of Peacekeeping Operations. Many other governments, including those affected by conflict, participated in the event and made statements in support of the guidelines. Buoyed by the event's success and with Ambassador Kongstad's strong support,

Norway agreed to champion a state-led process to finalize the guidelines and develop an avenue for states to commit formally to implementing them. Argentina agreed to partner with Norway. Working with GCPEA, the two countries created a core group of states representing all regions (Jordan, Liberia, Côte d'Ivoire, Philippines, Netherlands, and Nepal) to develop the process.

For some of the core activists who had worked to develop the guidelines, the transition to a state-led process was challenging. "When you care a lot about a process, you feel very invested, and losing that control can be very nerve-wracking," said Sheppard. "But that was an essential step, and I don't think it could be done in any other way."[61]

As Norway and Argentina worked with other states on the guidelines, resistance started building from some governments. At a December 2014 event to launch the final text, Germany, the United States, and others spoke out publicly against the guidelines. Germany was the most strenuous in raising objections, arguing that international humanitarian law already set standards for states to follow, and that by introducing so-called soft law, the guidelines created confusion regarding the standards legally binding on states.

According to Aubert, "I don't think that Norway nor the coalition expected such strong push-back from some states on a process seeking to ensure stronger protection for children and their education during armed conflict."[62] Aubert and Sheppard also believed Germany and other states were unhappy with the growing role of civil society in shaping military standards, including a new international treaty on cluster munitions and a new initiative that sought to regulate the use of explosive weapons in populated areas. "There was a sense that civil society people were taking too much space and stepping on military boundaries in a way they shouldn't," said Aubert.[63]

Norway announced that it would hold an international Safe Schools conference in Oslo in May 2015. Norway and Argentina then held a series of consultations to develop a Safe Schools Declaration as a vehicle for states to commit to the guidelines. Norway also urged GCPEA to resume contacts with capitals. Over the next few months, GCPEA representatives, including field staff for Save the Children and other members, held dozens of meetings with governments to discuss the guidelines and seek their support.[64] Norway also provided funding to support a Geneva-based coordinator, Filipa Guinote, to coordinate outreach to states, map out countries' positions, and develop talking points to respond to concerns that were raised.

In late May 2015, representatives from sixty countries gathered for the Oslo Conference on Safe Schools. Among the participants was Malala Yousafzai's father, Ziauddin Yousafzai. In a speech to the assembly, he described attacks on education in Pakistan, his own experiences as a teacher and principal, and how the military had used his own school. He told conference attendees, "We have to provide the same sanctity to our schools and educational institutions as we do to mosques, temples and churches. What has been done to our schools—it is unacceptable. It must be changed now."[65] Dozens of government representatives took the floor to condemn attacks on education and commit to the Safe Schools Declaration. Coursen-Neff said, "It was inspiring to hear people at the highest levels of government commit to addressing a human rights problem that no one was talking about less than a decade ago and that we put on the map."[66]

Advocates had hoped that at least thirty countries would endorse the Safe Schools Declaration in Oslo and commit to implementing the Guidelines for Protecting Schools and Universities from Military Use during Armed Conflict. In fact, thirty-seven did so.[67] Endorsers came from all regions of the world and included countries that had experienced firsthand the devastation of war and its impact on children, such as Afghanistan and Nigeria. After the conference, the number continued to grow, and by April 2017, sixty-three countries had endorsed the guidelines.[68]

Challenges

Like many other coalitions, GCPEA has struggled with limited human resources and competing priorities. Nijhowne, the director, observed that with only eight steering committee members and a handful of staff, it was difficult to move forward on all four of GCPEA's areas of work. The working group on the military use of schools worked well in large part because three GCPEA members— Human Rights Watch, Education above All, and Save the Children—made the working group a priority and invested significant staff resources. The other areas of work, however, did not get the same level of support. Nijhowne also felt that the coalition had produced excellent resources but needed to give more thought to follow-up advocacy and how the product could be used to promote change. "We now need to focus more on practical measures of what can be done to prevent attacks on education," she said.

The coalition's diverse membership also posed challenges. Human Rights Watch, for example, was known for publicly "naming and shaming" parties to armed conflict for their abuses, but other members, especially the UN agencies, were more cautious about criticizing perpetrators because of possible reprisals against their field staff. Coursen-Neff reflected, "I never thought we could pull this off. I went into it very skeptically, thinking we would try it. What has made it work is that we were lucky to get really good steering committee members who were really committed to the issue and having the right individuals who could move their agencies. We've been able to do things with the Coalition that we couldn't have done just as Human Rights Watch."

The effort to develop guidelines on the military use of schools faced unexpected obstacles, in particular, the vocal opposition from states including Germany, the United States, and the United Kingdom. Advocates were especially surprised by initial opposition from Germany, France, and Canada, since these states were otherwise seen as leaders on children and armed conflict. France and Germany had chaired the Security Council's working group on children and armed conflict, and Canada regularly convened a large informal group of states, Friends of Children in Armed Conflict, in New York.

GCPEA representatives went to Berlin to discuss the guidelines with Germany's ministries of defense and foreign affairs, but the response was negative and dismissive. Sheppard recalled, "Their opposition was clear and they did not seem open to support or engage."[69] As Germany became more outspoken in its opposition to the guidelines, the coalition was split on how to deal with its antagonism. Norway's approach was to ignore unsupportive states, and some GCPEA members believed that it would not be helpful to antagonize Germany further. Others wanted to shame Germany publicly for its opposition and work with German NGOs to put pressure on Germany to change its position.

Opposing states repeatedly raised concerns that the measures suggested in the guidelines went beyond existing legal obligations and that this could create confusion over what standards were legally binding and ultimately erode or weaken international humanitarian law. The coalition responded that international humanitarian law set the baseline for the minimum level of protection to be afforded to civilians, but nothing prohibited states from voluntarily adopting measures that could add to civilian protection. Advocates stressed that the guidelines were nonbinding and provided practical guidance to states that wanted to better protect children's right to education in conflict situations and incorporate good practices into their military operations.

Advocates believed that the guidelines' detailed language provided valuable guidance to armed forces, particularly in addressing the exceptional circumstances in which the laws of war allow the military use of schools. But in retrospect, at least one core member felt that a simpler, more straightforward pledge could have elicited stronger support. "To promote a voluntary practice, it may be easier to do if it's a simple message," said Guinote.[70] For example, Geneva Call chose to put a single line in its 2009 Deed of Commitment for the Protection of

Children in Armed Conflict, obliging signing parties to "avoid using for military purposes schools or premises primarily used by children." Jonathan Somer, who led the development of the deed for Geneva Call, explained that the term avoid was used to bypass a full legal obligation but still discourage the practice.[71]

The shift to a state-led process under Norway's leadership also brought advantages and disadvantages for the coalition. Coalition members had spearheaded the initiative and worked hard for several years to shape the guidelines, develop a strategy, and build state support. Turning that control over to Norway created understandable frustration, particularly when Norway made decisions that some members disagreed with. Advocates were unhappy when Norway cut off consultations with states on the text of the guidelines and did not respond to states that wanted to provide further inputs. Similarly, during the negotiations on the Safe Schools Declaration, some states had concerns on the text that advocates believed could have been successfully worked out through bilateral negotiations but were left unaddressed. As a result, many states complained about the lack of transparency in the process, and the support of some countries may have been lost. Despite some differences with Norway over strategy, however, coalition members still believed that its role as a champion was critically important to winning widespread support for the guidelines.

The Way Forward

At a policy level, GCPEA has identified seven key steps that government ministries can take to protect education from attack and prevent the military use of schools. The first is to conduct an analysis of the nature, scope, scale, and nature of attacks on schools and military use and to implement monitoring mechanisms. The analysis should assess issues such as which schools are at risk of attack and why and what protection measures are already in place. A second step is to strengthen the physical infrastructure of schools by constructing boundary walls, installing razor wire and adequate lighting, creating entry blockades, and taking other measures, particularly in areas at high risk of attack. Where children and teachers are in danger while traveling to and from school, governments can provide transportation or escorts or build boardinghouses to minimize travel for students.

A third step is to ensure education continuity during times of conflict by providing distance or informal learning, accelerated learning programs, and establishing flexible or temporary learning sites such as home schools. A fourth step is to provide support to local communities, often the first to respond to attacks on schools or military use. Governments can, for example, support school protection committees or efforts by community leaders to negotiate with local armed groups to establish schools as zones of peace.

A fifth step is to ensure that education is conflict sensitive by reviewing curricula to incorporate respect for diversity and human rights and ensure it does not promote community tension or violence. Conflict-sensitive education policies also ensure equal access to education and equitable resourcing to ensure that all identity groups benefit equally. Sixth is to systematize the protection of education, integrating it into government policies, planning, programming, budgeting, and evaluation.

Finally, government ministries can advocate for support through legal reforms to protect education, high-level political commitments, and appropriate military codes of conduct.[72]

In 2003, Katarina Tomasevski, the UN special rapporteur on the right to education, was asked whether the UN Commission on Human Rights could prioritize the protection of teachers in its work. She replied that the commission wouldn't act without pressure from a forceful, well-coordinated NGO campaign:

> What is needed here is the same growth of the human rights movement which we saw around freedom of expression or equal rights for women— good documents, sensible strategies and then well coordinated lobbying to get government delegations to move, but NGOs have to take the initiative. It is obviously not a job of diplomats to do human rights research, and to draw up alternative platforms.[73]

Only after Tomasevski's death in 2006 did the campaign she hoped for take shape. Over the course of a decade, NGOs, together with UN agencies, managed to bring attacks on education onto the international agenda and gain commitments from dozens of countries to avoid the use of schools by their armed forces. It was able to do so with a strong coalition, solid research, extensive consultation, strategic advocacy with states (including their militaries), and an alliance with committed government partners, Norway and Argentina.

The coalition that formed in 2010 was unique in bringing together both NGOs and UN agencies as full members and combining three areas of expertise: education, child protection, and international law. Sheppard found that the ability to highlight the involvement of major UN agencies helped bring credibility to the guidelines and made it easier to win support from states. Nijhowne agreed: "So much of our ability to be present at high-level meetings, be taken seriously, and have access to key decision makers is through the UN agencies." She added, "The organizations in the coalition are really the preeminent organizations in their field, which really gives the coalition legitimacy."[74]

The personal relationships among GCPEA members and their willingness to invest significant effort to achieving its goals also made a big difference. Individual members, particularly Education above All, Save the Children, and Human Rights Watch, invested considerable time and resources into the guidelines and were willing to do so under the GCPEA umbrella. Aubert said, "We have all been happy to work for GCPEA without promoting our own logos and names. That's been one of the successes."[75] Several GCPEA advocates highlighted the critical role that Sheppard played as the intellectual leader of the initiative and his skill in identifying strategic advocacy opportunities.

The research that Human Rights Watch, UNESCO, and GCPEA conducted to document attacks on education and military use of schools was essential for mobilizing attention, support, and action. Over several years, Human Rights Watch published ten country reports providing in-depth documentation of attacks on education and military use of schools. UNESCO published two global reports on attacks on schools in 2007 and 2010 before handing off its research and publication to GCPEA, which published another edition of *Education under Attack* in 2014. GCPEA also published two editions of *Lessons in War*, focused solely on the military use of schools worldwide. Sheppard reflected, "The findings on the ground, including the evidence of the negative consequences, the evidence of scale and prevalence, was really important. In my advocacy meetings, I was able to draw upon real world stories of individual experiences and the negative consequences for students' and teachers' safety, security, and education."[76] The survey Sheppard conducted in 2011 of the laws and practices of fifty-six countries on the military use of schools also proved very useful and helped GCPEA identify key states for advocacy.

Advocates found that documenting existing good practices by states was extremely valuable. "The fact that some countries already have good practices demystified it," said Guinote, the Geneva-based coordinator for the guidelines. "Countries could see that this is something that they could do something about."[77] The examples of Colombia and the Philippines were particularly powerful. Despite decades of internal armed conflict, both countries had explicitly prohibited their armed forces from using schools for military purposes. Sheppard said, "These examples allowed us to go into advocacy meetings with a basis for saying that this is not an unreasonable request of states. It's possible, because here are countries that have already done it."[78]

Extensive consultation with member states, particularly with ministries of defense, also influenced the guidelines. Consultation with armed forces "is not an approach that NGOs often take," said Sheppard, who believed that as a result, the guidelines were much more pragmatic than they would have been otherwise. Aubert found that ministries of defense from conflict countries had a strong interest in the guidelines because they had dealt with the issue firsthand.

Key stakeholders provided important support for the coalition's goals. For example, the decision of the UN Department of Peacekeeping Operations to include a prohibition on using schools in its infantry battalion training manual was significant in its own right, and advocates believed that could have a ripple effect. "All these troops being trained are being told they can't use schools, and they are taking it back to their own countries," said Sheppard. "Changing the behavior of these troops could have long-term benefits."[79] The involvement of Steven Haines, a former UK military commander, and technical advice from the ICRC also brought credibility to the drafting process and its outcome. The ICRC interprets international humanitarian law and what is acceptable behavior by parties to armed conflict. In meetings with states, the coalition found it helpful to cite the ICRC's support for the guidelines and its use of the guidelines in the field for their dialogue with parties to conflict.

The coalition was strategic in its advocacy with states. Members divided up lists of states among themselves, based on prior relationships and where they had staff who could make contacts. They targeted particular states for visits and op-eds based on their laws and practices, previous public statements, their stated commitment to children's rights, and the right to education, as well as other criteria, such as whether they were pursuing membership in the UN Security Council.

Meeting with government representatives in nearly thirty capitals made a real difference. According to Erwin, "It gave us a chance to talk directly with those that were making the decisions."[80] These country visits also allowed GCPEA to meet with local civil society organizations that could provide advice on how to tailor the advocacy approach for that particular government and help mobilize support for the guidelines. The majority of states GCPEA visited were among the first to endorse the guidelines and the Safe Schools Declaration. "The engagement with capitals really paid off," said Aubert.[81]

Finally, partnering with Norway and Argentina as champions for the Safe Schools Declaration and the guidelines was important to give credibility to the instrument and gain support from states that may not have taken it seriously otherwise. Ambassador Kongstad in particular brought personal commitment and extensive experience to the initiative, as well as valuable relationships with other ambassadors.

In reflecting on the final result, GCPEA members were understandably proud of their accomplishments. For Aubert, "It was positive and exciting. We were a very small group of actors and we all put a lot of our time and energy in. We worked hard, but it was worth it."[82] They also recognized that the work was still just beginning. Erwin said:

> A lot of these processes seem to focus on endorsement, but then that steam and emphasis and resources drop off once that's accomplished. This got much bigger than I imagined, but it doesn't end with guidelines and endorsement. I really hope just as much energy and resources go into continuing this engagement with states and making sure that they are implementing the guidelines.[83]

11 Lessons for the Future

IN SEPTEMBER 2015, governments adopted a new global agenda for sustainable development, pledging to end poverty, protect the planet, and ensure prosperity for all by the year 2030.[1] As part of their commitments, governments pledged to end all forms of violence against children, including sex trafficking and harmful traditional practices; end child labor and the use of child soldiers; and ensure that all children complete both primary and secondary school.

These goals are unquestionably ambitious. Governments have repeatedly failed to meet similar targets set in the past. Yet the evidence is clear that ensuring children's rights also ensures healthier, more productive, more educated, and more democratic communities. Ending abuses against children is not only a human rights imperative, but also an opportunity to alleviate a host of problems that impose significant social and economic costs on the nations of the world.

The past few decades have taught us a lot about the most effective ways to protect children and help them thrive. These strategies include strong laws, coupled with effective enforcement, and sound policies that provide children and their families with access to essential services. Perhaps most fundamental is ensuring free, quality education for all children. Children who are in school are much less likely to become engaged in child labor, be recruited as soldiers, marry young, or commit criminal offenses. At the same time, education expands children's opportunities, economic potential, and ability to engage in society as informed and active citizens.

Virtually every country has pledged to uphold children's rights as parties to the Convention on the Rights of the Child, but many fail miserably. They fail to enact legal protections for children and, even more often, fail to enforce their laws. In creating policy, they frequently ignore evidence-based arguments in favor of what is politically popular. Perpetrators of abuses against children often enjoy total impunity; only a tiny fraction of adults who exploit children sexually, recruit them as soldiers, employ them in hazardous child labor, facilitate child marriage, or subject them to violence are ever held to account.

Poor countries often lack the resources they need to provide universal education, effectively regulate the workplace, or maintain functioning judicial systems. Some governments simply fail to prioritize these measures, while in others, assistance from wealthier states falls far short of what is required. In either instance, children suffer.

The range of actors and technologies that bear on children's lives has grown and become more complex. In a global economy, multinational corporations are often complicit in child labor, and while new technologies can facilitate children's access to information, educate the public on children's rights, and mobilize people on children's behalf, they have also spawned new forms of sexual exploitation and abuse.

Changing practices that have prevailed for centuries, altering deeply ingrained attitudes toward children, and finding ways to stop abusers who exploit children is not easy. Yet with shrewd strategies and smart messages, persistent and resourceful advocates have won significant advances for children, prompting governments, corporations, and local communities to change their policies and practices to improve children's lives. The examples presented in this book point to several key strategies that can help advance children's rights.

Research and Documentation

Advocates must be able to show evidence of the nature and extent of violations in order to prompt action by decision makers, particularly when an issue is not well known. For example, when nongovernmental organizations (NGOs) first became aware that attacks on schools put children at risk and deprived them of education, they began documenting the number of affected countries in order to get this topic on the international agenda. The work of ECPAT International began with a study that for the first time revealed the extent of child sex tourism in Asia. For the Global Initiative to End All Corporal Punishment of Children, tracking legislation regarding corporal punishment in every country worldwide is an essential aspect of its advocacy.

Research on the harmful effects of practices like female genital cutting (FGM/C), child marriage, and corporal punishment has helped prompt international attention, new global commitments, and legal reforms. Juvenile justice advocates have used emerging neuroscience on adolescent brain development to persuade both state legislatures and the US Supreme Court to abolish the juvenile death penalty. South African juvenile justice advocates used research showing that alternatives to detention were cheaper than locking up juvenile offenders to build the case for a new child justice law. Similarly, the Global Coalition to Protect Education from Attack used positive examples of countries that prohibited the military use of schools to persuade other governments that such a policy was feasible.

Strategic Messaging

Effective advocates identify messages that will resonate with their advocacy targets. In South Africa, for example, juvenile justice activists highlighted traditional African values of restorative justice in order to promote the Child Justice Law. The Global Initiative to End All Corporal Punishment of Children presented a compelling argument that children should have no less protection from violence than adults do, while advocates for the Child Soldiers Prevention Act in the United States argued convincingly that tax dollars should not be used to support governments using child soldiers. US juvenile justice activists deliberately chose scientific arguments highlighting the physiological differences between juvenile offenders and adults to make the case that juvenile offenders should not be subject to the death penalty, believing that they would be more persuasive than moral or rights-based claims.

Community Dialogue

For abuses that are deeply embedded in social and cultural norms, community-level dialogue, involving gatekeepers such as village and religious leaders, is a powerful tool. Tostan in West Africa and Kembatti Mentti Gezzima in Ethiopia found that engaging villages in conversation regarding their goals and values helped prompt communities to reevaluate traditional practices such as FGM/C and make collective decisions to abandon them. The process took time, often three years, before a tipping point was reached, but it was much more likely to result in actual changes in practice compared to other strategies. The dialogue invested members of the community in the decision and ensured they were more likely to implement it. In India, Bachpan Bachao Andolan (BBA) successfully used community dialogue to establish child-friendly villages that were free of child labor. It engaged with influential members of the community over the course of a year to secure village commitments to remove children from child labor, ensure their education, and give them a voice in community decision making.

Advocates have also used community dialogue to combat child marriage. In particular, girls participating in empowerment groups have learned about their rights and sexual and reproductive health. They have influenced village leaders to oppose child marriage and their own parents to delay their marriage.

Broad Networks and Alliances

A hallmark of effective organizing is bringing organizations together to unify their voices and join forces around a single goal. Many of the cases explored in this book involve broad coalition efforts, including those of Girls Not Brides, the Global Campaign for Education, and the Global Coalition to Protect Education from Attack. The creation of these global networks ensured better access to global decision makers and greater impact. For these networks, sharing information among members on effective strategies helped expand their knowledge base and accelerate change.

Uniting diverse or even unlikely allies can be particularly powerful. The Global Campaign for Education, for example, found that bringing NGOs together with teachers' unions significantly strengthened its influence. ECPAT International partnered with travel agencies, hotels, and other actors in the tourism industry to combat child sex tourism. US juvenile justice advocates allied with the medical community to eliminate the juvenile death penalty. The Raise the Bar, Hershey! campaign successfully engaged the religious community, consumers, and, particularly, Hershey's business partners to win changes in Hershey's child labor policies.

Engaging New Governments

Political transitions and the election of new governments can provide opportunities to advance children's rights. In South Africa, for example, the end of apartheid and the election of Nelson Mandela as president heightened awareness of the number of children who had been imprisoned during the apartheid era and provided the opening for radical legal reforms to the juvenile justice system. Similarly, the end of Sierra Leone's war gave children the opportunity to participate in the national peace process and advocate for free education.

New governments are often eager to implement their campaign promises or bolster their reputation through new initiatives. For example, advocates working to end the military use of schools approached a new Norwegian government as a potential partner because it had criticized the previous government for not doing more on education. Norway subsequently became a strong and effective champion for safe schools. Similarly, ECPAT International approached the Swedish prime minister just days after he took office to propose that Sweden host a global conference on the commercial sexual exploitation of children. The prime minister agreed.

Individual Engagement

Campaigns that depend on mass mobilization to influence policymakers must find creative ways to engage individuals. The Global Campaign for Education found that its annual week of action was a powerful tool to rally activists worldwide around the right to education. By designating a specific theme and suggesting creative actions—such as making cut-out "buddies" to send to school or staging massive book readings—the campaign mobilized millions of people around the globe. Similarly, Stop the Traffik used chocolate fondue parties, Easter egg "hunts" for Fairtrade chocolate, and other imaginative campaigning ideas to raise awareness of child labor in the cocoa sector and mobilize people to take action.

Legal Reform

Legal reform is often one of the best avenues to advance children's rights. It can force changes in government practice and accelerate changes in attitudes and behaviors. Sweden's experience, for example, showed that the adoption of laws banning corporal punishment helped reduce the use of physical punishment significantly. In South Africa, the adoption of the Child Justice Law prompted profound reforms in the country's juvenile justice system and led to a dramatic drop in the number of children behind bars. In the United States, advocates saw an opportunity to use US military assistance as leverage to curb the use of child soldiers by other governments, and they partnered with members of Congress to win a groundbreaking law that influenced several countries to end child recruitment and demobilize child soldiers.

For issues that are strongly rooted in social custom, such as FGM/C and child marriage, legal reforms can complement other strategies, but they are rarely effective on their own. Families often perceive the benefits of traditional practices (e.g., social acceptance and marriageability in the case of FGM/C and economic benefits in the case of child marriage) as outweighing the possible risks of prosecution. But when communities begin to reevaluate these practices, legal reforms can provide legitimacy to new behaviors and facilitate change.

Use of the Courts

When governments fail to protect children, activists sometimes resort to the courts or other judicial bodies. In India, BBA used legal complaints against employers to win the freedom of children trapped in bonded child labor. Rather than pursue lengthy and tedious state-by-state campaigns to change laws allowing the use of the death penalty against child offenders, activists in the United States were able to gain a ruling from the US Supreme Court to abolish the practice nationwide.

Although the European Committee of Social Rights is not a formal court, fifteen European countries have accepted its jurisdiction to hear complaints under the European Social Charter. The Global Initiative to End All Corporal Punishment of Children took advantage of this avenue by bringing complaints against seven European countries. Ireland quickly responded with a commitment to ban corporal punishment, a dramatic turnaround from its public position just two years earlier. Slovenia subsequently banned corporal punishment as well.

UN Human Rights Mechanisms

The work of the Global Initiative to End Corporal Punishment of Children illustrates the potential impact of using the UN human rights mechanisms consistently and systematically. The Global Initiative briefed the Committee on the Rights of the Child on nearly every country in the world, prompting recommendations to governments to legally prohibit corporal punishment of children. In time, the Global Initiative also began briefing other treaty bodies, which meant that many governments received recommendations from multiple treaty bodies to enact a legal ban. When the universal periodic review was put in place, the Global Initiative used that avenue as well, submitting information and encouraging friendly states to recommend that other states ban corporal punishment of children. The Global Initiative credits these processes with the exponential increase in states enacting legal bans on all corporal punishment of children. In particular, the universal periodic review system, where states must respond publicly to the recommendations they receive, prompted commitments from dozens of states to prohibit all corporal punishment of children.

Children as Leaders

In many cases, children have taken the lead in advocating for their rights. Young activists like Malala Yousafzai, Chernor Bah, Om Prakash Gurjar, and Nujood Ali have brought new attention to children's rights and won victories related to education, child labor, child marriage, and other issues. In Sierra Leone, Bah and other children formed a national network of school-based clubs to identify their most urgent priorities. They drafted a Children's Manifesto and used radio and public forums with government officials to push their demands, ultimately winning new laws and policies guaranteeing free primary and junior secondary education for all children in Sierra Leone. Yousafzai has mobilized global support for the right to education, influencing government commitments to ensure free secondary education for all children by 2030. In India, Gurjar helped establish hundreds of child-friendly villages that are free of child labor and where all children attend school. In Malawi, girls trained as advocates persuaded sixty village chiefs to enact bylaws against harmful traditional practices. In numerous other countries, girls' empowerment groups and leadership training have led girls to refuse their parents' attempts to have them cut or married, intervene on behalf of other girls, and speak out publicly against FGM/C and child marriage.

Persistence

Creating change is often a slow process. Most of the campaigns described in this book took years. Many are ongoing. But perseverance can pay off. After three years of community dialogue facilitated by Tostan, many local villages decide to abandon harmful practices such as FGM/C and child marriage. In India, a year of engagement between local villages and BBA activists can result in a child-friendly village that is free of child labor. The Global Initiative to End All Corporal Punishment of Children began to see the greatest progress after working on the issue for five years. The rate of states prohibiting corporal punishment nearly tripled between 2007 and 2012 compared to 2001 to 2006. Advocates spent over fifteen years working to reform the juvenile justice system in South Africa, ultimately winning new laws that dramatically decreased incarceration rates for children.

Some advocates realized that what they initially perceived as a victory was simply the start of a new phase of work. After the Child Soldiers Prevention Act was adopted in the United States, for example, advocates were deeply disappointed in President Obama's implementation of the law, and they brought new pressure on the administration to use military assistance as leverage to prompt foreign governments to end the military recruitment of children. Similarly, although leading chocolate manufacturing companies pledged in 2001 to address child labor in the cocoa sector, it took years of additional campaigning to get them to make more meaningful commitments to certify all of their products as free of child labor by 2020.

Conclusion

Remarkable change for children takes place every day. In remote villages, girls advocate for their right to physical integrity and to marry when they please.

In military camps, commanders release children from their forces so they can go back to school. At corporate headquarters, executives adopt new policies to ensure their products are not made with child labor. In national capitals, lawmakers adopt reforms to end violence against children and the overuse of detention. These and other actions have brought significant gains for children, increasing their chances for education, health, decent livelihoods, freedom from exploitation and abuse, and the ability to shape their own lives and impact their communities.

Daily news reports will continue to feature unconscionable abuses against children. But there is no excuse to throw up one's hands and declare them inevitable. We have vast knowledge about the policies and strategies that can help children thrive and the strategies that can move people in power to act. The challenge is to act on that knowledge and demand the political will necessary to ensure all children the life they deserve. If we do, there is no limit to what we can accomplish.

Notes

Introduction

1. Nujood Ali with Delphine Minoui, *I Am Nujood, Age 10 and Divorced* (New York: Broadway Books, 2010).

2. UNICEF, *State of the World's Children 2015* (New York: UNICEF, November 2014), 88, http://www.unicef.org/publications/files/SOWC_2015_Summary_and_Tables.pdf.

3. Ali and Minoui, *I Am Nujood.*

4. UNFPA, United Nations Population Fund (UNFPA), *State of World Population 2016* (New York: UNFPA, 2016), 72, http://www.unfpa.org/sites/default/files/sowp/down loads/The_State_of_World_Population_2016_-_English.pdf.

5. International Labour Office, *Making Progress against Child Labour: Global Estimates and Trends 2000–2012* (Geneva: ILO, 2013), vii–viii.

6. UNESCO Institute for Statistics (UIS), "Leaving No One Behind: How Far on the Way to Universal Primary and Secondary Education?" (policy paper 27/fact sheet 37, July 2016), http://uis.unesco.org/sites/default/files/documents/fs37-leaving-no-one -behind-how-far-on-the-way-to-universal-primary-and-secondary-education-2016-en .pdf.

7. UNICEF, *Hidden in Plain Sight: A Statistical Analysis of Violence against Children* (New York: UNICEF, 2014), 96.

8. World Health Organization, "Female Genital Mutilation" (fact sheet, February 2016), http://www.who.int/mediacentre/factsheets/fs241/en/.

9. International Labour Office, *Making Progress against Child Labour.*

10. UIS, "Leaving No One Behind."

11. According to UNICEF, the percentage of girls aged 15 to 19 who had undergone FGM/C in the thirty countries where it is practiced dropped from 51 percent in 1985 to 37 percent in 2016. See UNICEF, *Female Genital Mutilation/Cutting: A Global Concern* (New York: UNICEF, 2016), http://www.unicef.org/media/files/FGMC_2016_brochure _final_UNICEF_SPREAD(2).pdf.

12. According to UNICEF, one in four young women alive in 2014 were likely to have married during childhood. In the 1980s, the proportion was one in three. See

UNICEF, *Ending Child Marriage: Progress and Prospects* (New York: UNICEF, 2014), http://www.unicef.org/media/files/Child_Marriage_Report_7_17_LR..pdf.

13. See Coalition to Stop the Use of Child Soldiers, *Child Soldiers Global Report 2001* (London: Coalition to Stop the Use of Child Soldiers, 2001) and United Nations, "Report of the Secretary-General to the UN Security Council on Children and Armed Conflict," S/2016/360, April 20, 2016.

14. UNESCO, "Education Is the Key to Lasting Development," 2011, http://www.unesco.org/fileadmin/MULTIMEDIA/HQ/ED/GMR/pdf/gmr2010/MDG2010_Facts_and_Figures_EN.pdf.

15. Ibid.

16. Anke Hoeffler and James Fearon, *Conflict and Violence Assessment Paper: Benefits and Costs of the Conflict and Violence Targets for the Post-2015 Development Agenda* (Lowell, MA: Copenhagen Consensus Center, August 2014), 16, http://www.copenhagenconsensus.com/sites/default/files/conflict_assessment_-_hoeffler_and_fearon_0.pdf.

17. Ibid., 39.

18. Global Partnership for Education, *Financing for Education* (fact sheet, 2016), http://www.globalpartnership.org/content/financing-education-factsheet.

19. Global military expenditures in 2015 were approximately US$1,676 billion. Stockholm International Peace Research Institute, SIPRI Yearbook 2016: Armaments, Disarmament, and International Security Summary (Stockholm: SIPRI, 2016), 17, https://www.sipri.org/sites/default/files/YB16-Summary-ENG.pdf.

Chapter 1

1. Clare Mulley, *The Woman Who Saved the Children: A Biography of Eglantyne Jebb, Founder of Save the Children* (Oxford: Oneworld Publications, 2009), 63.

2. Ibid.

3. Ibid, 249.

4. Declaration of the Rights of the Child, adopted by the League of Nations, September 26, 1924.

5. Judith Ennew, "Rethinking Childhood: Perspectives on Child Rights," *Cultural Survival* 24 (summer 2000): 44–48.

6. Global Nonviolent Action Database, "Philadelphian Mill Children March against Child Labor Exploitation, 1903," October 23, 2011, http://nvdatabase.swarthmore.edu/content/philadelpian-mill-children-march-against-child-labor-exploitation-1903.

7. Geraldine Van Bueren, *The International Law on the Rights of the Child* (The Hague: Martinus Nijhoff, 1998), 9.

8. Universal Declaration of Human Rights, Article 25.

9. Cited by Jadwiga Bińczycka, "Janusz Korczak—Champion of Children's Rights," paper presented in Warsaw, 2010, http://www.januszkorczak.ca/Prof_Binczycka.pdf.

10. Article 7.

11. Cynthia Price Cohen, "The Role of the United States in the Drafting of the Convention on the Rights of the Child," *Emory International Law Review* 20 (Spring 2006): 191.

12. Ibid., 188.

13. Ibid., 192.

14. Convention on the Rights of the Child, article 1.

15. Article 77(2) of the 1977 Additional Protocol I to the Geneva Conventions of 1949 states in part, "The Parties to the conflict shall take all feasible measures in order that children who have not attained the age of fifteen years do not take a direct part in hostilities and, in particular, they shall refrain from recruiting them into their armed forces."

16. Convention on the Rights of the Child, UN General Assembly resolution A/RES/44/25 (adopted November 20, 1989; entered into force September 2, 1990).

17. Article 12.

18. Article 13.

19. For a fuller discussion of opposition to US ratification of the convention, see Susan Kilbourne, "U.S. Failure to Ratify the U.N. Convention on the Rights of the Child: Playing Politics with Children's Rights," *Transnational Law and Contemporary Problems* 6 (1996): 437, 438.

20. Optional Protocol to the Convention on the Rights of the Child on the Involvement of Children in Armed Conflict, UN General Assembly resolution A/RES/54/263 (adopted May 25, 2000; entered into force February 12, 2002).

21. Optional Protocol to the Convention on the Rights of the Child on the Sale of Children, Child Prostitution and Child Pornography, UN General Assembly resolution A/RES/54/263 (adopted May 25, 2000; entered into force January 18, 2002).

22. Optional Protocol to the Convention on the Rights of the Child on a Communications Procedure, UN General Assembly resolution A/RES/66/138 (adopted December 19, 2011; entered into force April 14, 2014).

23. The general comments are available online at http://tbinternet.ohchr.org/_layouts/treatybodyexternal/TBSearch.aspx?Lang=en&TreatyID=5&DocTypeID=11.

24. See Osifunke Ekundayo, "Does the African Charter on the Rights and Welfare of the Child (ACRWC) only Underlines and Repeats the Convention on the Rights of the Child (CRC)'s Provisions? Examining the Similarities and the Differences between the ACRWC and the CRC," *International Journal of Humanities and Social Science* 5, no. 7 (July 2015): 143–58.

25. OAU Doc. CAB/LEG/24.9/49 (1990), entered into force November 29, 1999.

26. African Charter on the Rights and Welfare of the Child, articles 1, 11.

27. As of January 2017, ILO convention 182 was ratified by 180 countries, and convention 138 was ratified by 169.

28. Rome Statute, article 8(2)(b)(xxvi), (e)(vii).

29. Ibid., article 8(2)(b)(ix) and (e)(iv).

30. Ibid., 8(2)(b)(xxii) and (e)(vi). articles 7(1)(g).

31. Ibid., article 6.

32. *Situation in the Democratic Republic of the Congo, in the case of the Prosecutor v. Thomas Lubanga Dyilo*, ICC-01/04-01/06, International Criminal Court (ICC), March 14, 2012.

Chapter 2

1. Leyla Hussein, "Day of the Girl: A Survivor's Journey after Female Genital Mutilation," *Independent*, October 11, 2013, http://www.independent.co.uk/voices/comment/day-of-the-girl-a-survivors-journey-after-female-genital-mutilation-8874232.html.

2. Leyla Hussein, "Female Genital Mutilation Is Child Abuse. We Are Failing Young British Girls," *Guardian*, November 5, 2013. http://www.theguardian.com/commentis free/2013/nov/05/female-genital-mutilation-fgm-child-abuse-british-girls.

3. *A note on terminology:* In 1991, the World Health Organization recommended that the United Nations adopt the term *female genital mutilation.* However, the word *mutilation* can be perceived as unnecessarily judgmental and can alienate practicing communities. Some therefore prefer the term *female genital cutting.* UNICEF and the United Nations Population Fund use a hybrid term, *female genital mutilation/cutting* (FGM/C). This chapter also uses the hybrid term, FGM/C.

4. Hussein, "Female Genital Mutilation Is Child Abuse." See also Leyla Hussein, "Making Sure My Daughter Wasn't Cut Is My Greatest Achievement," *MumsNet Talk*, November 6, 2013, http://www.mumsnet.com/Talk/guest_posts/a1903396-Leyla-Hussein -on-FGM-Making-sure-my-daughter-wasnt-cut-is-my-greatest-achievement.

5. World Health Organization, *Female Genital Mutilation* (fact sheet 241, February 2014), http://www.who.int/mediacentre/factsheets/fs241/en/.

6. UNICEF, *Female Genital Mutilation/Cutting: A Global Concern* (New York: UNICEF, 2016), http://www.unicef.org/media/files/FGMC_2016_brochure_final_UNI CEF_SPREAD(2).pdf.

7. World Health Organization, *Female Genital Mutilation* (fact sheet, February 2016), http://www.who.int/mediacentre/factsheets/fs241/en/.

8. UNICEF, *Female Genital Mutilation/Cutting: A Statistical Overview and Explora-tion of the Dynamics of Change* (New York: UNICEF, 2013), inside cover and 52.

9. Ibid.

10. World Health Organization, *Female Genital Mutilation.*

11. Human Rights Watch, "Q&A on Female Genital Mutilation," June 10, 2010, http://www.hrw.org/news/2010/06/10/qa-female-genital-mutilation.

12. UNICEF, *Female Genital Mutilation/Cutting,* 43.

13. Ibid., 67.

14. Ibid., 8.

15. Ibid.

16. Ellen Gruenbaum, *The Female Circumcision Controversy: An Anthropological Perspective* (Philadelphia: University of Pennsylvania Press, 2001), cited in Gerry Mackie and John LeJeune, "Social Dynamics of Abandonment of Harmful Practices: A New Look at the Theory" (Innocenti working paper, UNICEF, Florence, 2009), 7–8.

17. Mackie and LeJeune, "Social Dynamics of Abandonment of Harmful Practices"; Gerry Mackie, "Ending Footbinding and Infibulation: A Convention Account," *Ameri-can Sociological Review* 61 (1996): 999–1017.

18. Ibid.

19. Sidney Gamble, "The Disappearance of Foot-Binding in Tinghsien" (1943), cited in Mackie, "Ending Footbinding and Infibulation," 1001.

20. Mackie and LeJeune, "Social Dynamics of Abandonment of Harmful Practices," 2009, 10.

21. Ibid., 11.

22. Tina Rosenberg, "Talking Female Circumcision Out of Existence," *New York Times*, July 17, 2013, http://opinionator.blogs.nytimes.com/2013/07/17/talking-female -circumcision-out-of-existence/.

23. Constitution of the Federal Democratic Republic of Ethiopia, article 35(4).

24. Criminal Code of the Federal Democratic Republic of Ethiopia 2004, articles 565–567.

25. UNICEF, *Female Genital Mutilation/Cutting: A Global Concern* (New York: UNICEF, 2016), http://www.unicef.org/media/files/FGMC_2016_brochure_final_UNI CEF_SPREAD(2).pdf.

26. Haile Gabriel Dagne, "Ethiopia: Social Dynamics of Abandonment of Harmful Practices: Experiences in Four Locations" (working paper, Innocenti, UNICEF, 2010).

27. Ibid., 9.

28. Ibid., 10.

29. UNICEF, *Statistical Overview*, 2013, 90.

30. Dagne, "Ethiopia," 4.

31. Rosenberg, "Talking Female Circumcision Out of Existence."

32. Dagne, "Ethiopia," 25–26.

33. Ibid., 17

34. Ibid., 20–21.

35. Rosenberg, "Talking Female Circumcision Out of Existence."

36. Dagne, "Ethiopia," 26.

37. Aimee Molloy, *However Long the Night: Molly Melching's Journey to Help Millions of African Women and Girls Triumph* (New York: HarperCollins, 2013), 56.

38. Diane Gillespie and Molly Melching, "The Transformative Power of Democracy and Human Rights in Nonformal Education: The Case of Tostan," *Adult Education Quarterly* 60 (2010): 477–98.

39. Molloy, *However Long the Night*, xi.

40. Mackie and LeJeune, "Social Dynamics of Abandonment of Harmful Practices," 19.

41. Ibid., 29.

42. http://www.tostan.org/blog/press-advisory-growing-human-rights-momen tum-west-africa.

43. UNICEF, *Case Studies on UNICEF Programming in Child Protection* (New York: UNICEF, 2013), 28.

44. Author interview with Molly Melching, August 5, 2014.

45. Hussein, "Making Sure My Daughter Wasn't Cut Is My Greatest Achievement."

46. Ibid.

47. Alison Macfarlane and Efua Dorkenoo, *Female Genital Mutilation in England and Wales: Updated Statistical Estimates of the Numbers of Affected Women Living in England and Wales and Girls at Risk: Interim Report on Provisional Estimates* (London: City University London and Equality Now, 2014), http://www.city.ac.uk/__data/assets/pdf_ file/0009/226287/FGM-statistics-report-21.07.14-no-embargo.pdf.

48. BBC News, "Female Genital Mutilation: London Hospitals Treat 4,000 Patients," March 19, 2014, http://www.bbc.com/news/uk-england-london-26639542.

49. RCM, RCN, RCOG, Equality Now, and UNITE, *Tackling FGM in the UK: Intercollegiate Recommendations for Identifying, Recording, and Reporting* (London: Royal College of Midwives, 2013), 11.

50. Leyla Hussein, "Cruel Cut Aftermath, Space for FGM Survivors," *Huffington Post*, February 6, 2014, http://www.huffingtonpost.co.uk/leyla-hussein/fgm-zero-toler ance-day_b_4733689.html.

51. www.leylahussein.com

52. Anna Davis, "What Happened When Anti-FGM Campaigner Asked People in the Street to Sign a Petition in Favour of Mutilating Girls," *London Evening Standard*, October 28, 2013, http://www.standard.co.uk/news/london/what-happened-when-anti fgm-campaigner-asked-people-in-the-street-to-sign-a-petition-in-favour-of-mutilat ing-girls-8908877.html.

53. RCM, RCN, RCOG, Equality Now, and UNITE, *Tackling FGM in the UK*, 11.

54. National Society for the Prevention of Cruelty to Children (NSPCC), *Female Genital Mutilation Fact Sheet* (May 2014), http://www.nspcc.org.uk/Inform/resources forprofessionals/minorityethnic/female-genital-mutilation_wda96841.html.

55. Keiran Corcoran, "Doctor and Second Man Accused of Being Involved in Female Genital Mutilation Plead Not Guilty as They Appear in Court," *Daily Mail Online*, July 31, 2014, http://www.dailymail.co.uk/news/article-2712285/Two-accused-involved -female-genital-mutilation-plead-not-guilty-appear-court.html.

56. RCM, RCN, RCOG, Equality Now, and UNITE, *Tackling FGM in the UK*.

57. House of Commons Home Affairs Committee, "Female Genital Mutilation: The Case for a National Action Plan: Second Report of Session 2013-2014," July 3, 2014, http://www.publications.parliament.uk/pa/cm201415/cmselect/cmhaff/201/201.pdf.

58. Ibid.

59. Prime Minister's Office, Department for International Development, Home Office, *PM Hosts Girl Summit 2014: A Future Free from FGM and Child and Forced Marriage* (press release, July 22, 2014), https://www.gov.uk/government/news/pm-hosts-girl-sum mit-2014-a-future-free-from-fgm-and-child-and-forced-marriage.

60. Mackie and LeJeune, "Social Dynamics of Abandonment of Harmful Practices," p 13.

61. Ibid.

62. Dagne, "Ethiopia," 39.

63. Ibid., 40.

64. Ibid., 48.

65. Author interview with Melching.

66. Bettina Shell-Duncan, Ylva Hernlund, Katherine Wander, and Amadou Moreau, "Legislating Change? Responses to Criminalization of Female Genital Cutting in Senegal," *Law and Society Review* 47 (2013): 803–35.

67. Mackie, "Social Dynamics of Abandonment of Harmful Practices," 23–24.

68. Author interview with Melching.

69. Ibid.

70. Ibid.

71. Ibid.

72. Shell-Duncan, Hernlund, Wander, and Moreau, "Legislating Change?"

73. Author interview with Melching.

Chapter 3

1. Human Rights Watch, *When I Die, They'll Send Me Home: Youth Sentenced to Life in Prison without Parole in California: An Update*, March 1, 2012, 14, https://www.hrw.org/sites/default/files/reports/crd0112webwcover.pdf.

2. Ibid.

3. UNICEF, *Progress for Children: A Report Card on Child Protection*, September 2009, 20, http://www.unicef.org/protection/files/Progress_for_Children-No.8_EN_081309(1). UNICEF believes that the 1 million figure is a significant underestimate of the actual number of children in detention, because the record-keeping systems in many countries are very poor.

4. Ibid.

5. Convention on the Rights of the Child, articles 37(b), 40(3)(b).

6. Child Rights Information Network, "Inhuman Sentencing" (n.d.), http://www.crin.org/en/home/campaigns/inhuman-sentencing/problem.

7. Human Rights Watch, *Adults before Their Time: Children in Saudi Arabia's Criminal Justice System* (New York: Human Rights Watch, 2008), http://www.hrw.org/reports/2008/03/24/adults-their-time-0.

8. US Department of Justice, Bureau of Justice Statistics, "Sexual Victimization in Juvenile Facilities reported by Youth, 2008–2009" (Bureau of Justice Statistics Special Report, January 2010).

9. Richard Mendel, *No Place for Kids* (Baltimore: Annie E. Casey Foundation, 2011), 9, http://www.aecf.org/resources/no-place-for-kids-full-report/.

10. Ibid.

11. Ibid., 10.

12. U. Gatti, R. E. Trembley, and F. Vitaro, "Iatrogenic Effect of Juvenile Justice," *Journal of Child Psychology and Psychiatry* 50, no. 8 (2009): 991–98.

13. Mendel, *No Place for Kids*, 17.

14. In Denmark, for example, rates of child incarceration in 2011 were only 1 in 100,000 (compared to 39.3 in 100,000 in Argentina). In New Zealand, only 66 children under the age of 18 were in custody in 2014.

15. Ann Skelton, "Freedom in the Making: Juvenile Justice in South Africa," in Franklin E. Zimring, Maximo Langer, and David S. Tanenhaus, eds., *Juvenile Justice in Global Perspectives* (New York: NYU Press, 2015), 344.

16. Ibid.

17. Neal Hazel, *Cross-National Comparison of Youth Justice* (New York: Youth Justice Board, 2008), 59, http://dera.ioe.ac.uk/7996/1/Cross_national_final.pdf.

18. Skelton, "Freedom in the Making."

19. World's Children's Prize Foundation, "Ann Skelton," *Globe Magazine*, 2012, http://issuu.com/wcprc/docs/2012_90-109_eng/1?e=1438407/10747187.

20. Author interview with Bob Schwartz, February 9, 2015.

21. Ann Skelton, R. Shapiro, and D. Pinnock, "Juvenile Justice for South Africa: Pro-

posals for Policy and legislative Change" (Cape Town: University of Cape Town Institute of Criminology, 1994).

22. Nelson Mandela, State of the Union Address, Houses of Parliament, Cape Town, May 24, 1994, http://www.sahistory.org.za/article/state-nation-address-president-south-africa-nelson-mandela.

23. South Africa Constitution, Act 108 of 1996, sec. 28(1(g).

24. Ann Skelton and Jacqui Gallinetti, "A Long and Winding Road: The Child Justice Bill and Civil Society Advocacy," *Crime Quarterly,* no. 25 (September 2008), 3–9.

25. World's Children's Prize Foundation, "Ann Skelton."

26. Carolyn Hamilton, "South Africa: The Fragility of the Children's Rights Agenda," Toolkit on Diversion and Alternatives to Detention (New York: UNICEF, 2010), https://www.unicef.org/tdad/index_56499.html.

27. Cited in Charmain Badenhorst, *Overview of the Implementation of the Child Justice Act, 2008* (Pinelands, South Africa: Open Society Foundation of South Africa 2011), 8. http://www.childjustice.org.za/publications/ImplementationCJA.pdf.

28. Conrad Barberton and John Stuart, *Costing the Child Justice Bill* (n.p.: AFReC, May 2001), http://www.childjustice.org.za/downloads/RecostingReport.pdf.

29. Hamilton, "South Africa."

30. Skelton and Gallinetti, "A Long and Winding Road."

31. Ibid.

32. Lukas Muntingh and Clare Ballard, *Report on Children in Prison in South Africa* (Cape Town: Community Law Centre, University of Western Cape, 2012), 3, http://cspri.org.za/publications/research-reports/report-on-children-in-prison-in-south-africa.

33. Department of Justice and Constitutional Development, *Annual Report on the Implementation of the Child Justice Act, 2008* (Act No. 75 of 2008), Pretoria, 2014, 20–22, 42.

34. Shaka Sankofa [Gary Lee Graham], "A Message to All Youth and Students: Stop the Violence, Stop the Executions" (n.d.), http://ccadp.org/Ssyouth.htm.

35. "Wife of Man Inmate Was Found Guilty of Killing Opposes Execution," *Kingman Daily Miner,* June 6, 1993.

36. ICCPR, article 6 (5) and Convention on the Rights of the Child, article 37(a).

37. Amnesty International, "Recorded Executions of Juvenile Offenders since 1990" (April 2016), https://www.amnesty.org/download/Documents/ACT5038322016ENGLISH.PDF. From 1990 to 2005, Iran executed eleven child offenders; Pakistan, three; China, two; Democratic Republic of the Congo, one; Nigeria, one; Saudi Arabia, one; and Yemen, one.

38. Author interview with Steven Drizin, December 17, 2014.

39. Ibid.

40. See, for example, Laurence Steinberg and Elizabeth C. Scott, "Less Guilty by Reason of Adolescence: Developmental Immaturity, Diminished Responsibility, and the Juvenile Death Penalty," *American Psychologist* 58 (2003): 1009, 1013.

41. Stephanie Chen, "States Rethink 'Adult Time for Adult Crime,'" CNN, January 15, 2010, http://www.cnn.com/2010/CRIME/01/15/connecticut.juvenile.ages/.

42. Author interview with Drizin.

43. Author interview with Lauren Girard Adams, December 22, 2014.

44. Endorsers of the call included three former US surgeons general, the American Academy of Child and Adolescent Psychiatry, the American Society for Adolescent Psychiatry, the International Pediatric Association, and chairs and other leaders in pediatrics, developmental medicine, psychiatry, psychology, and neuroscience at medical schools and medical centers throughout the United States. Physicians for Human Rights, *USA: Leading Health Professionals Call to End Execution of Juvenile Offenders* (press release, October 8, 2004), http://www.hrea.org/lists/psychology-humanrights-l /markup/msg00364.html. An earlier list was included in the Brief for Juvenile Law Center, Children and Family Justice Center et al. as Amici Curiae Supporting Respondent, Roper v. Simmons (No. 03-633), Appendix C.

45. Author interview with Drizin.

46. American Bar Association Juvenile Justice Center, "Cruel and Unusual Punishment: The Juvenile Death Penalty: Evolving Standards of Decency" (January 2004), http://www.americanbar.org/content/dam/aba/publishing/criminal_justice_section _newsletter/crimjust_juvjus_EvolvingStandards.authcheckdam.pdf.

47. Author interview with Bernardine Dohrn, December 8, 2014.

48. Victor Streib, "The Juvenile Death Penalty Today: Death Sentences and Executions for Juvenile Crimes, January 1, 1973–February 28, 2005" (2005), http://www .deathpenaltyinfo.org/juvdeathstreib.pdf.

49. Megan Freismuth, "Execution of Juvenile Offenders," blog post, *Prison Talk*, March 11, 2004, http://www.prisontalk.com/forums/showthread.php?p=496148.

50. See Death Penalty Information Center, "Recent Op-Eds Regarding Roper v. Simmons," n.d. http://www.deathpenaltyinfo.org/node/1083.

51. Death Penalty Information Center, "New Voices: Nobel Laureates Oppose Death Penalty, Decry Execution of Juvenile Offenders," December 3, 2003, http://www .deathpenaltyinfo.org/node/976.

52. Author interview with Adams.

53. Texas Department of Corrections, Napoleon Beazley, last statement, http:// www.tdcj.state.tx.us/death_row/dr_info/beazleynapoleonlast.html.

54. Streib, "The Juvenile Death Penalty Today."

55. Death Penalty Information Center, National Polls and Studies, various dates, http://deathpenaltyinfo.org/national-polls-and-studies#Harris1203.

56. Roper v. Simmons, 543 US 551 (2005).

57. Author interview with Dohrn.

58. Brief for Juvenile Law Center, Children and Family Justice Center et al. as Amici Curiae Supporting Respondent, Roper v. Simmons (No. 03-633).

59. Brief for President James Earl Carter Jr., President Frederik Willem de Klerk et al. as Amici Curiae Supporting Respondent, Roper v. Simmons (no. 03-633).

60. Brief for the American Medical Association et al., as Amici Curiae Supporting Respondent, Roper v. Simmons (no. 03-633). Others joining the brief included the American Psychiatric Association, the American Society for Adolescent Psychiatry, the American Academy of Child and Adolescent Psychiatry, the American Academy of Psychiatry and the Law, the National Association of Social Workers, the Missouri Chapter of the National Association of Social Workers, and the National Mental Health Association.

61. Death Penalty Information Center, "Editorials Regarding Roper V. Simmons," http://www.deathpenaltyinfo.org/node/1042.

62. Roper v. Simmons, 543 US 551 (2005).

63. Ibid.

64. Ibid.

65. Graham v. Florida, 560 U.S. 48 (2010) and Miller v. Alabama, 567 U.S. ___ (2012).

66. Senate bill 260, http://www.fairsentencingforyouth.org/wp/wp-content/uploads /2013/03/SB-260-9-10-13-with-highlights.pdf.

67. Author interview with Robert Schwartz, February 9, 2015.

68. John J. DiIulio Jr., "My Black Crime Problem, and Ours," *City Journal* (spring 1996). See also Equal Justice Initiative, "The Superpredator Myth, 20 Years Later," April 7, 2014, http://www.eji.org/node/893, and Jeffrey Fagan et al. as Amici Curiae, Miller v. Alabama, No. 10-9646, US Supreme Court, January 17, 2012.

69. Equal Justice Initiative, "The Superpredator Myth."

70. Author interview with Skelton.

71. Mendel, *No Place for Kids.*

72. Author interview with Skelton.

73. Postamble, Interim Constitution of South Africa, 1993.

74. Skelton, "Freedom in the Making."

75. Author interview with Skelton.

76. Author e-mail correspondence with Bernardine Dohrn, February 14, 2015.

77. Author interview with Stephen Harper, January 6, 2015.

Chapter 4

1. Nujood Ali with Delphine Minoui, *I Am Nujood, Age 10 and Divorced* (New York: Broadway Books, 2010).

2. Ibid.

3. Ibid.

4. Ibid.

5. Ibid. The French publisher of Nujood's 2010 memoir agreed to pay her school fees and a sum of $1,000 a month to support her upbringing. However, in 2013, she claimed her father had spent most of the funds to marry two more wives and that she had received very little of the money. See Joe Sheffer, "Yemen's Youngest Divorcee Says Father Has Squandered Cash from Her Book," *Guardian*, March 12, 2013, https://www .theguardian.com/world/2013/mar/12/child-bride-father-cash-spend.

6. UNICEF, *State of the World's Children 2015* (New York: UNICEF, 2014), 88; see also United Nations Population Fund (UNFPA), *State of World Population 2016* (New York: UNFPA, 2016), 72. http://www.unicef.org/publications/files/SOWC_2015_Sum mary_and_Tables.pdf.

7. UNICEF, "Ending Child Marriage: Progress and Prospects" (New York: Division of Policy and Research, Untied Nations, 2014), http://www.unicef.org/media/files /Child_Marriage_Report_7_17_LR..pdf.

8. UNFPA, *Marrying Too Young: End Child Marriage* (New York: UNFPA, 2012),6. https://www.unfpa.org/sites/default/files/pub-pdf/MarryingTooYoung.pdf.

9. World Health Organization, *Adolescent Pregnancy* (fact sheet 364, September 2014), http://www.who.int/mediacentre/factsheets/fs364/en/.

10. UNFPA, *State of World Population 2014*, 8, http://www.unfpa.org/sites/default /files/pub-pdf/EN-SWOP14-Report_FINAL-web.pdf.

11. World Health Organization, *Early Marriage, Adolescent and Young Pregnancy* (report to the World Health Assembly, A65/13, March 16, 2012), para. 11.

12. UNFPA, *Marrying Too Young*,11.

13. Ibid.

14. Dasra, *Marry Me Later: Preventing Child Marriage and Early Pregnancy in India* (2014), 15, https://www.dasra.org/sites/default/files/Marry%20Me%20Later.pdf.

15. Girls Not Brides, "Why Does Child Marriage Happen?" http://www.girlsnot brides.org/why-does-it-happen/.

16. Ibid.

17. "UNICEF, *State of the World's Children 2015.*

18. Human Rights Watch, *Marry before Your House Is Swept Away: Child Marriage in Bangladesh* (New York: Human Rights Watch, 2015).

19. Tahirih Justice Center, "Child Marriage in America," February 20, 2015, http:// www.tahirih.org/news/child-marriage-happens-in-the-u-s-too/.

20. Convention on Consent to Marriage, Minimum Age for Marriage and Registration of Marriages, adopted by General Assembly resolution 1763 A (XVII), November 7, 1962, articles 1, 2. The convention never gained a large number of states parties; as of January 2017, it had been ratified by fifty-five states.

21. Convention on the Elimination of All Forms of Discrimination against Women, article 16.

22. Convention on the Rights of the Child, article 24(3).

23. Committee on the Elimination of Discrimination against Women and the Committee on the Rights of the Child, "Joint General Recommendation/General Comment No. 31 of the Committee on the Elimination of Discrimination against Women and No. 18 of the Committee on the Rights of the Child on Harmful Practices," CEDAW /C /GC/31-CRC/C/GC/18, November 4, 2014.

24. Ibid., para. 55(f).

25. Anita Raj and Ulrike Boehmer, "Girl Child Marriage and Its Association with National Rates of HIV, Maternal Health, and Infant Mortality across 97 Countries," *Violence against Women* 19 (2013): 536–51.

26. A. Savadogo and Q. Wodon, "Simulating the Impact of Child Marriage on Labor Force Participation and Earnings in Niger," mimeo. (Washington, DC: ICRW-World Bank Economic Impacts of Child Marriage Project, 2015).

27. Q. Wodon, "What Would Be the Effect of the Elimination of Child Marriage on Demographic Growth?" mimeo. (Washington, DC: ICRW-World Bank Economic Impacts of Child Marriage Project, 2015).

28. UNFPA, *Marrying Too Young*, 51–52. See also Anju Malhotra, Ann Warner, Allison McGonagle, and Susan Lee-Rife, *Solutions to End Child Marriage: What the Evidence Shows* (Washington, DC: International Center for Research on Women, 2011).

29. Girls Not Brides, "Integrated Project for Empowering Adolescent Girls," http://

www.girlsnotbrides.org/child-marriage-theory-of-change/interactive/#casestudies-em
powering -adolescent-girls.

30. International Center for Research on Women, "Child Marriage and Education"
(Washington, DC: International Center for Research on Women, 2006), http://www
.icrw.org/files/images/Child-Marriage-Fact-Sheet-Education.pdf.

31. Sarah Baird, Ephraim Cherwa, Craig McIntosh, and Berk Ozler, "The Short-
Term Impacts of a Schooling Conditional Cash Transfer Program on the Sexual Behavior of Young Women," *Health Economics* 19 (2010): 55–68.

32. UNFPA, *Marrying Too Young.*

33. Ibid.

34. Nancy Williamson, *Motherhood in Childhood: Facing the Challenge of Adolescent
Pregnancy, State of World Population 2013* (New York: UNFPA, 2013),63.

35. Belinda Maswikwa, Linda Richter, Jay Kaufman, and Arijit Nandi, "Minimum
Marriage Age Laws and the Prevalence of Child Marriage and Adolescent Birth: Evi-
dence from Sub-Saharan Africa," *International Perspectives on Sexual and Reproductive
Health* 41 (2015): 58–68.

36. Farah Mohamed, "She-Lanthropy: Mabel van Oranje on Ending Child Marriage," *World Post,* July 29, 2013, http://www.huffingtonpost.com/farah-mohamed/shel
anthropy-mabel-van-or_b_3664893.html

37. Madeleine Brand, "Mabel van Oranje of Girls Not Brides Wants to End Child
Marriage in One Generation," *America Abroad,* March 23, 2015, http://www.pri.org
/stories/2015-03-23/ending-child-marriage-one-generation-extended-interview-mabel
-van-oranje-girls.

38. Mohamed, "She-lanthropy."

39. Girls Not Brides, "About Girls Not Brides," n.d., http://www.girlsnotbrides.org
/about-girls-not-brides/.

40. Girls Not Brides, *Girls Not Brides—A New Global Partnership to End Child Marriage Announced at 2011 Clinton Global Initiative Annual Meeting* (press release, September 20, 2011), http://www.girlsnotbrides.org/girls-not-brides-announced-at-2011
-clinton-global-initiative-annual-meeting/.

41. *Girls Not Brides Blog,* "Joining Hands: Why Ending Child Marriage Needs a
Global Partnership," blog entry by Lakshmi Sundaram, June 21, 2013. http://www.girls
notbrides.org/joining-hands-why-ending-child-marriage-needs-global-partnership/.

42. UNICEF, *State of the World's Children 2015,* 86.

43. Howard Mlozi, "Information on GENET Malawi's Work in the Fight to End
Child Marriage" (December 2013), www.ohchr.org/Documents/Issues/Women/...
/ForcedMarriage/.../GENETMalawi.docx. See also Denise Dunning and Joyce Mkanda-
wire, "How Girl Activists Helped to Ban Child Marriage in Malawi," *Guardian,*
February 26, 2015, http://www.theguardian.com/global-development-professionals-
network/2015/feb/26/girl-activists-child-marriage-malawi-let-girls-lead. Although the
new law is a step forward, it does not change Malawi's constitution, which still includes
the parental exception for child marriage.

44. See www.girlsnotbrides.org.

45. Girls Not Brides, *Summary Report: Girls Not Brides Member and Other Activities*

to Highlight Child Marriage on Inaugural International Day of the Girl Child, October 11, 2012, http://www.girlsnotbrides.org/wp-content/uploads/2012/10/Summary-Report -Girls-Not-Brides-member-activities-On-International-Day-of-the-Girl-2012-child -marriage-gains-global-attention1.pdf.

46. Ibid.

47. OHCHR, "Joint Statement by a Group of UN Human Rights Experts to Mark the First International Day of the Girl Child," October 11, 2012, http://www.un.org/en /events/girlchild/2012/hrexperts.shtml.

48. UN General Assembly, "Child, Early, and Forced Marriage," resolution A/RES /68/148, adopted December 18, 2013; UN Human Rights Council, "Strengthening Efforts to Prevent and Eliminate Child, Early and Forced Marriage: Challenges, Achievements, Best Practices and Implementation Gaps," resolution A/HRC/RES/24/23, adopted September 27, 2013.

49. UN General Assembly, "Child, Early and Forced Marriage," resolution A/RES /69/156, adopted December 18, 2014.

50. Ommera Zafar, "Sustainable Development Goals: Why Ending Child Marriage Should Be a Target," *Guardian Global Development Professionals Network,* April 10, 2015, http://www.theguardian.com/global-development-professionals-network/2015/apr/10 /sustainable-development-goals-ending-child-marriage-target.

51. Girls Not Brides, *Girls Not Brides Members Co-Sign Letter to Ban Ki-Moon Stressing That Child Marriage Target Must Be Included in Sustainable Development Goals* (press release, October 2, 2014, http://www.girlsnotbrides.org/girls-brides-members-co -sign-letter-ban-ki-moon-stressing-child-marriage-target-must-included-sustainable -development-goals/.

52. Girls Not Brides, "Ending Child Marriage Will Help Us Achieve the Global Goals for Development. Here's How," blog post, May 15, 2016, http://www.girlsnotbrides.org /ending-child-marriage-will-help-us-achieve-the-global-goals-heres-how/.

53. UN General Assembly, "Transforming Our World: The 2030 Agenda for Sustainable Development," resolution A/RES/70/1, adopted September 25, 2015, goal 5.3.

54. Luke Waller, "The 28 People from 28 Countries Who Are Shaping, Shaking, and Stirring Europe," *Politico,* n.d., http://www.politico.eu/list/politico-28/princess-mabel/.

55. *Girls Not Brides Blog,* "Taking a Stand by Sitting Down: Ending Child Marriage in Pakistan," October 29, 2015, http://www.girlsnotbrides.org/taking-a-stand-by-sitting -down-ending-child-marriage-in-pakistan/.

56. Brand, "Mabel van Oranje."

57. Annie Bunting, "Stages of Development: Marriage of Girls and Teens as an International Human Rights Issue," *Social and Legal Studies* 14, no. 1 (2005): 17–38.

58. Ibid., 18.

59. *Girls Not Brides Blog,* "Joining Hands: Why Ending Child Marriage Needs a Global Partnership," blog entry by Lakshmi Sundaram, June 21, 2013, http://www.girls notbrides.org/joining-hands-why-ending-child-marriage-needs-global-partnership/.

60. Population Council, "Building an Evidence Base to Delay Marriage in Sub-Saharan Africa," n.d., http://www.popcouncil.org/research/building-an-evidence-base -to-delay-marriage-in-sub-saharan-africa.

61. TEDX Talk by Mabel van Oranje, Amsterdam, November 20, 2011, https://www.youtube.com/watch?v=nunqwMN2g7g.

62. Graca Machel, "Why We Are Building an Alliance to End Child Marriage," June 7, 2011, http://www.girlsnotbrides.org/why-we-are-building-an-alliance-to-end-child-marriage/.

63. Brand, "Mabel van Oranje."

Chapter 5

1. UNICEF, "Om Prakash Gurjar: My Identity, My Rights: From Child Laborer to Child Rights Activist," UNICEF, http://www.unicef.org/rightsite/364_559.htm.

2. Author interview with Om Prakash Gurjar, November 14, 2014.

3. Ibid.

4. "Victory at Last: Child 'Slave' Gets Peace Prize," *Times of India*, November 21, 2006. http://timesofindia.indiatimes.com/india/Victory-at-last-Child-slave-gets-peace-prize/articleshow/498510.cms?.

5. International Labour Office, *Making Progress against Child Labour: Global Estimates and Trends 2000–2012* (Geneva: ILO, 2013), vii.

6. Ibid. The service industry includes work in hotels, restaurants, retail trade, transportation, and domestic work.

7. International Labour Office, *World Report on Child Labour: Economic Vulnerability, Social Protection and the Fight against Child Labour* (Geneva: ILO, 2013).

8. See Patrick Emerson and André Portela Souza, "Is Child Labor Harmful? The Impact of Working Earlier in Life on Adult Earnings" (discussion paper 3027, Institute for the Study of Labor, Bonn, September 2007); see also Nadeem Ilahi, Peter Orazem, and Guilherme Sedlacek, "The Implications of Child Labor for Adult Wages, Income and Poverty: Retrospective Evidence from Brazil," mimeo. (Ames: Iowa State University, 2001).

9. International Labour Office, *Investing in Every Child: An Economic Study of the Costs and Benefits of Eliminating Child Labour* (Geneva: ILO, 2003).

10. Ruth Levine, Cynthia B. Lloyd , Margaret Greene, and Caren Grown, *Girls Count: A Global Investment and Action Agenda* (Washington, DC: Center for Global Development, 2009), 19.

11. ILO, *Making Progress against Child Labour*.

12. ILO, *World Report on Child Labour*, 19.

13. Uma S. Kambhampati and Nigar Hashimzade, *Growth and Inverted U in Child Labour: A Dual Economy Approach* (Reading: Centre for Institutional Performance and School of Economics, University of Reading, May 2009), http://www.henley.ac.uk/web/FILES/management/080-09.pdf.

14. Convention on the Rights of the Child, article 32 (1).

15. ILO Convention 182 Concerning the Prohibition and Immediate Action for the Elimination of the Worst Forms of Child Labour (1999). (Worst Forms of Child Labor Convention.)

16. ILO Convention 138 Concerning Minimum Age for Admission to Employment (1973).

17. ILO, *Making Progress against Child Labour*, 9.

18. See also ILO, *What Is Child Labor?* (fact sheet), n.d., http://www.ilo.org/ipec/facts/lang—en/index.htm.

19. Morocco High Commission for Planning, "Information Note of the High Commission for Planning on the Occasion of the World Day against Child Labour" (Note d'information du Haut-Commissariat au Plan à l'occasion de la Journée mondiale contre le travail des enfants), June 12, 2012.

20. Sarah Baird, Francisco H. G. Ferreira, Berk Özler, and Michael Woolcock, "Relative Effectiveness of Conditional and Unconditional Cash Transfers for Schooling Outcomes in Developing Countries: A Systematic Review," *Campbell Systematic Review* 9, no. 8 (2013).

21. ILO, *World Report on Child Labour*, xvii, 20.

22. Author interview with Florencia Devoto, researcher, Poverty Action Lab, April 17, 2012.

23. ILO, *World Report on Child Labour*, 30.

24. Nora Boustany, "A Lifelong Crusader against Child Labor," *Washington Post*, July 23, 2004, http://www.washingtonpost.com/wp-dyn/articles/A7518-2004Jul22.html.

25. ILO, *New ILO Study on Child Labor in South Asia*, press release, February 25, 2015, http://www.ilo.org/newdelhi/info/public/pr/WCMS_346673/lang—en/index.htm.

26. Goodweave, "A Journey of One Blazes a Trail of Freedom for Many," n.d., http://www.goodweave.org/index.php?pid=9439.

27. Government of India, Department of Social Welfare, Bonded Labour System (Abolition) Act, Act No. 19, enacted February 9, 1976, http://indiacode.nic.in/fullact1.asp?tfnm=197619

28. See, for example, Child Rights and You (CRY) and Committed Action for Relief and Education (CARE), *Developing a New Perspective on Child Labour: Exploring the Aftermath of Mumbai Raids Conducted 2008 Onwards* (June 2014), http://www.cry.org/resources/pdf/CRY-CARE-report-on-Child-Labour-2014.pdf.

29. BBC, "Asia-Pacific Global March against Child Labor Begins," January 17, 1998, http://news.bbc.co.uk/2/hi/asia-pacific/48267.stm.

30. "From the Global March International Secretariat," archived material, http://www.iearn.org.au/clp/archive/update2.htm.

31. Basu Rai, *From the Streets of Kathmandu* (New Delhi: Vitasta Publishing, 2014), 212.

32. Melanie Gow, "The Global March against Child Labor Arrives in Geneva," May 30, 1998, http://www.iearn.org.au/clp/archive/geneva.htm.

33. ILO, "The End of Child Labour: Millions of Voices, One Common Hope," *World of Work*, no. 61, December 3, 2007, 4. http://ilo.org/global/publications/magazines-and-journals/world-of-work-magazine/articles/WCMS_090028/lang—en/index.htm.

34. Harriet Alexander and Dean Nelson, "Nobel Peace Prize: Who Is Kailash Satyarthi?" *Telegraph*, October 10, 2014, http://www.telegraph.co.uk/news/worldnews/asia/india/11153539/Nobel-Peace-Prize-Who-is-Kailash-Satyarthi.html.

35. Author interview with Gurjar.

36. Alexander and Nelson, "Nobel Peace Prize."

37. Author interview with Gurjar.

38. Bachpan Bachao Andolan, *Annual Report, April 2012–March 2013* (2013), http://bba.org.in/sites/default/files/Annual-Report-12-13.pdf.

39. ICF International, *Program and Practices Report: Research on Children Working in the Carpet Industry in India, Nepal, and Pakistan* (Calverton, MD: ICF International, 2012), http://www.dol.gov/ilab/iclre/Downloads/Research/Report/PPR_Regional_Report.pdf.

40. Business for Social Responsibility (BSR) and FUNDEMAS, *Eradicating Child Labor: Because a Better World Is Possible: The Experience of the Sugar Industry in El Salvador and FUNDAZUCAR*, n.d., 25.

41. Human Rights Watch, *Turning a Blind Eye: Hazardous Child Labor in El Salvador's Sugarcane Cultivation* (New York: Human Rights Watch, 2004).

42. UL, "The Sugar Association of El Salvador Case Study," 2013, http://www.ul.com/global/documents/verificationservices/businesssegments/RS/MC202_AAES_Case Study_F_Web.pdf.

43. BSR and FUNDEMAS, *Eradicating Child Labor*, 24–26.

44. Human Rights Watch, *Turning a Blind Eye*, 10.

45. BSR and FUNDEMAS, *Eradicating Child Labor*, 15.

46. Ibid.

47. Michael G. Schechter and Michael Bochenek, "Working to Eliminate Human Rights Abuses of Children: A Cross-National Comparative Study," *Human Rights Quarterly* 30 (2008): 579–606.

48. Ibid.

49. US Department of Labor, "Technical Cooperation Project Summary," n.d. http://www.dol.gov/ilab/projects/summaries/El_Salvador_TBP_PhaseI_CLOSED.pdf

50. BSR and FUNDEMAS, *Eradicating Child Labor*, 49.

51. Author interview with Benjamin Smith, January 26, 2015.

52. ILO, "Private Sector Contributions to Combating Child Labour in Sugarcane in El Salvador" (fact sheet, October 1, 2010), http://www.ilo.org/ipec/Informationresources/WCMS_IPEC_PUB_14355/lang—en/index.htm.

53. UL, "The Sugar Association of El Salvador Case Study."

54. ILO, "Elimination of the Worst Forms of Child Labour in Sugarcane Sector: A Different World Is Possible (El Salvador)," 2010 (published as a case study by the III Global Conference on Child Labor in 2013); http://unpan1.un.org/intradoc/groups/public/documents/icap/unpan043527.pdf.

55. Ibid.

56. Ibid.

57. True Vision Productions, *Slavery: A Global Investigation by Brian Woods and Kate Blewett* (2000), http://truevisiontv.com/films/details/90/slavery-a-global-investigation.

58. Ibid.

59. KPMG, *A Taste of the Future: The Trends That Could Transform the Chocolate Industry* (June 2014), http://www.kpmg.com/Global/en/IssuesAndInsights/ArticlesPublications/Documents/taste-of-the-future.pdf.

60. *ICCO Quarterly Bulletin of Cocoa Statistics* 42 (February 26, 2016), http://www

.icco.org/about-us/international-cocoa-agreements/cat_view/30-related-documents
/46-statistics-production.html; World Cocoa Foundation, *Cocoa Market Update*, April 1,
2014, http://www.worldcocoafoundation.org/wp-content/uploads/Cocoa-Market-Update
-as-of-4-1-2014.pdf.

61. International Labor Rights Forum, *The Fairness Gap: Farm Incomes and Root Cause Solutions to Ending Child Labor in the Cocoa Industry* (Washington, DC: IRLF, 2014), http://www.laborrights.org/sites/default/files/publications/Fairness%20gap_low _res.pdf.

62. Tulane University School of Public Health and Tropical Medicine, *Final Report: 2013/2014 Survey Research on Child Labor in West African Cocoa Growing Areas* (July 30, 2015), 4.

63. Datamonitor Industry Market Research, cited in Sarah Grossman-Greene and Chris Bayer, "A History of Child Labor, Child Rights, and the Harkin-Engel Protocol" (Tulane University, November 2009),11.

64. Chocolate Manufacturers Association and World Cocoa Foundation, "Protocol for the Growing and Processing of Cocoa Beans and Their Derivative Products in a Manner That Complies with ILO Convention 182 Concerning the Prohibition and Immediate Action for the Elimination of the Worst Forms of Child Labor," September 19, 2001, http://www.cocoainitiative.org/wp-content/uploads/2016/10/Harkin_Engel_Pro tocol.pdf.

65. Responsible Cocoa, "The Harkin-Engel Protocol," n.d., http://responsiblecocoa .com/about-us/the-harkin-engel-protocol/.

66. Tom Harkin and Eliot L. Engel, "Taking Child Slavery out of Valentine's Day," *Los Angeles Times*, February 14, 2005, http://articles.latimes.com/2005/feb/14/opinion/oe -harkin14.

67. In 2006, the US Congress charged the Department of Labor with creating an oversight process for the protocol, resulting in a $5.5 million grant to Tulane University to assess progress and conduct independent surveys in Ghana and Côte d'Ivoire.

68. Payson Center for International Development and Technology Transfer, "Oversight of Public and Private Initiatives to Eliminate the Worst Forms of Child Labor in the Cocoa Sector in Côte d'Ivoire and Ghana," Tulane University, March 31, 2011, http:// www.childlabor-payson.org/Tulane%20Final%20Report.pdf.

69. Author interview with Bama Athreya, July 31, 2015.

70. See www.fairtrade.net, https://www.utzcertified.org, and http://www.rainforest -alliance.org.

71. IRLF, "The Cocoa Protocol: Success or Failure?" July 30, 2008. http://www.labor rights.org/sites/default/files/publications-and-resources/Cocoa%20Protocol%20Suc cess%20or%20Failure%20June%202008.pdf.

72. International Labor Rights Forum, Americans for Informed Democracy, Co-op America, Dominican Sisters of Springfield, IL, Equal Exchange, Global Exchange, Kopali Organics, Ithaca Fine Chocolates, New York State Labor-Religion Coalition, Oasis USA, Organic Consumers Association, et al., NGO letter to Senator Tom Harkin, June 17, 2008. Appendix to IRLF, "Broken Hearts: A Review of Industry Efforts to Eliminate Child Labor in the Cocoa Industry," January 25, 2010.

73. IRLF, "The Cocoa Protocol."

74. Stop the Traffik, *Stop the Traffik demands Traffic-Free Chocolate* (press release, February 13, 2008), http://www.stopthetraffik.org/press/article/41-stop-the-traffik-de mands-for-traffik-free-chocolate.

75. Author interview with Ruth Dearnley, September 22, 2015.

76. Ruth Dearnley, "A Glass Half-Full," *Tablet*, March 14, 2009, http://www.colum ban.org.au/publications/the-far-east/2009/the-far-east-jun-2009/a-glass-and-a-half.

77. Author interview with Dearnley.

78. Stop the Traffik, *20% Increase in Fair Trade Chocolate Worldwide* (press release, March 3, 2008), http://www.stopthetraffik.org/press/article/38-20-increase-in-fair-trade -chocolate-worldwide.

79. Ibid.

80. Statement from Stop the Traffik CEO Ruth Dearnley, *Cadbury Goes Traffik-Free!* (press release, November 20, 2008), http://www.stopthetraffik.org/press/article/35 -cadbury-goes-traffik-free.

81. Ibid.

82. *Stop the Traffik Blog*, "The March Is Working (Already!)" April 9, 2009, https:// stopthetraffik.wordpress.com/2009/04/09/the-march-is-working-already/.

83. Ibid.

84. Author interview with Dearnley.

85. Global Exchange, Green America, and International Labor Rights Forum, *Still Time to Raise the Bar, Hershey! The Real Corporate Social Responsibility Report for the Hershey Company*, September 2011, http://www.globalexchange.org/sites/default/files /HersheyReport2011.pdf.

86. Global Exchange, Green America, IRLF, and Oasis USA, *Time to Raise the Bar: The Real Corporate Social Responsibility Report for the Hershey Company*, September 2010, http://www.globalexchange.org/sites/default/files/HersheyReport2010.pdf.

87. Global Exchange et al., *Still Time to Raise the Bar, Hershey!*

88. Author interview with Elizabeth O'Connell, August 5, 2015.

89. Green America, *Costumed Activists to Give Hershey More Than 100,000 Signa-tures Demanding a Commitment to Child-Labor-Free Cocoa by Halloween* (press release, October 25, 2011), http://www.greenamerica.org/about/newsroom/releases/2011-10-25 -Costumed-Activists-to-Give-Hershey-More-Than-100000-Signatures-Demanding-a -Commitment-to-Child-Labor-Free-Cocoa-by-Halloween.cfm.

90. Author interview with O'Connell.

91. *Change.org Blog*, "Hershey: Raise the Bar—Victory," January 30, 2012, https:// www.change.org/p/hershey-raise-the-bar.

92. United Methodist Women, "United Methodist Women Call on Hershey's to Raise the Bar!" 2012, https://lms.manhattan.edu/pluginfile.php/52265/mod_resource /content/1/UMW_Talking_Points—_Hershey_6-12-12.pdf.

93. Green America, *Consumer-Owned Grocery Retailers Call on Hershey to Address Child Slave Labor in Cocoa* (press release, August 23, 2012), http://www.greenamerica .org/about/newsroom/releases/2012-08-23-Consumer-Owned-Grocery-Stores-Push -Hershey-on-Child-Slave-Labor.cfm.

94. Green America, "Raise the Bar, Hershey! Campaign Welcomes Hershey Announcement to Source 100 Percent Certified Cocoa by 2020" (statement, October 3, 2012). http://www.greenamerica.org/about/newsroom/releases/2012-10-03-Green-America -Welcomes-Hershey-Announcement-to-Source-100-percent-certified-cocoa.cfm.

95. Hershey Company, *Hershey to Source 100% Certified Cocoa by 2020* (press release, October 3, 2012), http://www.thehersheycompany.com/newsroom/news-release .aspx?id=1741328.

96. Ibid.

97. Ibid.

98. Author interview with O'Connell.

99. Green America, "Raise the Bar, Hershey!"

100. Hershey Company, *Hershey '21St Century Cocoa Plan' Outlines Commitment to Sustainable Cocoa and Improving Cocoa Communities* (press release, March 21, 2013), http://www.thehersheycompany.com/newsroom/news-release.aspx?id=1798984.

101. Hershey Company, *2015 Corporate Responsibility Report* (2015), https://www .thehersheycompany.com/content/dam/corporate-us/documents/csr-reports/hershey -2015-csr-report.pdf.

102. Michael Bourdillon, Deborah Levison, William Myers, and Ben White, *Rights and Wrongs of Children's Work*, (New Brunswick, NJ: Rutgers University Press, 2010), xv.

103. Code for Children and Adolescents, LAW NO. 548, adopted July 17, 2014, published in the Official Gazette of the Government of Bolivia on July 23, 2014.

104. Author interview with Benjamin Smith, January 26, 2015.

105. Tulane University School of Public Health and Tropical Medicine, *Final Report: 2013/2014 Survey Research on Child Labor in West African Cocoa Growing Areas*, July 30, 2015, 4, 84–86.

106. International Labor Rights Forum, *The Fairness Gap*.

107. Author interview with O'Connell.

108. Author interview with Athreya.

109. Ibid.

110. Payson Center for International Development and Technology Transfer, "Oversight of Public and Private Initiatives to Eliminate the Worst Forms of Child Labor in the Cocoa Sector in Cote d'Ivoire and Ghana" (Tulane University, March 31, 2011), 72, http://www.childlaborcocoa.org/images/Payson_Reports/Tulane_Final _Report.pdf.

111. Author interview with Athreya.

112. Author interview with O'Connell.

113. Author interview with Dearnley.

Chapter 6

1. Tracy Sabo and Ashley Hayes, "Texas Judge's Daughter: Violence Was Regular Occurrence," *CNN*, November 3, 2011, http://edition.cnn.com/2011/11/02/justice /texas-video-beating/.

2. "Family Law Judge Exposed for Beating His Daughter, 16, in a Video She Posted Online Loses His Re-Election Bid," *Daily Mail*, March 6, 2014, http://www.dailymail

.co.uk/news/article-2574863/Family-law-judge-caught-beating-16-year-old-daughter
-video-posted-online-2011-losses-election-bid.html.

3. Ibid.

4. In Texas, the statute of limitations for inflicting bodily harm on a child was five years.

5. *Reddit*, "I'm Hillary Adams," 2011, https://www.reddit.com/comments/mvc95/im_hillary_adams_the_girl_in_the_judge_william/.

6. UNICEF, *Hidden in Plain Sight: A Statistical Analysis of Violence against Children* (New York: UNICEF, September 2014), 96.

7. Ibid., 94.

8. Committee on the Rights of the Child, General Comment no. 8 (2006), "The Right of the Child to Protection from Corporal Punishment and Other Cruel and Degrading Treatment," CRC/C/GC/8, March 2, 2007, para. 11.

9. UNICEF, *Hidden in Plain Sight*, 96

10. C. C. Aniand S. Grantham-McGregor, "Family and Personal Characteristics of Aggressive Nigerian Boys: Differences from and Similarities with Western Findings," *Journal of Adolescent Health* 23 (1998): 311–17; C. H. Hart, G. W. Ladd, and B. R. Burleson, "Children's Expectations of the Outcomes of Social Strategies: Relations with Sociometric Status and Maternal Disciplinary Styles," *Child Development* 61(1990): 127–37.

11. See Elizabeth Gershoff, "Corporal Punishment by Parents and Associated Child Behaviors and Experiences: A Meta-Analytic and Theoretical Review," *Psychological Bulletin* 128(2002): 539–79; Elizabeth Gershoff, *Report on Physical Punishment in the United States: What Research Tells Us about Its Effects on Children* (Columbus, OH: Center for Effective Discipline, 2008), http://www.nospank.net/gershoff.pdf.

12. Tracie O. Afifi, Natalie P. Mota, Patricia Dasiewicz, Harriet L. MacMillan, and Jitender Sareen, "Physical Punishment and Mental Disorders: Results from a Nationally Representative US Sample," *Pediatrics*, July 2, 2012.

13. Anke Hoeffler and James Fearon, *Conflict and Violence Assessment Paper: Benefits and Costs of the Conflict and Violence Targets for the Post-2015 Development Agenda* (Lowell, MA: Copenhagen Consensus Center, August 2014), 16, http://www.copenhagenconsensus.com/sites/default/files/conflict_assessment_-_hoeffler_and_fearon_0.pdf.

14. E. G. Krug, J. A. Mercy, L. L. Dahlberg, and A. B. Zwi, *World Report on Violence and Health* (Geneva: World Health Organization, 2002).

15. Global Initiative to End All Corporal Punishment of Children, "Corporal Punishment of Children: Review of Research on Its Impact and Associations" (working paper, June 2016), http://www.endcorporalpunishment.org/assets/pdfs/research-summaries/Review-research-effects-corporal-punishment-June-2016.pdf.

16. Convention on the Rights of the Child, article 19.

17. Committee on the Rights of the Child, General Comment no. 8 (2006), The Right of the Child to Protection from Corporal Punishment and Other Cruel and Degrading Treatment, CRC/C/GC/8, March 2, 2007, para. 18.

18. Sweden, Finland, Norway, Austria, Cyprus, Denmark, Latvia, Croatia, Bulgaria, Israel, and Germany.

19. Global Initiative to Prohibit All Corporal Punishment of Children, "Countdown to Universal Prohibition," n.d., http://www.endcorporalpunishment.org/progress /countdown.html.

20. Author interview with Peter Newell, October 14, 2010.

21. Hammarberg also served as Sweden's ambassador on humanitarian affairs and, later, as commissioner for human rights for the Council of Europe.

22. Author interview with Thomas Hammarberg, November 16, 2015.

23. Sweden official website, "Smacking Banned since 1979," https://sweden.se/so ciety/smacking-banned-since-1979/.

24. See the list at http://www.endcorporalpunishment.org/supporting-prohibition /supporters.html.

25. Carol Bower, *Evaluation of the Global Initiative to End All Corporal Punishment of Children*, April 2015, 21, http://www.endcorporalpunishment.org/assets/pdfs/miscel laneous/GI-evaluation-2015.pdf.

26. Author interview with Peter Newell, November 10, 2015.

27. These treaty bodies included the Human Rights Committee, the Committee against Torture, the Committee on Economic, Social and Cultural Rights, the Committee on the Rights of Persons with Disabilities, and the Committee on the Elimination of Discrimination against Women.

28. Bower, *Evaluation of the Global Initiative*, 54.

29. Global Initiative to End All Corporal Punishment of Children, "States Actively Pursuing the Issue of Corporal Punishment of Children in the Universal Periodic Review: Analysis of Sessions 1–22 (2008–2015)," October 2015, paper provided to the author by the Global Initiative.

30. Bower, *Evaluation of the Global Initiative*, 33.

31. Author interview with Newell, November 10, 2015.

32. Ibid.

33. For example, "Do not withhold discipline from a child; if you punish them with the rod, they will not die" (Proverbs 23:13) and "A rod and a reprimand impart wisdom, but a child left undisciplined disgraces its mother" (Proverbs 29:15).

34. Author interview with Newell, November 10, 2015.

35. Author interview with Chris Dodd, November 25, 2015.

36. Ibid.

37. Churches' Network for Non-Violence, "Faith-Based Support for Prohibition and Elimination of Corporal Punishment of Children—A Global Overview," May 2015, http://churchesfornon-violence.org/wp/wp-content/uploads/2012/02/Global-faith -support-summary-2015.pdf.

38. "A Multi-Religious Commitment to Confront Violence against Children," adopted at the Religions for Peace VIII World Assembly, Kyoto, Japan, August 28, 2006, http://www.unicef.org/violencestudy/pdf/Final%20Declaration%20VAC-28%20Aug -Kyoto.pdf.

39. E-mail communication from Chris Dodd to author, November 26, 2015.

40. UNICEF, "Religious Leaders Call for Ending Corporal Punishment in Mauritania," May 6, 2009, http://www.unicef.org/protection/mauritania_49593.html.

41. New Zealand's 1961 Crimes Act, section 59: (1) Every parent of a child ... is justified in using force by way of correction towards the child, if the force used is reasonable in the circumstances.

42. Author interview with Beth Wood, November 29, 2015.

43. Ibid.

44. Beth Wood, Ian Hassall, George Hook, and Robert Ludbrook, *Unreasonable Force: New Zealand's Journey towards Banning the Physical Punishment of Children* (Wellington: Save the Children New Zealand, 2008), 128.

45. Statement by Phil Goff, minister of justice, May 19, 2000, quoted in ibid., 172.

46. James Gardiner, "How Williams Killed Coral after Night on P," *New Zealand Herald*, December 11, 2003, http://www.nzherald.co.nz/nz/news/article.cfm?c_id=1&object id=3538849.

47. UNICEF Innocenti Research Center, *A League Table of Child Maltreatment Deaths in Rich Nations* (Florence: UNICEF, 2003), http://www.unicef-irc.org/publica tions/pdf/repcard5e.pdf.

48. Wood et al., *Unreasonable Force*, 204.

49. Author interview with Wood.

50. Beth Wood, "A Report from New Zealand: Four Years Post Law Change" (paper presented to the Global Summit on Ending Corporal Punishment of Children, Dallas, June 2011), http://epochnz.org.nz/images/stories/pdfs/NZ_4_year_%20post_law _change.pdf (October 15, 2015).

51. Author interview with Wood.

52. Ibid.

53. T. Dobbs, *Insights: Children and Young People Speak Out about Family Discipline* (Wellington: Save the Children New Zealand, 2005), 44.

54. Ibid.

55. Wood et al., 128.

56. "Ngongotaha Working to Be NZ's First Smack Free Zone," *Family and Community Services News*, Ministry of Social Development (April 2004).

57. Author interview with Wood.

58. Ibid.

59. Vernon Small, "Labour Takes It on the Chin," *Dominion Post*, May 29, 2007, www.pressreader.com/new-zealand/the-dominion-post/20070529/281578056236606.

60. Public Health Association of New Zealand, "Physical Punishment of Children in New Zealand—An Update," *Bulletin 391* (February 2014), http://www.pha.org.nz /documents/PPInformationSheet-FF.pdf,.

61. Author interview with Hammarberg.

62. Newell brought the complaints on behalf of APPROACH (Association for the Protection of All Children), a UK-based NGO that formally runs the Global Initiative to End All Corporal Punishment of Children.

63. CRIN, "Europe: Progress on Corporal Punishment of Children after Collective Complaints," September 28, 2015, https://www.crin.org/en/library/publications /europe-progress-corporal-punishment-children-after-collective-complaints.

64. The committee found that Italy was not in breach of the convention because

of a 1996 Supreme Court decision outlawing violence against children, including in child rearing. APPROACH argued that the court case was not sufficient and that explicit changes needed to be made in law.

65. See Complaints nos. 98/2013, 97/2013, 96/2013, No. 95/2013, 94/2013, 93/2015, 92/2015, and corresponding decisions, http://www.coe.int/t/dghl/monitoring/social charter/Complaints/Complaints_en.asp.

66. Global Initiative to Prohibit All Corporal Punishment of Children, "Countdown to Universal Prohibition," n.d., http://www.endcorporalpunishment.org/progress/countdown.html. In December 2016, the French parliament adopted a law stating that parental authority excluded "all cruel, degrading or humiliating treatment, including any use of corporal violence." The Global Initiative to End All Corporal Punishment of Children has stated that the law would not constitute a full ban unless a *décret d'application,* a governmental document that gives interpretative guidance of the law, made clear that "corporal violence" included all corporal punishment. At the time of writing, the *décret d'application* had not been issued. Global Initiative to End All Corporal Punishment of Children, "France Passes Law Prohibiting the Use of 'Corporal Violence' against Children," January 9, 2017, http://www.endcorporalpunishment .org/news/01/2017/france-passes-law-prohibiting-the-use-of-%E2%80%9Ccorporal -violence%E2%80%9D-against-children.html.

67. "L'amendement contre la fessée censuré par le Conseil constitutionnel," January 26, 2017. http://www.lemonde.fr/politique/article/2017/01/26/fessee-ecole-hors-contrat -hlm-le-conseil-constitutionnel-censure-des-dispositions-du-texte-egalite-et-citoyen nete_5069736_823448.html#VSTPdKc1ihG5iTg0.99

68. Harris Poll, "Four in Five Americans Believe Parents Spanking Their Children Is Sometimes Appropriate," September 26, 2013, http://www.theharrispoll.com/health -and-life/Four_in_Five_Americans_Believe_Parents_Spanking_Their_Children_is_ Sometimes_Appropriate.html.

69. Author interview with Hammarberg.

70. Author interview with Newell, November 10, 2015.

71. Author interview with Hammarberg.

72. Bower, *Evaluation of the Global Initiative,* 38.

73. Author interview with Hammarberg.

74. Author interview with Newell, November 10, 2015.

75. Ibid.

76. Author interview with Wood.

Chapter 7

1. US Immigration and Customs Enforcement, *Canadian John Wrenshall Sentenced on Child Porn Charges* (press release, January 31, 2011), http://www.ice.gov/news /releases/canadian-john-wrenshall-sentenced-child-porn-charges.

2. Ibid.

3. Ibid.

4. Precise figures are impossible to obtain. A 2012 ILO report estimates that 4.5 million individuals were engaged in forced sexual exploitation and that 22 percent of victims

of forced labor are children. See ILO, "Global Estimate of Forced Labour 2012: Results and Methodology," June 2012, http://www.ilo.org/global/topics/forced-labour/publica tions/WCMS_182004/lang—en/index.htm.

5. Angela Hawke and Alison Raphael, *Offenders on the Move: Global Study on the Sexual Exploitation of Children in Travel and Tourism* (ECPAT International and Defense for Children-ECPAT Netherlands, 2016), 20.

6. Helena Karlén, *The Commercial Sexual Exploitation of Children* (Stockholm: ECPAT Sverige and Jure Forlag AB, 2011), 25.

7. Unpublished history of ECPAT, author's files.

8. Donna M. Hughes, "The Internet and Sex Industries: Partners in Global Sexual Exploitation," IEEE *Technology and Society Magazine* (spring 2000) 35–42.

9. Muireann O'Briain, Milena Grillo, and Helia Barbosa, "Sexual Exploitation of Children and Adolescents in Tourism," contribution of ECPAT International to the World Congress III against Sexual Exploitation of Children and Adolescents, 2008, http://www.ecpat.net/sites/default/files/Thematic_Paper_CST_ENG.pdf.

10. Ron O'Grady, *The Child and the Tourist: The Story behind the Escalation of Child Prostitution in Asia* (ECPAT, 1992), 15.

11. United Nations, "Report of the Special Rapporteur on the Sale of Children, Child Prostitution and Child Pornography, Najat Maalla M'jid," A/HRC/22/54, December 24, 2012, http://www.ohchr.org/Documents/HRBodies/HRCouncil/RegularSession /Session22/A.HRC.22.54_en.pdf.

12. Ibid.

13. Convention on the Rights of the Child, article 34.

14. The Ecumenical Coalition on Third World Tourism.

15. Author interview with Amihan Abueva, March 12, 2015.

16. Ibid.

17. Australia, Canada, England, France, Germany, Japan, the Netherlands, Sweden, Switzerland, and the United States.

18. Unpublished history of ECPAT.

19. Author interview with Helena Karlén, March 18, 2015.

20. Ibid.

21. See "Declaration and Agenda for Action," First World Congress against Commercial Sexual Exploitation of Children, Stockholm, Sweden, August 27–31, 1996, http: //www.ecpat.org/wp-content/uploads/legacy/stockholm_declaration_1996.pdf.

22. See "ECPAT International: What We Do," http://www.ecpat.net/what-we-do.

23. Author interview with Karlén.

24. Ibid.

25. Ibid.

26. See www.thecode.org/about.

27. Author interview with Karlén.

28. "The Code: Why Join," http://www.thecode.org/join/.

29. Unpublished history of ECPAT.

30. Author interview with Theo Noten, March 11, 2015.

31. UNICEF, *Assessing "The Code of Conduct" for the Protection of Children from*

Sexual Exploitation in Travel and Tourism (Florence: UNICEF Innocenti Research Centre, 2012).

32. Philip Wright, "Sex Tourism: Lessons Learned in Costa Rica," BBC, June 18, 2004, http://news.bbc.co.uk/2/hi/programmes/this_world/3818871.stm.

33. Author interview with Milena Grillo, March 9, 2015.

34. Ibid.

35. Ibid.

36. Ibid.

37. UNICEF, *Assessing "The Code of Conduct."*

38. Author interview with Grillo.

39. Ibid.

40. Hawke and Raphael, *Offenders on the Move*, 14.

41. Author interview with Dorothy Rozga, March 12, 2015.

42. Hawke and Raphael, *Offenders on the Move*, 14.

43. Author interview with Rozga.

44. UNICEF, *Assessing "The Code of Conduct."*

45. Author interview with Grillo.

46. Hawke and Raphael, *Offenders on the Move*, 14

47. Ibid., 106.

48. Ibid., 109.

49. United Nations, "Report of the Special Rapporteur."

50. Author interview with Grillo.

51. Author interview with Rozga.

52. Child Exploitation and Online Protection Centre, "Threat Assessment of Child Sexual Exploitation and Abuse" (London: CEOP, June 2013),14, https://ceop.police.uk/Documents/ceopdocs/CEOP_TACSEA2013_240613%20FINAL.pdf.

53. James McNicol and Andreas Schloenhardt, "Australia's Child Sex Tourism Offences," *Current Issues in Criminal Justice* 23 (2012): 369–92, http://www.austlii.edu.au/au/journals/CICrimJust/2012/5.html.

54. US Immigration and Customs Enforcement, *Operation Predator—Targeting Child Exploitation and Sexual Crimes* (fact sheet, June 25, 2012), http://www.ice.gov/factsheets/predator.

55. Interpol, "INTERPOL Network Identified 10,000 Child Sexual Abuse Victims," January 9, 2017, https://www.interpol.int/News-and-media/News/2017/N2017-001.

56. United Nations Resolution A/RES/70/1, September 25, 2015, para. 54.

Chapter 8

1. Author interview with "Aruna" (name changed for her safety), Batticaloa, Sri Lanka, August 2004.

2. For more information about the LTTE's use of child soldiers, see Human Rights Watch, *Living in Fear: Child Soldiers and the Tamil Tigers in Sri Lanka* (New York: Human Rights Watch, 2004).

3. Author interview with "Aruna."

4. United Nations, "Report of the Secretary-General to the UN Security Council

on Children and Armed Conflict," S/2016/360, April 20, 2016. The secretary-general reported the recruitment and use of child soldiers in Afghanistan, the Central African Republic, Colombia, the Democratic Republic of the Congo, India, Iraq, Lebanon, Mali, Myanmar, Nigeria, Pakistan, Philippines, Somalia, South Sudan, Sudan, Syria, and Yemen.

5. Human Rights Watch, *Early to War: Child Soldiers in the Chad Conflict* (New York: Human Rights Watch, 2007), 20–21.

6. See Mark A. Drumbl, *Reimagining Child Soldiers in International Law and Policy* (Oxford: Oxford University Press, 2012), for a discussion of the discourse around child soldiers and a critique of the portrayal of child soldiers as passive victims who are not responsible for their actions.

7. Human Rights Watch, *You'll Learn Not to Cry: Child Combatants in Colombia* (New York: Human Rights Watch, 2003),4.

8. Ibid., 35.

9. Ibid.

10. Ibid.

11. During Sri Lanka's conflict, for example, UNICEF kept a comprehensive database of children who had been recruited by the LTTE. Girls accounted for approximately 40 percent of cases.

12. Author interview, Gulu, Uganda, February 2003.

13. Protocol Additional to the Geneva Conventions of 12 August 1949, and Relating to the Protection of Victims of International Armed Conflicts (Protocol I), article 77, 1125 U.N.T.S. 3, and Protocol Additional to the Geneva Conventions of 12 August 1949, and Relating to the Victims of Non-International Armed Conflicts (Protocol II), article 4, 1125 U.N.T.S. 609.

14. Convention on the Rights of the Child, article 38.

15. Article 8(2)(e)(vii) of the Rome Statute for the International Criminal Court defines "conscripting or enlisting children under the age of fifteen years into armed forces or groups or using them to participate actively in hostilities" as a war crime under the court's jurisdiction, UN document A/CONF.183/9 of July 17, 1998.

16. ILO Convention 182 Concerning the Prohibition and Immediate Action for the Elimination of the Worst Forms of Child Labour (1999). (Worst Forms of Child Labor Convention.)

17. For a full discussion of the campaign, see "Campaigning to Stop the Use of Child Soldiers," in Jo Becker, *Campaigning for Justice: Human Rights Advocacy in Practice* (Stanford: Stanford University Press, 2013), 11–31.

18. Optional Protocol to the Convention on the Rights of the Child on the Involvement of Children in Armed Conflict, adopted May 25, 2000, G.A. resolution 54/263, Annex I, 54 U.N. GAOR Supp. (no.49) at 7, U.N. document A/54/49, vol. III (2000).

19. International Criminal Court, "Cases," https://www.icc-cpi.int/en_menus/icc/situations%20and%20cases/cases/Pages/cases%20index.aspx.

20. International Criminal Court, *The Prosecutor v. Thomas Lubanga Dyilo*, https://www.icc-cpi.int/en_menus/icc/situations%20and%20cases/situations/situation%20icc%200104/related%20cases/icc%200104%200106/Pages/democratic%20republic%20of%20the%20congo.aspx.

21. Child Soldiers International, "Children in Armed Conflict: A War Crime We Have the Responsibility to Prevent," March 26, 2015, http://www.child-soldiers.org/news _reader.php?id=820.

22. See Coalition to Stop the Use of Child Soldiers, *Child Soldiers Global Report 2001* (London: Coalition to Stop the Use of Child Soldiers, 2001), for estimates of child soldier use during the 1990s, and United Nations, "Report of the Secretary-General to the UN Security Council on Children and Armed Conflict," S/2016/360, April 20, 2016, for child soldier use in 2015.

23. In 2016, the following governments were listed by either the US State Department or the UN secretary-general, or both, for using children as soldiers in violation of international standards: Afghanistan, Burma, the Democratic Republic of the Congo, Iraq, Nigeria, Rwanda, Somalia, South Sudan, Sudan, Syria, and Yemen. All but Burma, Somalia, and South Sudan have ratified the optional protocol.

24. Between 2001 and 2017, members of the steering committee of the Watchlist included CARE, the Coalition to Stop the Use of Child Soldiers, Human Rights Watch, International Refugee Council, the Norwegian Refugee Council, Save the Children, International Federation Terre des Hommes, War Child, Women's Refugee Commission, and World Vision.

25. Author interview with Julia Freedson, August 18, 2015.

26. Security Council resolution 1379, S/RES/1379, adopted November 20, 2001.

27. United Nations, "Report of the Secretary General to the Security Council on Children and Armed Conflict," S/2003/1053, November 10, 2003.

28. Security Council 1539, S/RES/1539, adopted April 22, 2004.

29. Author interview with Freedson.

30. Ibid.

31. Security Council resolution 1539, S/RES/1539, adopted April 22, 2004, para. 2.

32. Watchlist on Children and Armed Conflict, "Violations against Children in Armed Conflicts: An Action Plan for Monitoring, Reporting and Response," October 2004, http://watchlist.org/violations-against-children-in-armed-conflicts-an-action-plan -for-monitoring-reporting-and-response/.

33. Author interview with Freedson.

34. Jean-Marc de la Sablière, "Security Council Engagement on the Protection of Children and Armed Conflict: Progress Achieved and the Way Forward," June 15, 2012, 6, https://childrenandarmedconflict.un.org/publications/Delasablierereport_en.pdf.

35. Letter dated September 8, 2006, from the Permanent Representative of France to the United Nations addressed to the President of the Security Council, S/2006/724, September 11, 2006.

36. Security Council Working Group on Children and Armed Conflict, "Conclusions on Children and Armed Conflict in Sri Lanka," S/AC.51/2007/9, June 13, 2007, http://www .un.org/ga/search/view_doc.asp?symbol=S/AC.51/2007/9&Lang=E&Area=UNDOC.

37. See the website of the Special Representative to the Secretary General on Children and Armed Conflict, https://childrenandarmedconflict.un.org/our-work/sanctions/.

38. Olara Otunnu served from 1998 to 2005 as the first SRSG on children and

armed conflict. He was succeeded by Radhika Coomeraswamy, who served from 2006 to 2012, and Leila Zerrougui, who served from 2012 to 2017.

39. United Nations, "Report of the Secretary General to the Security Council on Children and Armed Conflict," S/2007/757, December 21, 2007, para. 17.

40. Sablière, "Security Council Engagement," 12.

41. Communication with the author from a representative from the Permanent Mission of Germany to the United Nations.

42. Author interview with Freedson.

43. Human Rights Watch, *Early to War*, 22.

44. Ibid., 23.

45. Ibid., 29–30.

46. Meeting between Rima Salah and the Watchlist on Children and Armed Conflict, March 12, 2012.

47. Ibid.

48. United Nations, "Report of the Secretary General to the Security Council on Children and Armed Conflict," S/2010/181, April 13, 2010, para. 21.

49. Office of the SRSG on Children and Armed Conflict, *Chad Signs an Action Plan to End Recruitment and Use of Children in Its National Army and Security Forces* (press release, June 16, 2011), https://childrenandarmedconflict.un.org/press-release/16jun11/.

50. United Nations, "Report of the Secretary General to the Security Council on Children and Armed Conflict," S/2012/261, April 26, 2012, para. 24.

51. United Nations, "Report of the Secretary General to the Security Council on Children and Armed Conflict," S/2013/245, May 15, 2013, para. 46–47.

52. See, for example, Child Soldiers International, *Chad: Grasping a New Opportunity to End Child Recruitment into the Armed Forces* (press release, June 25, 2013), http://www.child-soldiers.org/news_reader.php?id=682.

53. Watchlist on Children and Armed Conflict, *Where Are They? The Situation of Children and Armed Conflict in Mali*, June 2013, http://watchlist.org/wordpress/wp-content/uploads/Watchlist_Mali.pdf.

54. United Nations, "Report of the Secretary General to the Security Council on Children and Armed Conflict," S/2014/267, May 14, 2014, para. 46–50.

55. See Child Soldiers International, *Efforts to Put a Definitive End to Child Recruitment in Chad Should Continue* (press release, July 1, 2015), http://www.child-soldiers.org/news_reader.php?id=769; Conflict Dynamics International, *Children and Armed Conflict Accountability Framework: A Framework for Advancing Accountability for Serious Violations against Children in Armed Conflict*, June 2015, 32–33. http://cacaccountability.org/framework.

56. Child Soldiers International, *Efforts to put a Definitive End to Child Recruitment in Chad Should Continue*.

57. United Nations, *The Future of United Nations Peace Operations: Implementation of the Recommendations of the High-Level Independent Panel on Peace Operation Report of the Secretary-General*, S/2015/682, September 2, 2015, para. 127. This commitment was later welcomed by the Security Council in resolution S/Res/2242, October 13, 2015, para. 10.

58. For more information, see "Campaigning to Stop the Use of Child Soldiers," in Becker, *Campaigning for Justice.*

59. Author interview with Rachel Stohl, August 13, 2015.

60. Foreign Relations Authorization Act of FY03 (HR 1646) (2002).

61. US State Department, *2004 Country Reports on Human Rights Practices* (February 2004), http://www.state.gov/j/drl/rls/hrrpt/2004/.

62. Author interview with Stohl.

63. Author interview with Joe Mettimano, August 20, 2105.

64. Ibid.

65. Child Soldiers Prevention Act, S. 1175, introduced April 19, 2007.

66. Rachel Stohl of the Center for Defense Information worked on the bill in her own capacity.

67. Ishmael Beah, *Long Way Gone: Memoirs of a Boy Soldier* (New York: Farrar, Straus, and Giroux, 2007).

68. E-mail from a congressional staffer to the author, July 23, 2007.

69. E-mail to author, July 23, 2007.

70. Author interview with Mettimano.

71. The William Wilberforce Trafficking Victims Protection Reauthorization Act of 2008, Pub. L. No. 110–457. The Child Soldiers Prevention Act was incorporated as Title IV of the act.

72. Burma received no US aid, and Somalia received peacekeeping assistance that was not covered by the Child Soldier Prevention Act.

73. Author interview with Stohl.

74. Mary Beth Sheridan, "Obama Waiver Allows US Aid to 4 Countries Using Child Soldiers," *Washington Post,* October 27, 2010, and Brian Knowlton, "4 Nations with Child Soldiers Keep US Aid," *New York Times,* October 28, 2010.

75. White House spokesman Tommy Vietor, quoted in Knowlton, "4 Nations with Child Soldiers Keep US Aid."

76. Open Letter to President Obama regarding waivers to the Child Soldiers Prevention Act, November 5, 2010, signed by twenty-eight nongovernmental organizations. Author's files.

77. Chuck Neubauer, "US Gives Military Aid to Nations with Child Soldiers," *Washington Times,* August 8, 2011, http://www.washingtontimes.com/news/2012/aug/8/us -gives-military-aid-to-nations-with-child-soldie/?page=all.

78. US State Department, "Democratic Republic of Congo," *2016 Trafficking in Persons Report* (June 2016), http://www.state.gov/j/tip/rls/tiprpt/countries/2016/258747.htm.

79. Human Rights Watch, *DR Congo: M23 Rebels Committing War Crimes* (press release, September 11, 2012), https://www.hrw.org/news/2012/09/11/dr-congo-m23 -rebels-committing-war-crimes.

80. United Nations, "Report of the Secretary-General to the UN Security Council on Children and Armed Conflict," S/2013/245, May 15, 2013, para. 137.

81. UNICEF, "UNICEF and LGen Dallaire Call for Urgent Action to Protect Children from Becoming Soldiers," November 12, 2015, http://www.unicef.org/esaro/5440 _ss2015_dallaire.html.

82. United Nations, "Report of the Secretary-General to the UN Security Council on Children and Armed Conflict," S/2016/360, April 20, 2016.

83. Author interview with Freedson.

84. Leila Zerrougui, "Twenty Years for Children" (statement, December 12, 2016), https://childrenandarmedconflict.un.org/twenty-years-for-children/.

85. Watchlist interviewed forty-nine members of the UN Security Council Working Group on Children and Armed Conflict, UN agencies and offices at UN headquarters and at the country-level, nongovernmental organizations, diplomatic missions, and independent experts. It examined six country situations: Chad, DRC, South Sudan, Afghanistan, Nepal and the Philippines.

86. Watchlist on Children and Armed Conflict, "Action Plans to Prevent and End Violations against Children" (discussion paper, April 2013), http://watchlist.org/word press/wp-content/uploads/FINAL-Discussion-Paper-Action-Plans.pdf.

87. Author interview with Mettimano.

88. Author interview with Stohl.

Chapter 9

1. Human Rights Watch interview with Bara'a (full name withheld), February 16, 2016.

2. Ibid.

3. Ibid. See also Josh Wood, "In Lebanon's Refugee Camps, Syrian Girls Start Outdoor Schools," *National*, March 22, 2015, http://www.thenational.ae/world/middle-east /in-lebanons-refugee-camps-syrian-girls-start-outdoor-schools#full.

4. UNESCO Institute for Statistics (UIS)and Global Education Monitoring Report, "Leaving No One Behind: How Far on the Way to Universal Primary and Secondary Education?" (policy paper 27/fact sheet 37, July 2016), http://uis.unesco.org/sites/default/files /documents/fs37-leaving-no-one-behind-how-far-on-the-way-to-universal-primary-and -secondary-education-2016-en.pdf.

5. UNESCO, "Education Is the Key to Lasting Development," 2011, http://www .unesco.org/fileadmin/MULTIMEDIA/HQ/ED/GMR/pdf/gmr2010/MDG2010_Facts _and_Figures_EN.pdf.

6. UNESCO, *Education for All 2000–2015: Achievements and Challenges* (Paris: UNESCO, 2015), ii, http://unesdoc.unesco.org/images/0023/002322/232205e.pdf.

7. Convention on the Rights of the Child, articles 28, 29.

8. International Covenant on Economic, Social and Cultural Rights, article 13.

9. Convention on the Rights of Persons with Disabilities, article 24.

10. The six goals related to early childhood care and education, universal primary education, youth and adult skills, adult literacy, gender parity and equality, and quality of education.

11. UIS and Global Education Monitoring Report, "Leaving No One Behind," and UNESCO, *Education for All 2000–2015*, 15.

12. Ibid.; UNESCO, *Education for All 2000–2015*, 226.

13. UIS and Global Education Monitoring Report, "Leaving No One Behind," and UNESCO, *Education for All 2000–2015*, xiii.

14. UNESCO, *Education for All 2000–2015*, 80.

15. Ibid., 157.

16. World Bank and UNICEF, *Abolishing School Fees in Africa: Lessons from Ethiopia, Ghana, Kenya, Malawi, and Mozambique* (2009), 162, http://www.unicef.org/publi cations/files/Aboloshing_School_Fees_in_Africa.pdf.

17. Victor Chinyama, "Kenya's Abolition of School Fees Offers Lessons for Rest of AFRICA," UNICEF, April 2006, http://www.unicef.org/education/kenya_33391.html).

18. UNESCO, *Education for All 2000-2015*, 86.

19. Ibid., 260.

20. Jody Heymann, with Kristen McNeill, *Children's Chances: How Countries Can Move from Surviving to Thriving* (Cambridge, MA: Harvard University Press, 2013), 23.

21. UNESCO, *Education for All 2000–2015*, 90.

22. Ibid.

23. Human Rights Watch interview with Florencia Devoto, researcher, Poverty Action Lab, April 17, 2012.

24. UNESCO, *Education for All 2000–2015*, 24.

25. Ibid., 89.

26. Ibid.

27. Ibid., 88.

28. Ibid., 92.

29. Ibid.

30. Ibid.

31. In some African countries, 12 to 22 percent of school dropouts among girls are due to early marriage. See Heyman, *Children's Chances*, 78.

32. UNESCO, *Education for All 2000–2015*, 164.

33. Author interview with Chernor Bah, April 20, 2015.

34. Ibid.

35. Chernor Bah, "A Personal Reflection on Children's Role in Peacebuilding and Governance in Sierra Leone," Beyond Intractability, n.d., http://www.beyondintracta bility.org/reflection/childrens-role-in-peacebuilding.

36. UNESCO, *Sierra Leone Education Country Status Report* (Dakar: UNESCO, 2013). Primary enrollment increased from 634,000 in 2000 to 1.2 million in 2004–2005.

37. Ibid., 18.

38. Ibid. Junior enrollment increased from 60,000 to 244,000 between 2000 and 2010, and senior secondary increased from 23,000 to 108,000.

39. In 2007, the World Bank estimated that the cost of uniforms doubled the costs associated with school for families in Sierra Leone. UNESCO, *Education for All Global Monitoring Report 2010*, 166.

40. Author interview with Bah.

41. Ibid.

42. The founding aim was to "ensure that the World Education Forum in Dakar, April 2000, would result in concrete commitments and viable policies to implement the Education for All (EFA) goals, including gender equity by 2005, universal enrolment in and completion of free primary education by 2015 and a 50% reduction in adult literacy by 2015."

43. Global Campaign for Education Constitution, November 27, 2001.

44. Author interview with Anne Jellema, August 5, 2015.

45. Ibid.

46. Ibid.

47. Carolyn Culey, Andy Martin, and Dan Lewer, *Global Campaign for Education: 2007 Mid-term Review* (London: Firetail Limited, n.d.), 51.

48. Campaña Latinoamericana por el Derecho a la Educación (CLADE), *Society Advocating for the Right to Education: Stories and Lessons Learned from Latin America and the Caribbean* (São Paulo: CLADE, 2012), 13.

49. United Nations, Sustainable Development Goals, Goal 4, http://www.un.org/sustainabledevelopment/education/.

50. Author interview with Camilla Croso, August 26, 2015.

51. Education for All Global Monitoring Report, "Pricing the Right to Education: The Cost of Reaching New Targets by 2030," Policy Paper 18, (July 2015 update), 1, http://unesdoc.unesco.org/images/0023/002321/232197E.pdf.

52. UIS and Global Education Monitoring Report, *A Growing Number of Children and Adolescents Are out of School,* 7.

53. Ibid., 1.

54. United Nations, *With 4 Million Syrian Children out of School, $1.4 Billion Sought by UN to Save "Lost Generation"* (news release, February 2, 2016, 2, http://www.un.org/apps/news/story.asp?NewsID=53145#.V73bCGWN2FY.

55. UNESCO, *Education for All 2000–2015,* 101.

56. Kishore Singh, "Report of the UN Special Rapporteur on the Right to Education to the UN General Assembly," UN document A/69/402, September 24, 2014, para. 67.

57. Global Campaign for Education, *Time to Get It Right: Lessons from EFA and the MDGs for Education, 2016–2030* (London: GCE, 2015).

58. Author interview with Croso.

59. Culey et al,, "Global Campaign for Education," 33.

60. Ibid., 39.

61. Ibid.

62. Ibid., 30.

63. Author interview with Jellema.

64. Author interview with Croso.

65. Author interview with Jellema.

66. Camilla Croso, "Address to the Education 2030 Special High Level Meeting," Paris, November 4, 2015, http://www.campaignforeducation.org/docs/statements/Speech%20FFA_Paris%202015_CAMILLA_CROSO_FINAL_INT.pdf.

Chapter 10

1. Malala Yousafzai, Nobel Lecture, Oslo, Norway, December 10, 2014, http://www.nobelprize.org/nobel_prizes/peace/laureates/2014/yousafzai-lecture_en.html.

2. Rick Westhead, "Brave Defiance in Pakistan's Swat Valley," *Toronto Star,* October 26, 2009, http://www.thestar.com/news/world/2009/10/26/brave_defiance_in_pakistans_swat_valley.html.

3. Irin News, "Pakistan: Militants Announce Ban on Girls' Education in Swat," January 1, 2009, http://www.irinnews.org/report/82161/pakistan-militants-announce-ban-on-girls-education-in-swat.

4. BBC, "Diary of a Pakistani Schoolgirl," January 19, 2009, http://news.bbc.co.uk/2/hi/south_asia/7834402.stm.

5. Global Coalition to Protect Education from Attack (GCPEA), "Pakistan Country Profile," *Education under Attack 2014* (New York: GCPEA, 2014), 169.

6. Malala Yousafzai, *I Am Malala* (New York: Little, Brown, 2013).

7. Michelle Nichols, "Pakistan's Malala, Shot by Taliban, Takes Education Plea to U.N.," Reuters, July 12, 2013, http://www.reuters.com/article/2013/07/12/us-malala-un-idUSBRE96B0IC20130712.

8. GCPEA, *Education under Attack 2014*, 168.

9. Ibid., 8.

10. Ibid., 9.

11. Human Rights Watch, *"They Set the Classrooms on Fire": Attacks on Education in Northeast Nigeria* (New York: Human Rights Watch, 2016).

12. As of August 2016, 57 of the 276 abductees had managed to escape, but the fate of more than 200 was unknown.

13. United Nations, "Report of the Secretary-General to the UN Security Council on Children and Armed Conflict," S/2016/360, April 20, 2016.

14. See Scholars at Risk, *Free to Think: Report of the Scholars at Risk Academic Freedom Monitoring Project* (June 2015), http://www.right-to-education.org/sites/right-to-education.org/files/resource-attachments/SAR%20Free%20to%20Think.pdf.

15. See Jean-Marie Henckaerts and Louise Doswald-Beck, eds., *Customary International Humanitarian Law* (Cambridge: Cambridge University Press, 2005), rules 7, 9.

16. Rome Statute of the International Criminal Court, art. 8(b)(ix), UN document A/CONF.183/9 (1998)

17. Convention on the Rights of the Child, article 28.

18. UNESCO Institute for Statistics (UIS)and Global Education Monitoring Report, "Leaving No One Behind: How Far on the Way to Universal Primary and Secondary Education?" (policy paper 27/fact sheet 37, July 2016), 4, http://uis.unesco.org/sites/default/files/documents/fs37-leaving-no-one-behind-how-far-on-the-way-to-universal-primary-and-secondary-education-2016-en.pdf.

19. UNESCO, *EFA Global Monitoring Report—The Hidden Crisis: Armed Conflict and Education* (Paris: UNESCO, 2011), 132.

20. UNICEF e-mail to Human Rights Watch, March 27, 2003, cited in Human Rights Watch, *"Killing You Is a Very Easy Thing for Us": Human Rights Abuses in Southeast Afghanistan* (New York: Human Rights Watch, 2003), 96.

21. Human Rights Watch, *Lessons in Terror: Attacks on Education in Afghanistan* (New York: Human Rights Watch, 2006), 3.

22. Ibid., 103.

23. Author interview with Mark Richmond, July 31, 2015.

24. Ibid.

25. The results of the seminar, including a set of papers written by participants,

were included in *Protecting Education from Attack: A State-of-the-Art Review*, published by UNESCO in early 2010. See http://unesdoc.unesco.org/images/0018/001867/186732e .pdf. One of the participants was Gregory Bart, commander in the Judge Advocate General's Corps, US Navy, who had written an article in 2009, highlighting the discrepancy in international protections for schools, as compared to hospitals and religious institutions. See Gregory Bart, "The Ambiguous Protection of Schools under the Law of War: Time for Parity with Hospitals and Religious Buildings," *Georgetown Journal of International Law* 40 (2009), 321–58.

26. The initial steering committee included CARA (Council for Assisting Refugee Academics), Education above All (later renamed Protect Education in Insecurity and Conflict, as a program of an enlarged Education Above All Foundation), Education International, Human Rights Watch, Institute of International Education/IIE Scholar Rescue Fund, Save the Children, UNICEF, and UNESCO. The Office of the United Nations High Commissioner for Refugees (UNHCR) joined later. Education International withdrew from the steering committee in 2012.

27. See GCPEA, "Initiatives," http://www.protectingeducation.org/initiatives.

28. The workshop resulted in the publication of "Report from the Knowledge Roundtable on Programmatic Measures in Prevention, Intervention, and Response to Attacks on Education, November 8–11, 2011, Phuket, Thailand," http://www.protect ingeducation.org/sites/default/files/documents/study_on_field-based_programmatic _measures_to_protect_education_from_attack_0.pdf.

29. Author interview with Richmond.

30. GCPEA defined a "significant pattern" as including at least five or more incidents or victims, including at least one direct attack on a school or the killing of at least one teacher, student, or academic.

31. GCPEA, *Education under Attack 2014.*

32. Author interview with Diya Nijhowne, July 30, 2015.

33. Security Council resolution 1998, S/RES/1998, adopted July 12, 2011.

34. Author interview with Bede Sheppard, July 23, 2015.

35. Ibid.

36. Ibid.

37. Human Rights Watch, *Sabotaged Schooling: Naxalite Attacks and Police Occupation of Schools in India's Bihar and Jharkhand* (New York: Human Rights Watch, 2009).

38. Author interview with Sheppard.

39. Human Rights Watch, *No Place for Children: Child Recruitment, Child Marriage, and Attacks on Schools in Somalia* (New York: Human Rights Watch, 2012), 67–68.

40. GCPEA, *Lessons in War 2015: Military Use of Schools and Universities during Armed Conflict* (New York: GCPEA, 2015),44.

41. GCPEA, *Lessons in War 2012: Military Use of Schools and Other Educational Institutions during Conflict* (New York: GCPEA, 2012),37.

42. Protocol Additional to the Geneva Conventions of August 12, 1949, and relating to the Protection of Victims of International Armed Conflicts (Additional Protocol I), June 8, 1977, article 58; Protocol Additional to the Geneva Conventions of August 12,

1949, and relating to the Protection of Victims of Non-International Armed Conflicts (Additional Protocol II), June 8, 1977, article 4.

43. Author interview with Sheppard.

44. Human Rights Watch, *Schools and Armed Conflict: A Global Survey of Domestic Laws and State Practice Protecting Schools from Military Use* (New York: Human Rights Watch, 2011).

45. Author interview with Sheppard.

46. GCPEA, *Lessons in War 2015*, 6.

47. GCPEA, *Education under Attack 2014*, 193; Syrian Network for Human Rights, "A Report on the Destruction of Schools Its Consequences."

48. GCPEA, *Lessons in War 2012*, 30.

49. Department of Peacekeeping Operations, Department of Field Support, *United Nations Infantry Battalion Manual*, 2012, sec. 2.13.

50. Deed of Commitment under Geneva Call for the Protection of Children from the Effects of Armed Conflict. http://www.genevacall.org/wp-content/uploads/dlm_up loads/2013/12/DoC-Protecting-children-in-armed-conflict.pdf.

51. For a complete list of signatories, see http://www.genevacall.org/how-we-work /armed-non-state-actors/.

52. Author interview with Courtney Erwin, August 18, 2015.

53. Governments represented included Argentina, Canada, Côte d'Ivoire, Finland, Liberia, Nepal, Norway, Philippines, Qatar, and Switzerland. The International Committee of the Red Cross, UN agencies, and nongovernmental organizations, including Geneva Call and Amnesty International, also attended.

54. Author interview with Sheppard.

55. The full Guidelines for Protecting Schools and Universities from Military Use during Armed Conflict can be found at http://www.protectingeducation.org/sites/de fault/files/documents/guidelines_en.pdf.

56. Author interview with Véronique Aubert, July 21, 2015.

57. Author interview with Erwin.

58. See www.emuscampaign.org.

59. E-mail to author from Pamela Bruns, July 30, 2015.

60. Author interview with Sheppard.

61. Ibid.

62. Author interview with Aubert.

63. Ibid.

64. Countries that GCPEA representatives visited at capital level between 2012 and 2015 included Argentina, Austria, Canada, Côte d'Ivoire, the Democratic Republic of the Congo, Finland, France, Germany, Greece, Ireland, Italy, Japan, Jordan, Ireland, Liberia, Lithuania, Luxembourg, Mexico, Nepal, Netherlands, Norway, Philippines, Poland, Portugal, Qatar, South Africa, Switzerland, the United Kingdom, and Uruguay.

65. Louis Belanger, "Ziauddin Yousafzai Speaks Out against Military Use Of Schools at Oslo Conference," *Malala Fund Blog*, June 1, 2015, http://community.malala.org/zi auddin-yousafzai-speaks-out-against-military-use-of-schools-at-oslo—1177958552 .html.

66. Author interview with Zama Coursen-Neff, July 14, 2015.

67. GCPEA, *37 Countries Start Process of Protecting Schools and Universities during Conflict* (press release, May 29, 2015), http://www.protectingeducation.org/news/coun tries-join-safe-schools-pact#sthash.4UR9GHUh.dpuf.

68. The full list of endorsing states can be found at http://www.protectingeduca tion.org/guidelines/support.

69. Author interview with Sheppard.

70. Author interview with Filipa Guinote, July 23, 2015

71. Author interview with Jonathan Somers, July 22, 2015.

72. For more detail, see GCPEA, *What Ministries Can Do to Protect Education from Attack and Schools from Military Use: A Menu of Actions* (December 2015), http://www .protectingeducation.org/sites/default/files/documents/what_ministries.pdf.

73. Katarina Tomasevksi, interviewed in *Human Rights Features*, April 5–12, 2004, cited in UNESCO, *Education under Attack 2007* (Paris: UNESCO, 2007), 92–93.

74. Author interview with Nijhowne.

75. Author interview with Aubert.

76. Author interview with Sheppard.

77. Author interview with Guinote.

78. Author interview with Sheppard.

79. Ibid.

80. Author interview with Erwin.

81. Author interview with Aubert.

82. Ibid.

83. Author interview with Erwin.

Chapter 11

1. See United Nations, Sustainable Development Goals, http://www.un.org/sustain abledevelopment/sustainable-development-goals/.

Index

Lightning Source UK Ltd.
Milton Keynes UK
UKHW010040061119
352919UK00012B/168/P